Darker Shade of Pale uncovers the hidden story of global migration from the Jewish territories of the Russian Empire to the far-flung British colony of South Africa at the turn of the twentieth century. Following the life of the author's grandfather Maurice Posel, an ordinary man whose struggles and disappointments mirror those of countless others, the book belies the common narrative of Jewish immigrant success in South Africa. It brings the psychodramas of immigration into focus in the traumas of dislocation; in the pressures to succeed and the shame of failure; in the ironies of this journeying for literate, working women from the shtetl; in the version of whiteness that South Africa assigned to Jews from Eastern Europe as well as the prejudicial punches that they had to take from both the British and the already assimilated English-speaking Jewish community. Through one man's unfulfilled hopes, we discover what was given and what was taken, as immigrants sought to build new lives in a strange land.

DARKER SHADE OF PALE

Shtetl to Colony

DEBORAH POSEL

WITS UNIVERSITY PRESS

Published in South Africa by:
Wits University Press
1 Jan Smuts Avenue
Johannesburg 2001

www.witspress.co.za

Copyright © Deborah Posel 2025
Images © Copyright holders

First published 2025

http://dx.doi.org.10.18772/12025119711

978-1-77614-971-1 (Paperback)
978-1-77614-972-8 (Hardback)
978-1-77614-973-5 (Web PDF)
978-1-77614-974-2 (EPUB)

All rights reserved. No part of this publication may be reproduced, stored in a retrieval system, or transmitted in any form or by any means, electronic, mechanical, photocopying, recording or otherwise, without the written permission of the publisher, except in accordance with the provisions of the Copyright Act, Act 98 of 1978.

All images remain the property of the copyright holders. The publishers gratefully acknowledge the publishers, institutions and individuals referenced in captions for the use of images. Every effort has been made to locate the original copyright holders of the images reproduced here; please contact Wits University Press in case of any omissions or errors.

Project manager: Inga Norenius
Copyeditor: Alison Lowry
Proofreader: Alison Paulin
Cover design: Carina Comrie

Typeset in 10.5 point Crimson

For Jess, Ilan and Asher

Contents

List of images	xiii
Note on terminology	xv

Part One   1

1	Longing	3
2	On the move	4
3	The glitter of gold	6
4	Conversations with Carruthers	9
5	Living with lack	11
6	A structure of life	15
7	The *farribel*	18
8	The ticket	25
9	Two more fragments	28
10	Many lives are possible	30
11	Ordinary stories	32
12	The myth of Jewish exceptionalism	34

Part Two — 37

13	Shtetl	39
14	Prospects in the Pale of Settlement	41
15	Schisms and fault-lines	44
16	Posels in Pumpian	46
17	Posel prospects	48
18	Sitting and standing	51
19	Taverning	54
20	Itsyk	58
21	Singles	60
22	Pushy daughters	66
23	*Stille chuppah*	70
24	Conversion to Christianity	73
25	Margin of margins	75
26	A boy child	77
27	Veins of violence	81

Part Three — 87

28	Leaving Pumpian	89
29	At sea	94
30	'They came with nothing'	98
31	Those who stayed	100
32	The 'East' of the 'West'	103

CONTENTS

Part Four   **105**

33	Rats	107
34	24 June 1902	111
35	Towards District Six	114
36	A shtetl that wasn't	116
37	'Squat-bodied'	120
38	Shapeshifting	122
39	At risk	125
40	Upstanding work	129
41	28 Longmarket Street	133
42	Choices	136
43	Carrier	140
44	Smous	142
45	Good eggs and bad eggs	147
46	Nothing ventured, nothing gained	150
47	Business in the mix	154
48	Ways for women	157
49	Love and marriage	162
50	One of those who froze	166
51	What's left behind	169
52	Mothers of loss	173
53	Longing to be let in	175
54	A colonial education	177
55	Carruthers Beattie	180
56	What a shame	183

Part Five — 187

57 Brothers — 189
58 Modern Jews — 191
59 Money — 194
60 'Like insects to the light' — 196
61 Jews in front — 199
62 Chatzkel's luck — 204
63 Whose gold — 208
64 Jews and 'the Blacks' — 210
65 Chatzkel on the move — 214
66 Obscene extremes — 217
67 A deferent retort — 224
68 Ferreirastown — 228
69 Prospering in Ferreirastown — 232
70 The *farribel* undone — 238
71 Max — 242

Part Six — 245

72 A Johannesburg man — 247
73 'One man with four girls' — 250
74 'Little Vienna' — 253
75 Jews in the Austro-Hungarian Empire — 255
76 Czernowitz and the Jews — 259
77 Bakers for the emperor — 263

CONTENTS

78	Family ties	266
79	Leaving	269
80	Lourenço Marques	271
81	Doornfontein	274
82	World War I	277
83	A darker world	281
84	Cernauti	284
85	A Johannesburg 'spinster'	286

Part Seven		**289**
86	Marriage	291
87	Jewish suburbia	294
88	Set in stone	297
89	Archives	302
90	*Farribels* revisited	306
91	Dear Maurice	308
	Notes	310
	Acknowledgements	335
	Bibliography	337

List of images

Posel family tree	xvi
Maurice Posel. Author's collection.	12
Erna Posel. Author's collection.	13
Map of the Pale of Settlement. Redrawn by Janet Alexander.	42
Beila Posel's signature. Permit for entry to the Cape Colony, 1902. Author's photograph of original document in author's possession.	159
Official form for settling Bere Posel's estate with Beila's X. Western Cape Archives and Records Service. Author's photograph.	160
Bere's gravestone, Jewish Cemetery, Maitland, Cape Town. Beila's looks exactly the same. Author's photograph.	171
Inscription on Beila's gravestone, Jewish Cemetery, Maitland, Cape Town. Author's photograph.	172
Maurice Posel's signature, taken from a letter in the author's possession. Author's photograph.	179
Maurice Posel as a bachelor in Johannesburg. Author's collection.	248

Map showing Czernowitz in Bukovina, Austro-
    Hungarian Empire. Redrawn by Janet Alexander.   260
Mayer family outing in Czernowitz (1). Author's
    collection.   266
Mayer family outing in Czernowitz (2). Author's
    collection.   267
Maurice and Erna Posel on their wedding day, 1930.
    Author's collection.   292

Note on terminology

I have reproduced the racial terminology of the time, in the interests of historical authenticity. 'White' and 'Black' have been capitalised for two reasons: first, because this accords with the usage in several of the historical texts I have used, and second, because using capital letters underlines the artifice involved in these racial categories. I have chosen not to censor the racially offensive terms of the day, to confront readers with the contempt and dehumanisation that informed them. It is my intention to discomfort, but not to offend.

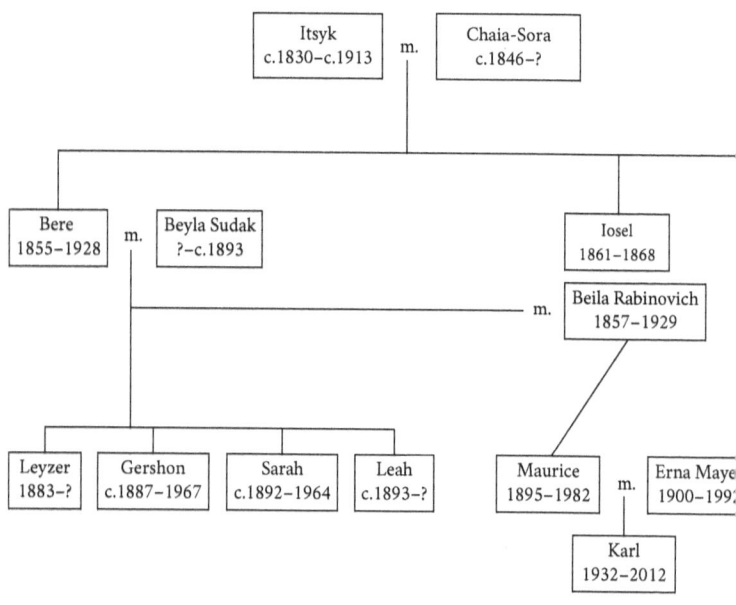

Posel family tree

Note: This is a partial family tree. I have omitted details that are not centrally relevant to the book, as well as information that is not reasonably reliable. Many of the dates included should be read as provisional (as indicated by the c.) Although I have used available archival sources for births and deaths, these are sometimes inconsistent.

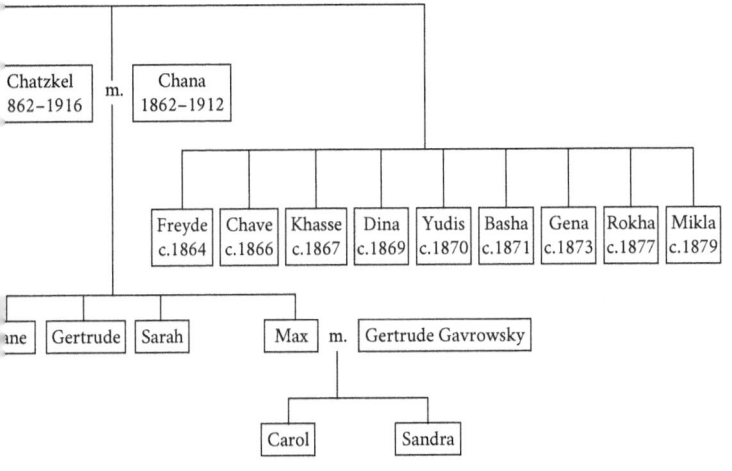

Part One

1 | Longing

Migration stories – like this one – are biographies of longing.[1]

Longing to outgrow the pain of departure.
Longing not to be punished for the audacity of arriving.
Longing to be recognised and rewarded.
Longing to love the new face in the mirror.
Longing to belong.

2 | On the move

From the mid- to late-nineteenth century, mass migration fired up on an unprecedented scale. Steamships moved hundreds at a time from one part of the globe to another, in weeks rather than months. Many millions would relocate as the new century advanced: 'the greatest migration in human history'.[2]

It wasn't just the wealthy who travelled. The journeying became an option for multitudes of ordinary folk imagining themselves starting again in an entirely new and strange place. Populations would be reconfigured; economies would be reorganised; societies would be rearranged. The world would transform.

Of course, not all doors were open, not all were permitted to arrive. This was the age of Empire; terms and conditions applied. But for those allowed in, opportunities would multiply.

Yet it would not be easy, each journey a heavy-hearted departure from all that was familiar, even if there was little comfort left in what home could offer. Even for an enthusiastic adventurer, the journey took the courage to risk a new life, to start again, make mistakes, and not look back.

Staring ahead, daring for a better future, an emigrant surely strove to leave the past behind and move on. Yet if all imprints of the past disappeared, like footprints on a beach, how much was lost? How whole could a person feel if the past was washed away?

Ships could offload throngs of immigrants at a time, but this is not to say they were all welcome. New arrivals often had to bear the burden of strangeness, and the distaste it provoked. Their foreign dress, culture, ways of walking and talking, would present a sometimes wrenching challenge: how much to give up, how far to go to blend in.

Nor was it easy for those on the receiving end. It would be the first time that settled populations would have to deal with tens of thousands of strangers – often even more – set on becoming part of them, without ever being the same as them. Anxiety, suspicion, uncertainty, anger too, were common reactions. What would these aliens take, what would they give? This predicament – or was it an unsettling opportunity? – would become one of the defining features of the twentieth century.

My grandfather Maurice and his family – Jews on the long haul from a blip of a town in the Russian empire to the South African tip of the British empire – were one tiny flicker in the thick, pulsing surge. They would have to confront the borders of their bodies and minds, just like all the others.

3 | The glitter of gold

The discovery of diamonds (1867) and gold (1886) in South Africa produced a deluge of immigrants, bigger than any other gold rush in the world around that time.[3] A territory languishing on the margins of international attention suddenly lit up on global maps as a destination of note.

Dreams of shimmering wealth – or of burgeoning opportunities to find work, at the very least – drew rushes of hopefuls from all over. Unsurprisingly, most came from Great Britain, the imperial motherland that claimed the place as its own. Arrivals from India were the second most numerous (mostly labourers, not all of whom stayed).

Surprisingly – surely – the third largest grouping that headed to these southern parts was Jews. Between 1880 and 1914, the Jewish exodus to South Africa brought around forty thousand men, women and children to this distant land.

This Jewish stream had many currents. Some came from Western Europe, Britain, Canada and the USA, a handful from Palestine. Much bigger numbers came from different places in what Westerners considered to be 'the East': places deemed by Great Britain and its colonial territories to be culturally lesser, diminished by lower orders of civilisation.

The large majority of these 'Eastern' Jews arrived from parts of the then Russian Empire, and most of those from northern areas of what is now Lithuania. Others came from the Russian territory that became Latvia, Belarus, Ukraine and part of Poland, and from Poland as it was then. Smaller numbers arrived from eastern parts of the then Austro-Hungarian Empire – Romania, Galicia, Hungary and Bukovina.

Their backgrounds varied. Some came from large, relatively sophisticated, modernising cities like Minsk, Vilnius, Odessa, Riga and Warsaw. Some were from lesser towns like Kaunus, Bialystok, Rovno. And many others made their way from small market towns – more traditionalist and parochial – known as shtetls.

Most immigrants were youngish men – in their twenties, or even younger – some not yet married, others with wives and young children either accompanying them or waiting to receive tickets to make the journey themselves. Some men and women were in their thirties, with teenage or young adult children; a few were older, in their forties or fifties.

Typically, a family's first foray southwards was made by one of its men, alone or with other male kin or friends, who scouted the place out, and then sent for others in the family to join him. One of the distinctive features of this Jewish migration was the high proportion of families involved – a sign of the longing to settle and stay.

This book traces the arc of the Jewish immigrant journey from the 'East' to South Africa and the terms of absorption into its society: what was given, what was taken. It's a story I tell largely through the prism of my grandfather's experiences, together with those of his immigrant family, and their contrast with the journeying of my grandmother and her family.

I do so not because my family's experiences can stand in for or typify the lives of others. The family optic sheds a particular light on the broader picture that is otherwise more difficult to see. Unremarkable people – like my family and most of the other immigrants – don't show up in the bigger story without a deliberate search that brings them resolutely into the frame. And their subjective interiors stay hidden if the focus of the story remains on the outside, limited to a more impersonal account of historical forces and their social impacts.

Yet these personal insides have already taken the outside in, which makes a keen view of that historical exterior equally necessary. Here is an instance, then, of how individual psyches and the wider society knitted together, patterned by the shift from the conditions of Jewish life in Russia, in my grandfather's case, and in Austro-Hungary in my grandmother's case, to those of a British colony preoccupied with its wealth and Whiteness; a story of how these Jews moved from one version of Empire to another, and the personal and collective repercussions of those moves.

4 | Conversations with Carruthers

I grew up with the name Sir Carruthers Beattie ringing in my young ears. When my grandfather Maurice and my grandmother Erna came to my childhood home in Johannesburg for tea, Sir Carruthers came too. I had no idea then who he was or what he did, where he came from or where he lived, whether he was alive or dead, real or imagined. I didn't ask, and I wasn't told. But his special place in the life of my grandfather's mind was unmistakable.

Maurice's conversation was sparse, just as his presence was reserved. When he did speak, Sir Carruthers Beattie made his presence felt. It was Sir Carruthers Beattie this, Sir Carruthers Beattie that. I don't remember any of the this or that; just the awed repetitions, the relish in uttering the name of the man, as if the name alone carried weight and spoke volumes.

Even as a child, I sensed something bizarre in these ramblings. They were as opaque as they were resolute, repetitions without direction, obviously meaningful to Maurice yet senseless to others. The adults in the room ignored him, apparently showing no interest whatsoever in the said Carruthers, real or not. Yet Maurice was undeterred; he would keep Sir Carruthers Beattie in the room, at his side, regardless. A constant interlocutor, even as others disengaged.

My siblings and I would joke incredulously at what we saw as the baroque implausibility of the name: so formal, so difficult to abbreviate, impossible to say with any intimacy or affection. Who, I would ask, could possibly have named their young child Carruthers? 'Carr-u-thers, supper is ready!' 'I'm going to ca-a-tch you, Carruthers!' we laughed. But Maurice savoured the pomposity, slowly rolling each and every syllable around his tongue.

Many decades later, I unexpectedly ran into Sir Carruthers Beattie again. I discovered, to my surprise, that he had indeed been a real person, the first vice-chancellor of the University of Cape Town, in fact, appointed in 1918. Ninety years after that, I would find myself living in Sir Carruthers' house, lying in his bed, so to speak, married to the ninth vice-chancellor of this university.

Maurice's strange chatter came back to me then, along with my youthful bemusement, but now my adult curiosity was more seriously piqued. I wondered what had driven his odd preoccupation. Why had an undistinguished and modestly educated Russian Jew become so fixated with a lofty British man at the helm of a colonial university?

5 | Living with lack

My grandfather's presence did not light up a room. He was rather stiff, entirely awkward in the presence of strangers, and usually showed little interest in the lives of those he had already met. He had never mastered the art of conversation and the habits of social etiquette.

Thinking back, I suspect he knew that others did not take to him, and he reacted brusquely, his defences up; a man anticipating social alienation and acting to produce it.

To his grandchildren, Maurice was warm in the only way he knew how. Smiling, eyes lit up, lines of affection creasing his face. He enjoyed being in our presence. But he had no idea how to move on from there: unable to make child-friendly conversation, incapable of play. I don't recall ever seeing him throw a ball, run or hide. He never read us any books, never asked to see anything we had drawn or built. Maurice's way was to detach, just sitting and watching. A small man, taking up little space in a room with boisterous others, he would sit with his head tilted to the side, his wide mouth on the brink of a smile as the grandchildren criss-crossed his field of vision; otherwise, his expression was more impassive, on the verge of a frown, revealing little. As he sat there, it would have been just as unthinkable for us children to jump into his lap as it was for him to offer us a hug, even a stray touch or stroke of the hair. His body was a fort, walled and guarded; spontaneous incursions were impossible.

My grandmother Erna was a lot warmer, adoring in fact. He grimaced, she beamed. A woman eager to please, sometimes overly so, she radiated joy in the presence of her only son, the daughter-in-law she loved as a daughter, and four grandchildren. A skilled baker, and irrepressibly generous, Erna invariably

Maurice Posel. Author's collection.

arrived at our house laden with tarts and biscuits, made – she would say – the Austrian way. It thrilled her that we devoured them with glee, as if this was a delighted affirmation of her: the grandmother who made us light up.

She asked about others, disinclined to speak about herself. Still, even to us children, it was clear that she relished whatever attention we were willing to give her. Ever keen to participate in whatever ways she could, she gave as much of her time and enthusiasm as we were willing to take. I suspect she longed for more, a woman quietly in need.

LIVING WITH LACK

Erna Posel. Author's collection.

Maurice's presence unsettled her. He seemed to diminish her energy, as she anxiously monitored him, watching herself, watching him, watching herself watching him, because he disapproved of much of what she said and did. We children preferred the days when our other grandparents came to tea; there was less tension in the air.

It went without saying – at least to us children – that our two sets of grandparents would never arrive on the same day. These were two separate sides of the family; seldom did their lines cross. We knew that our other grandparents warmed to Erna. They admired her tenacity and forbearance, and her unmistakable devotion to her son, daughter-in-law and grandchildren. It was clear that they felt sorry for her too, married to a man whom they found entirely unappealing. It was not as if their own marriage glowed; it created its own climate of cold and wind. But to us children, the differences and barriers were self-evident.

My mother's parents were more stylish, more sophisticated, more worldly. They had a regular social life, playing bridge and *klaberjass*,[4] with weekend tennis games, and friends over for dinner. Sometimes they went on cruises overseas and sent us postcards from exotic places.

Maurice eschewed all such things. We children pitied Erna. Her horizons were so limited, living with a man who felt alarm at the prospect of a big wide world out there. I suspect we were also a bit ashamed of him, the grandfather who we knew lived a life of lack.

6 | A structure of life

As I grew older, a picture of my grandfather Maurice took shape in my mind, put together from bits and pieces of what I picked up about him, partly through my experience and partly in the back and forth of family conversations.

It was obvious that Maurice was a man of sober habits and rigorous routine. Punctual and punctilious, he ensured that each day had a well-defined and largely unwavering rhythm. For much of his working life, Maurice contracted his services as a shipping clerk and did his work from home. Breakfast at seven, tea at eleven, lunch at one, tea at four, supper at six, early to bed. I remember him as obsessively tidy, and as meticulous about his dress as his daily ablutions. His nails were perfectly manicured, his hair kept neat and short, and his shirts – always white – were sternly ironed.

Maurice insisted on a household defined by norms of moderation and temperance – which he took as the basis of the Victorian propriety to which he aspired. Extravagances or indulgences were not permitted, not for him, nor for his wife and child. This was partly a reflection of his strained finances, but also a firm personal predilection. It seeped into all his personal habits – such as the food he liked to eat (bland, without unnecessary condiments) and his disdain for hot baths as an undesirable excess. I recall listening incredulously to Erna tell us grandchildren that when my father was a child, she had to use a thermometer to ensure the precisely specified temperature of his bathwater.

Maurice was an ardent anglophile, drawing inspiration from (his idea of) Great Britain and (his interpretation of) quintessentially British ways and values. He spoke only English, with great relish for the kind of circumlocution that would display his vocabulary and command of English grammar. It was a contrived pomposity that he wielded against his Austro-Hungarian-born wife Erna, who never lost her Germanic accent and whose proficiency in English was more hesitant. Erna also spoke a bit of Yiddish, which Maurice never did, despite this having been his parents' first language and the language of his childhood home.

It was Maurice's handwriting – a preposterous Victorian flourish – that demonstrated his infatuation with Great Britain most vividly. I recall watching him dip his treasured fountain pen into his ink well, blotting paper to hand, and then slowly and deliberately take to the page, with careful upward sweeps and downward turns. With his tongue slipping out of the corner of his mouth, a sign of his intense concentration, his process of writing was an act of love.

Maurice cultivated a Victorian stiff upper lip too. Much like other advocates of militant emotional control, this did not prevent an aggressive streak that was not entirely under wraps. The targets of his anger may have been strangers who clumsily nudged him on the pavement, or customers who failed to appreciate his services fully. And Maurice was as likely to unleash his temper at home. He would lash out at Erna – a verbal, not a physical assault; there was some measure of restraint – even if for trivial transgressions of his orderly scheme of things. Perhaps she came home a few minutes late to prepare his tea at exactly four pm (not something he would ever have considered doing himself), or she might have failed to follow his instructions exactly. He was also a strict and punitive father, particularly when it came to my father's schoolwork and athletic performance. Unless excellent at all times, his son Karl had to endure Maurice's raging disappointment.

Quick to take offence and unlikely to let it go, Maurice did not breathe easily in the world.

7 | The *farribel*

By the mid-1970s, I was a student at the University of the Witwatersrand, living in Johannesburg, leaving my parents and three siblings in Westville, close to Durban. I visited my grandparents in their apartment in the modestly middle-class suburb of Yeoville, usually for afternoon tea. The heavy wooden dining table, squashed into the entrance hall, was always already laid with Erna's treasured Austrian porcelain tea cups, a plate of butter biscuits and a jam tart (which Erna had baked at the crack of dawn), covered in white muslin cloths with crocheted edges, to keep the flies away.

To be honest, I went to see her, but Maurice was always there – and in the way, I felt, preventing more open conversations with her. He was unfailingly polite, and warm – in his way. But talk was stiff and barren, with a predictable litany: the weather, bits of 'news' about my family back home, whether I was doing well in my studies, then maybe some exchange about the traffic noise outside.

I never asked him any personal questions, because then I wasn't interested. For me, these were heady days of student awakenings. After the political quiescence of the late 1960s, the first waves of political protest were rising, taking university students like me into unfamiliar waters: a more urgent sense of injustice than I had grown up with, an intense discomfort with the racial order of things and searching for ways of articulating that. Of all my extended family members, Maurice was the most obvious instance of the problem: an embarrassingly reactionary White South African, who resented all 'trouble-makers' and insisted that Black people – *shwartzes*, to use the derogatory Yiddish term of the time – should know their place, very much below his. It was another reason to pull away from him, and to leave him in that dark space of absence and lack.

In my family circles, there was never any talk of Maurice's background, nor of his extended family – other than one story that was told and retold, in his absence. It concerned his feud – a *farribel*, to give it its Yiddish name – with his first cousin, and its harsh and immutable repercussions.

It went like this. Maurice's uncle had one son, Max Posel, who became a well-respected physician in Johannesburg. And he married into social eminence, taking Gertrude Gavronsky – daughter of an affluent businessman, and sister of Helen, soon to be Suzman and later a prominent politician – as his wife. But Max inflicted a terrible injustice on Maurice that would relegate him to the lower reaches of Jewish society. Neither Maurice's nor Max's fathers could afford to send their sons to university. The understanding between these two brothers was that after Maurice matriculated, he would work to pay for Max's years at medical school, and then Max would reciprocate so that Maurice would have his turn at university. Maurice dutifully obliged, but the dastardly Max reneged on the deal, and Maurice never got to university. Deeply wounded and angry, Maurice then wanted nothing to do with anyone and everyone associated with his uncle's side of the family.

In my experience – having grown up and lived most of my life in South Africa – many, maybe most, South African Jewish families have *farribels*: stories of heartfelt grudges preserved and nurtured in the telling and retelling, passed down from one generation to the next. To have and to hold, for better and for worse. These are tales of hurt and indignation, of family or community members falling out, rifts with fellow Jews that have never healed, the scars of wounds that injured the muscles of kin or broke the bones of connection altogether. At their most potent, *farribels* are stories forged through trauma.

The phenomenon is not unique to Jews, of course. But Jews have their own special attachment to it; in South Africa, so much so that it has its own Yiddish name. And there's a joke that makes the point. *What's the Jewish definition of Alzheimer's? To forget everything except the farribel.* Most versions of Yiddish elsewhere in the Jewish diaspora from Eastern Europe don't have the word, perhaps because it's associated specifically with Lithuanian Yiddish, dominant among the South African immigrants from the East. What it refers to, however, is ubiquitously familiar.

A *farribel* can be a small or large part of a family's emotional inheritance. The grievances – always involving other Jews – will vary. Perhaps not having received an invitation to a wedding, or bearing the brunt of a rude remark; feeling diminished by another's act of snobbery or social rejection. More often than not, a *farribel* is stoked by issues of money, status or betrayal – or, most painfully, a combination of all three. A loan never repaid, a lack of financial support or reciprocity during hard times from one who could afford it; feeling depleted or diminished by someone else's successes; feeling let down, undermined or betrayed by supposedly loyal or close others; feeling unseen or unrecognised by others who should know better. In an intensely status-conscious community, with a throbbing drive for upward mobility, such injuries would be keenly felt.

Farribels are often vague, the details of exactly what went wrong and what one family member or fellow Jew holds against another remaining opaque. Asking for clarity may feel inappropriate, as if the strength of feeling and its resilience over time are explanation enough. Or it may be that no one knows more than what is already told. Either way, imprecision doesn't get in the way of the conviction that an offence was committed sufficient to sustain rifts and animosities over many generations.

Maurice's *farribel* involved all of the big three – money, status and betrayal. It captured his life, framing his shame at what he never became. He felt bereft at his failures to achieve success or prominence, and laid the blame squarely at Max's door, in having deprived him of the opportunity to go to university.

He, Erna and my father Karl – their only child – were stuck in a small apartment that was cramped and dank. He never owned a car, and remained a lowly accounting clerk, on the edge of financial hardship through much of his life. It was a life of enduring constraint and uncomfortable constriction.

In the national scheme of things, his situation, though sparse, was not that bad. This was apartheid South Africa, in which living spaces and job opportunities were racially assigned. Maurice's pinched dwelling sprawled in comparison to the Black equivalent; he lived in a place reserved for Whites only. The clerical job that embarrassed him, as he yearned for greater accomplishment, was out of the reach of almost all Black people in those times. But Maurice looked up, not down; that's what kept him small and bitter.

He was not an especially materialistic man: he did not aspire to great wealth or an abundance of things. It was recognition and status that he craved, particularly among fellow Jews. Yet this was not disconnected from his lack of means. He felt deeply wounded at being unable to afford the cost of a reserved seat, marked with his name, in the synagogue that he attended regularly, every Friday night and Saturday morning. In his mind's eye, ever envious, he never stopped seeing Max, by contrast, enjoying fame and fortune, revelling in the generous spaces of a large suburban mansion, becoming a big *macha* – a man of note – in the Jewish community, comfortably affording a seat in the biggest synagogue in town. And married to the sister of Helen Suzman, who became the only woman in parliament and a well-known public figure. Maurice despised her liberal politics, but took grudging note of her professional stature and the prominence it conferred on her and her family in Jewish circles.

My father and mother repeated the story of the *farribel* to us children, and we in turn absorbed the mix of outrage and shame that came with it. It seemed to explain the financial austerity in our grandparents' lives, and why Maurice had achieved so little; also, why his extended family was a blank, why we had no contact with any aunts, uncles or cousins related to him; why we didn't even know who they were or where they lived; why there were no family gatherings, weddings or bar mitzvahs, none of the exuberance of extended family, on Maurice's side; why absence was the biggest presence in his life.

In retrospect, it was always an abbreviated narrative, with many gaps. Did Max not have any siblings, or other relatives, who could have contributed to his education? Why was this Maurice's responsibility alone? Were there no other means to provide for Maurice's studies other than through Max's reciprocity? But these questions were never asked; the *farribel* seemed fully formed and evidence enough.

So complete was the ostracism produced by the *farribel* that it took decades of adulthood and an exhibition in the Gertrude Posel Gallery at the University of the Witwatersrand in 1994 for me to meet Max's ex-wife Gertrude (by then, they were long divorced). A colleague Hilton Judin had invited Susan Parnell and me – all academics at that university – to work with him on an exhibition of original archival documents, to depict how Johannesburg's inner city had been remade, beginning in the 1930s, from what was regarded as a dirty, blackened slum to a zone of clean, respectable Whiteness. During one of many archival forays, we alighted upon a scrap of paper, its contents a handwritten listing of tenants living in part of that slum, noting the rentals paid or defaulted. The document was headed 'Posel's Yard'.

I remember my astonishment – this was the first time I had found any trace of a Posel preserved in the official archival record – and my nauseous disquiet at what the document signified. At that stage, I had no idea which Posel this was, or how he had become a rack-renting slumlord. But I was not aware of other Posel families in the country, so I had to assume that this seemingly unsavoury individual was linked to me in some way or other.

The document was duly included in the exhibition, in the gallery also bearing the Posel name – for me, a pithy serendipity. I had never met Gertrude before, but knew that she had been married to Max, and that her fulsome contributions to the university's art collection had been acknowledged with a gallery established in her name. Gertrude attended the opening of the exhibition, which presented me with the opportunity to meet her.

I went over to her and introduced myself. She was stylishly dressed and struck a confident, no-nonsense pose. I felt a flicker of doubt, suddenly uncomfortable in my more informal garb and lack of poise. Like me, Maurice, I thought, would surely have found her intimidating. We exchanged a few niceties, sufficient for me to ask her to walk with me to the document that somehow implicated us both. She took one look at it, and then exclaimed, with vehement distaste, 'All Posel men are dogs!' Then she strode off, and no further conversation ensued. I was left standing, wondering what had produced such undiscriminating scorn.

Being a Posel – previously of no historical consequence whatsoever – was suddenly more engaging. There I was, in the Posel Gallery, a Posel woman by birth, stunned by a Posel woman by marriage abruptly turning away, and both puzzled and intrigued by her blistering excoriation of Posel manhood. Who were these men, where did they come from, were they really that bad? But this was a fleeting curiosity; at that time I was not inclined to pursue it.

As it turns out, the accusation at the heart of Maurice's *farribel* was specious. In the sparse family canon, here was a monumental fabrication, a myth of suffering and injury. But it would take many more years for me to realise that – beginning with my father's death in 2012 and the emergence of the ticket.

8 | The ticket

My father Karl's death, in 2012, took me by surprise. He had been living alone in a house in Kloof, outside Durban, with his beloved Maltese poodle. We spoke every week, in short, somewhat uncomfortable conversations. He would relay the absence of any activity in his solitary life – 'peace and quiet', he would say, to shut down any further exchange on the subject. I would give a very brief update on each of my children and my husband and reassure him that all was well with me.

He had been ailing for many years – mainly the result of invasive skin carcinomas that had not been excised. Karl refused to get any medical help; he did not trust doctors, he would say. But I hadn't realised that he was in any mortal danger.

We think he died peacefully and quickly. He had been watching TV and eating chocolate, a piece of which was still in his mouth when he passed away. It was likely a stroke or heart attack.

After the funeral, my siblings and I steeled ourselves for the challenge of clearing out his house. Over decades, he had accumulated dusty mounds of paper on every available surface. After a long academic career as an engineer and applied mathematician, he had continued researching and writing into his retirement, building up this voluminous and untamed paper trail: reams of paper photocopies of every academic article he had written, reviews of the various books he had written, newspaper columns and letters to editors he had penned, articles of financial and scientific interest, other texts that had struck some sort of chord. There was no order in the assemblages, no system in their storage, just a chaotic jumble.

Confronted by these many indeterminate piles, my brothers suggested we simply gather the paper in garbage bags and throw it away. But I was reluctant. I am a historian, after all, and I had a vague, lingering hope that I would discover a relic or two of my father's past, hidden somewhere in the mess. I knew so little about his side of the family; maybe I would find a clue, a trace, that would relieve some of its dogged darkness.

I began sifting through the sheets of paper, one by one. The faint smell of the years of dust disturbed by my movements seeped into the room. I washed my hands repeatedly. The painstaking process of dismantling the piles seemed endless. But then, after a few fruitless hours, there was indeed a moment of revelation. Lo and behold, one of the piles magically yielded a ticket, for passage by sea from Southampton to Cape Town, leaving on 7 June 1902.

Five passengers were listed: Mrs B. Posel, aged forty-four, travelling with four children, aged eight, seven, six and five. They were booked to travel steerage class on the steamship *The Briton*, one of the Union Castle liners. Pinned to the ticket was a flimsier sheet of paper, an official permit, issued by the British Consul in Libau (on the Baltic Sea), granting Mrs Posel and her children admission to the Cape Colony on the grounds that her husband was already there, living in Longmarket Street in Cape Town.

The circumstances of this discovery astounded me. There was no envelope or folder clothing the ticket and permit, just the naked documents. How did they get into the inauspicious pile? The ticket – the sturdier of the two pieces of paper – was well preserved, considering its age, which suggested that a succession of custodians had taken meticulous care of it, since 1902. Who had been so invested in its conservation? And why?

On this side of the family, almost no photographs, and no letters or diaries had been treasured and passed down. There was nothing to convey anything at all about Maurice's ancestry, nor his relationships with any members of his family; just the fact of that nothingness, which made its own statement. My father had had no memorabilia from Maurice's side of the family: no artefacts, big or small, no gifts given and retained, to pass on. His relationship with Maurice had been embattled from childhood onwards. Even if there had been anything resembling a family archive – which I doubt – Karl would have likely been uninterested and disinclined to keep it alive.

Yet here was a ticket, back to back with an official permit opening the door to a life in the Cape Colony of old, that had been deemed worthy of retention for more than a century – and then ending up precariously submerged in a dusty heap on the cusp of disappearance. A token of a past that had long ceased to live but refused to die altogether.

Now it was in my possession and immediately threw a faint light on that hidden past. I had known that Maurice's parents were Jews who had come from somewhere in Eastern Europe – just that. I had been told nothing about the size or circumstances of his family, nor when and why they came to South Africa. Now, I suddenly knew that Maurice had had at least three siblings (he had never acknowledged the existence of more than one). I knew when his mother had arrived in the country, and that her husband was already living in Longmarket Street in Cape Town. It wasn't much, just the tiniest beginnings of a story completely untold.

9 | Two more fragments

Not long after the ticket presented itself, Erna's old Austro-Hungarian passport emerged, just as inauspiciously, from the same pile. Inserted into it were two more surprises, carefully stowed.

The first was a notice in the Deaths column of a newspaper in 1928.

> POSEL – Barnard, on 28 April, at Cape Town, beloved husband of Betsy and father of Sarah, Gershon, Leah and Mannie. Deeply mourned. M.H.D.S.R.I.P

The year 1928 was handwritten underneath, in Maurice's unmistakable script.

I assumed that Mannie was Maurice; it sounded suitably ethnic. Gershon, Sarah and Leah sounded a similar note. But Barnard? Betsy? I chuckled at the waspish anglicisation of what I knew would have to have been Yiddish names. We know that the bureaucrats who opened the gates to the colonial compound sometimes reassigned and invented names that sounded less foreign, more English. Was this what had happened here? Or was the renaming an act of assimilation on Maurice's parents' part, to designate how they wished to be seen by others – and, through endless repetition, with their own eyes too? Or was this Maurice's doing, a declaration of sorts of his parents' colonial propriety?

Then I read the prayers. Two of them, handwritten, on small pieces of paper, in Maurice's signature swirl.

> Almighty and merciful father.
> I beseech Thee, help me in my

business, guard me, guide me,
put wisdom into me.
Amen and Amen.

<u>A nightly prayer</u>
Almighty and merciful father! I
humbly beseech Thee help us.
Help Erna, help Chookie,[5] and help
myself.
Help us to walk in the paths of right-
eousness, give us our daily bread,
keep our enemies away from us,
keep us free from disease. I again
beseech thee. Amen and Amen.

I felt I had stumbled into Maurice's bedroom. There he was, undressed and exposed, vulnerable and insecure, beseeching his God for help and support in a hostile world beyond those walls. A small man steeped in his faith, crying out in fear. I felt a surge of sadness; I hadn't known how very sorely beleaguered he had felt.

But why was I given that unexpected access? Maurice had died before Erna, so it must have been she who had decided to keep these little texts and pass them on to my father, intent on their preservation. Hers had been a trying, unfulfilling marriage; it had bequeathed no mementoes of happy occasions or meaningful connections. She had chosen these prayers as the only residue of her life with Maurice to leave for future generations. What message was she sending?

10 | Many lives are possible

Before the ticket presented itself to me, as if a cryptic parting gift from my father, I had had little interest in delving into Maurice's life, nor that of his extended family. The ticket and the permit attached – a totem of sorts – changed that, and compelled me to know more. Suddenly, there were the beginnings of a story to tell. Maurice, a young child, all of five years old, was leaving home forever, taking to the seas with three siblings and their mother. Sailing towards a father, already far away.

I had never previously imagined my grandfather as a child, nor given any thought to the conditions under which he had grown up. I couldn't have seen him with an impish skip in his step, or running free with the curiosity to explore. But the ticket opened an entirely new vista. I glimpsed Maurice for the first time as an innocent, not yet fully formed. Arriving in a new and strange place, his future would have been indeterminate; his life could have taken many different turns.

On that ship in 1902, Mrs Posel and her children were journeying into a modernising world churning with change. Historian Christopher Bayly calls it 'the great acceleration':[6] more people, money and things were criss-crossing the globe, faster than ever before.

Experiences of time and place changed, as the pace and scope of travel – on railways and steamships, and then motor cars – broke the barriers of the more stolid past. The exhilaration of speed and motion shaped the zeitgeist of the times, signs of a new world in progress. And as the heaving capitalist machine cranked up its intensity, and the greed of empires grew, markets heated up, near and far. The world grew smaller in its connectedness, and larger in its possibilities.

And yet, as a sense of connection accelerated, so too did anxieties about borders and boundaries. Who belonged where, at whose behest and under what conditions, would become more vexed and contested. Nationalisms grew more vigorous, and divisive. Social Darwinism – a notoriously useful accompaniment to the project of imperial conquest – invented a purportedly scientific classification of human variability. It produced a hierarchy of races, with White Europeans at the apex of civilisation and intelligence; the darker the skin, the more inferior the mind, supposedly. The twentieth century would become obsessed with – and wounded by – the differences that race made. Jews would become both victims and beneficiaries of that obsession.

Jews had been on the move for centuries – peripatetic people, to be sure – be it to escape persecution, advance their trade, or pursue an elusive sense of belonging somewhere else. In many Christian depictions, the archetypal Wandering Jew is a stranger, rootless and cosmopolitan. These restless migrations would produce networks and linkages between disparate communities long before the late nineteenth century. But the modern era would trigger the largest movement of Jews ever, a tumultuous upheaval for those who were leaving and for the Jews who would receive them. From 1881 to 1914, over two and a half million would migrate from all over the Russian Empire and Eastern Europe at large, to various destinations around the globe. Proportionately more Jews were on the move during these years than any other ethnic or national group in the world.

Maurice's story would have to capture how his prospects took shape amidst all this turbulence, and how he made his own way from one version of the world to another. As I see it; from where I stand.

11 | Ordinary stories

Writer Njabulo Ndebele exhorts us South Africans to look beyond the flaming spectacles of our history – the political conflagrations, often violent, ignited by the brutality of apartheid – and to delve into the minutiae of ordinary lives.[7] The small subplots of the everyday unfold in the crevices of the bigger drama, and in there many lives are possible. Modest and motley, these are the quieter stories of most of us – no less engaging or complex for being ordinary.

The same could be said about how South Africa's Jewish history has been remembered and told. Typically, it's spectacles of suffering and its redemption that loom large and dominate attention, in dramas of resilience and accomplishment against often formidable odds. Less visible are the marginals and the misfits, the little people who in the big scheme of things have no history, at least nothing of any apparent significance. All the more so if these lives tell stories of mediocrity or failure: the envious, diminished, shameful ordinary, rather than the stoically robust, incrementally triumphant, or tenaciously cheerful ordinary.

It's mainly Maurice's life, entirely on the margins, that I'm intent on retrieving. This has puzzled others in my family: why him? they have asked, incredulously; he was so embittered, so much at odds with the world. It's exactly these qualities that have drawn me to Maurice's story: as the marks of a man who did not make what he had hoped of himself and who never recovered from the ignominy of that, acutely aware of the Jewish preoccupation with achievement. A man surely not unlike many other Jewish immigrants who have, for that reason, faded into historical insignificance.

The task is made difficult, however, by Maurice's ephemeral trace: the lack of letters, diaries or other family memorabilia, and a minimal archival imprint. I have to make do with fragments. Where there is bulk, it may be stuffed with silence; where there is form, it sometimes has more shadow than light.

My sense of how he became the man he was takes shape intermittently then, and partly in counterpoint, contrasted and connected to others: his parents and grandparents, the few I can trace in his extended family, as well as many unrelated, unknown others who embarked on similar journeys from the East, into alien territory. Maurice's parents, and then Maurice himself, come into view partly through the options they discounted, the choices that eluded them, the people they could not have become.

Confronted by a citadel of power and privilege, the Eastern European Jews who arrived in South Africa from the late nineteenth century took different routes in. Some stayed low and struggled to breathe in the strange colonial air. Others flourished, either playing proudly by the rules, or taking a more experimental approach, pushing boundaries and taking risks, as their prospects rose and fell. Some were so offended by the system they encountered that they devoted themselves to the fighting against it. These were variegated lives, never a homogenous mass. Maurice was just one among the ordinary, insignificant many, moving in and out of focus.

12 | The myth of Jewish exceptionalism

All the Jews heading to South Africa did not slip into the country unnoticed. The impact of their immigration would be prominent, and decisive at times. In the national population at large, Jews were never more than a small minority (peaking at just short of five per cent of the White population), but one that was disproportionately conspicuous.

Initially, Jews made their presence felt most strongly at the economic frontier. Several became leading pioneers, among the country's richest and most entrepreneurial. In the early days of industrialisation, with gold-mining in the driving seat, Jews were in the financial vanguard, pouring money in and taking even more out. Lionel Phillips, Otto Beit, Barney Barnato and Sammy Marks were among the mining magnates who helped set the course for the country's industrial development, vexed as it was. Others made their mark as commercial innovators, perhaps none as formatively as Isidore Schlesinger, who set up early insurance and entertainment businesses – including the first radio and film studios – that dominated these sectors for decades. Gustav Ackerman and Morris Mauerberger were among those who would set up the first giant retail food enterprises, with many others following suit.

Jews also stood out in the professions, particularly medicine and law. By the late 1920s, 'nearly forty percent of graduands and diplomates at the University of the Witwatersrand were Jewish ... At the University of Cape Town, Jews often made up more than twenty percent of the graduating classes in arts, law and medicine.'[8] At the time, Jews comprised a little over four per cent of the country's White population at large.[9] The trend towards professionalisation accelerated, so that by 1960 around twenty per cent of the economically active Jewish population were professionals. Around twenty-three per cent of doctors in general practice were Jewish; the proportion of specialists was higher, at around thirty-three per cent.[10]

For those of us looking back on that history, the disproportion of these accomplishments has made it discomforting to write the Jews into the wider story of South Africa from the late nineteenth century. It risks reanimating the familiar antisemitic tropes that circulated in the Western world in those times and that have never entirely disappeared. I'm thinking, for example, of the supposed Jewish conspiracy to seize control and steer the course of history in line with selfish Jewish interests. And then there's one or other version of the alleged obsession with making money above all else, on the part of all Jews, be they lowly or more elevated, professional or not.

One response for the writer is to turn away, disconcerted and unsettled. Some evidence of that strategy lies, perhaps, in the relatively scant scholarly history of Jewish immigration to these parts. What there is has been written almost entirely by Jewish authors, and largely as an ethnic story written for and by insiders. And even then, there are chunks of that history that haven't been opened up.

Another response has been a redemptive writing-back to antisemitic prejudices, affirming Jewish achievements to the fullest. Typically this is a triumphalist narrative of Jewish advance in this country: a series of rags-to-riches stories, overcoming adversity, attaining extraordinary successes – as if a characteristically Jewish thing. A myth of Jewish exceptionalism became a strongly held belief, a motivating tenet of communal identity.

This myth may have been comforting, but it is also inaccurate and misleading. Alongside the internally reassuring – if externally uncomfortable – feature of sometimes extraordinary Jewish attainment, the majority of the Jewish population remained middling to mediocre, neither more nor less successful than others who had put down roots here.

It must be possible to hold both facets of the immigration narrative in the frame. If anything, the ordinary mass makes the triumphant minority all the more striking, but not then as a characteristically or uniquely Jewish phenomenon. Some Jews did exceedingly well; most did not. The mix requires an explanation that extends beyond the fact of Jewishness.

Part Two

13 | Shtetl

It didn't take me long to discover that Maurice and his family had come from the shtetl of Pumpian, as it was known in Yiddish (Pumpenai, in Lithuanian), in the north-east of what is now Lithuania.

When I started out in pursuit of Maurice's life, I knew nothing about shtetls. Still, I had naively made the assumption – perhaps like many Western Jews with Eastern European roots – that most of the Jews who emigrated from the Russian Empire came from shtetls: as if this was the archetypal, authentic, beginning.

I had absorbed the romance of the shtetl. Imagine a small market town, happily huddled, even as the cold wind blows. It's untainted by the outside; a place where all Jews are believers, 'steeped in piety and poverty';[11] where everyone speaks Yiddish; where traditions of old are lovingly preserved, even if they are mocked and sabotaged sometimes; where the buildings are ramshackle, but communal life is sturdy and inclusive, centred in the synagogue; where most of the men devote themselves to religious study, while the women shrewdly navigate the marketplace, making a living, helping each other out.

I know now that this is a shtetl of the mind, crafted in the chit-chat about family origins among Jews who hailed from those parts. It's a fiction that grew from the nostalgic stories that the emigrants told of what they had left behind, giving comfort in the aftermath of the dislocation of long journeys and foreign destinations – unchallenged by the irony that it was life in the shtetl that the emigrants were fleeing. And then, for subsequent generations, the fictional shtetl came alive in books, theatrical productions and musicals. Historian Markus Krah writes of the 'almost obsessive preoccupation of American Jews with the East European Past', that was 'evoked, retold, romanticized, in works of fiction and memoirs, sermons and political pamphlets'.[12] An idea of the shtetl was distilled as if the spiritual and cultural essence of the old life in the Russian homeland.

The symbolic shtetl marked an origin, a point from which to measure the social and emotional distance travelled in reaching the West. Typically, this was depicted as a progression from poverty to prosperity, and from abjection to dignity. In the collective Western Jewish imagination, the Russian overlords had condemned their Jewish subjects to unrelenting deprivation and hardship; the shtetl was uniformly poor and downtrodden. It was the West – and the USA in particular – that opened doors to abundance and success. 'Tradition' – the cultural mainstay of everyday life in this shtetl – was static, frozen in time. The journey Westwards would heat it up, making Jews modern for the first time.

The reality, I discovered, was different. Shtetl life was far more fluid and fractious than in the idealised imaginings. Real shtetls spanned the gamut of prosperity and poverty, and the fires of cultural and social change had ignited within.

14 | Prospects in the Pale of Settlement

The lot of Russian Jews was certainly confined and constrained. From the early nineteenth century, almost all Jews within the Russian Empire were limited to an area known as the Pale[13] of Settlement. This included all of what is now Lithuania, Belarus, Moldova, much of Ukraine, eastern and central Poland, and some of Latvia. Approximately ninety-five per cent of the Jews in Russia – nearly half of the world's Jews – lived there.[14]

The Pale was not only a means of territorial segregation; it was also the site of some onerous restrictions placed on Jewish economic life. Initially, Jews were prohibited from settling in some of the larger cities in the Pale, as well as in agricultural communities in villages. Most had to put down roots in the small towns – the advent of what would become known as the shtetls – where the men would primarily become artisans, shopkeepers and merchants, if not devoted full-time to religious study.

As the nineteenth century wore on, economic life in the Pale diversified. A Jewish population developed in larger towns and cities – such as Vilnius (Lithuania), Minsk (Belarus), Riga (Latvia) and Odessa (Ukraine) – which offered a wider range of economic options than the shtetls. A few Jews became financiers and bankers; some established flourishing trades, even as the majority eked out a more precarious living. In the shtetls, too, economic prospects varied. Many struggled in menial occupations; others did better, some dramatically so.

Sharp inequality was the yield of economically good times. The fifty years between the 1790s and the 1840s, writes historian Yohanan Petrovsky-Shtern, were the 'golden age' of the shtetls, which shone with 'prosperity and stability, economic and cultural opportunity'.[15] The small size of these towns belied the

Map of the Pale of Settlement. Redrawn by Janet Alexander.

reach of their markets. Entrepreneurial shtetl Jews had traded across a surprisingly wide canvas, local and international; above and below board.[16] The most successful among them had crossed the border of the Russian Empire regularly, bringing back a miscellany of whatever they could imagine as 'marketable merchandise'.[17]

By the mid-nineteenth century, in most shtetls a small stratum of wealthy merchants and property owners sat atop the social ladder, looking down upon the lesser shopkeepers and artisans below them, with the water carriers and other manual labourers relegated to the bottom, above the vagrants and beggars.

By the end of the nineteenth century, however, living conditions in the Pale had taken a dramatic turn for the worse. Tsar Alexander II, who ascended to power in 1855, had relaxed some of the existing restrictions, allowing Jews with 'useful' skills to leave the Pale for other parts of the Russian Empire. But this did not last. After Alexander II's assassination in 1881 – falsely blamed on revolutionary Jews – his son, who was far more aggressive and punitive, took over. The notorious May Laws reinscribed the borders and strictures of the Pale with renewed vengeance. The regime was now intent on limiting Jewish commercial successes and capturing sources of wealth contained within the Pale.

As antisemitic anger escalated, violence surged, with particular vehemence in the pogroms of 1881 to 1884, centred around Kiev and Odessa. The economic pressures of a constricted Pale worsened too. Although the Pale was a large chunk of land, the Jewish concentrations there would become increasingly overcrowded as the population ballooned, and the economic competition between those within its borders intensified.

As the twentieth century beckoned, the number of Jews unable to secure fixed employment or income swelled, as did the ranks of the destitute, struggling to survive on meagre contributions from Jewish charities.[18] And the creamy layer – the more prosperous Jews at the top of the darkening brew – had become thinner. The search for more promising economic prospects elsewhere would be one of the main drivers of emigration.

15 | Schisms and fault-lines

There were other divides and differences too; even the smallest shtetl was a fractious place. Ideological schisms criss-crossed the fissures of class and social status, unsettling the old rhythms of traditional religious life. Argument and conflict were hallmarks of the times, as Jews grappled with the challenges of modernisation that the nineteenth century threw at them.

The first powerful ruptures were triggered by the *Hasidic* movement which gathered momentum in Eastern Europe from the mid-eighteenth century. Its mysticism and emphasis on inner religious ecstasy challenged Orthodox versions of Jewish spirituality and religious leadership. *Hasidism* was less powerful in Lithuania than in other parts of the Pale, but Pumpian was one among other Lithuanian shtetls that had a *Hasidic* synagogue, of the Lubavitch variety.[19]

The *misnagdim* were Orthodox Jews who spoke out in defence of their traditional versions of the faith, opposed both to the ways of the *Hasids* and the tenets of the *Haskalah*. The *Haskalah* – the so-called Jewish Enlightenment – had originated in Germany in the mid-eighteenth century, then spread to Eastern Europe from the early nineteenth century, taking various forms, all vehemently opposed to both *Hasidism* and the Orthodox traditions. Its proponents – the *maskilim* – urged a process of spiritual and cultural renewal, moving away from traditional modes of Jewish education, embracing Hebrew rather than Yiddish, and enabling more freedom in contracting marriage.[20] In Lithuania, the *Musar* movement offered yet another way of life, rejecting the modernising force of the *Haskalah*, and creating its own spiritual enclaves, secluded from the mainstream of shtetl orthodoxy.

All this philosophical and spiritual turbulence created political waves too. From the late nineteenth century, communist and Zionist ideals, drawing on precepts of the *Haskalah*, set religious preoccupations aside and offered secular, modern options for radically new futures – differently though, and sometimes at odds with each other. From the early 1880s, the *Chovevei Zion* (Lovers of Zion) movement took root across the Pale, more than a decade before Theodor Herzl published what would become his defining Zionist tract, *Judenstaat*. And socialist ideas flourished among Jewish workers as well as intellectuals, most influentially in the *Yiddisher Arbeter Bund* (General Jewish Workers' Union), as the century drew to a close.[21]

'*Hasidic* sects, *misnagdim*, Communists, Jewish socialists, and Zionists of various orientations all inhabited the same communities; indeed, they could even be found in the same families',[22] writes historian Nathaniel Deutsch.

The Jewish diaspora from the Pale would be a scattering of people who felt simultaneously connected and divided. There wasn't – and would never be – one version of the Jew replicated all over; no single essential idea of Jewishness. Not in leaving, nor in arriving.

16 | Posels in Pumpian

The shtetl of Pumpian was paltry and nondescript. By the 1880s, its population had peaked at around one thousand five hundred. As in many of the shtetls, Jews were in the majority – about two thirds of Pumpian's people. Residents made their living mainly in trade or artisanship. The Pale was slowly industrialising, but with uneven effects on the shtetls within. Since Pumpian was remote from one of the bigger economic hubs, its prospects plateaued. As its population swelled, their collective opportunities shrank.

I find many Posels in Pumpian, going back at least as far as the mid-eighteenth century. The timing aligns with the advent of Jewish surnames. It was more or less from this time that Jews were pressed by the Russians – intent on surveying and classifying them – to take permanent surnames.[23]

Posel, I discover, was not originally a Jewish surname. From the fifteenth century, there were many Catholics with that name, in France, Spain, Germany and Britain.[24] The name must have moved eastwards after that. The meaning of the word varied in different languages, but in Russian a 'posel' was a messenger or ambassador of some sort, and therefore also an interlocutor with foreign others. Jewish surnames were assigned or chosen. If the latter, there is no way of knowing what appealed to the original Posels in alighting upon this name. I like the idea of border-crossing that it connotes, a person on the move. Perhaps way back, a Posel ancestor went on a mission. But this was not a particularly apt descriptor for the more recent forebears I find.

Jewish genealogy sites reveal to me that several Posels in Pumpian had had large families with elders who had lived long lives – some into their seventies, one or two into their eighties.[25]

A few Posels had moved off to elsewhere in the Pale, but most had stayed in Pumpian, eventually watching their small world explode as the wider world went to war.

One of these elders was Maurice's grandfather, Itsyk, who was born around 1830 and likely died around 1913 (when I lose sight of him in the available archives). He married Chaia-Sora, and they never strayed from Pumpian, along with most of their eleven offspring. Of these, only three would emigrate to South Africa: Maurice's father Bere, Bere's brother Chatzkel (father of Max), and sister Chave, who left for South Africa some years after her brothers, husband in tow.

17 | Posel prospects

My grandfather Maurice's life, as I have mentioned, was abidingly modest. In my memory, money in his and Erna's household was sparse; luxuries were unthinkable. I had imagined, then, that Maurice's family, too, must have had humble origins, enduring the rigours of shtetl poverty. To my surprise, I discovered that this was not the case.

Jewish genealogical archives tell me that Russian efforts to survey and classify the population in the Pale, along with records of the payment of various local taxes, distinguished between three categories of people: the 'well-to-do'; the 'middle class'; and the 'poor'. They didn't offer – or at least, I couldn't find – the amounts of income or other criteria that constituted the dividing lines, so the classifications remain somewhat impressionistic.

In the four generations of Posels preceding Maurice, family patriarchs had made the transition from 'poor', through 'middle class', to 'well-to-do'. Records of tax collection provide one window on these transitions. Jews were required to pay two taxes, the box tax (on kosher meat) and the candle tax (levied on candles used routinely for all Jewish rituals) – both supposedly collected for the purposes of financing local Jewish institutions and services (although these monies were sometimes siphoned off by the Russian authorities for their own use). One way of recognising the poor was through their recorded inability to pay these taxes. Itsyk's grandfather had been among them. By the mid-1800s, however, Itsyk's father was a middle-aged man who could pay both taxes and was duly recorded as 'middle class'. And forty years later, by the early 1890s, Itsyk and two of his brothers had done even better: all were classified as 'well-to-do'.

Itsyk was a tavern-keeper, and by that means had become a property owner too. By the 1890s he had accumulated a little over one thousand rubles in his postal savings account. Establishing the relative value of this amount is difficult; earnings and costs varied a lot between parts of Imperial Russia and within the Pale.[26] Still, from what I have read, Itsyk's savings – while far less than the amounts that wealthy merchants could have achieved – were impressive. A reasonable house would likely have cost around two hundred rubles; six hundred would have provided for an impressively substantial dwelling in any shtetl.[27]

By that time, some of Itsyk's children, too, had proven their economic prowess. His second son Chatzkel must have made Itsyk proud as a 'well-to-do flax trader'. To my surprise, several of Itsyk's daughters seemed to have made their own mark – more modest, but noteworthy. The most enterprising was his second-youngest daughter Rokha. By 1912, she was listed as a 'well-to-do tradeswoman' and a box taxpayer, with nearly five hundred rubles in the bank and a house to her name too. There she lived with three other women, who were most likely some of her sisters. An older sister, Khasse, also a 'tradeswoman', had notched up savings of around one hundred rubles, and the youngest sister, Mikla, had accumulated three hundred rubles in her savings account. These were not large amounts of money, but they showed that these women – then aged forty-two, thirty-six and thirty-three – were independent and resourceful in their own right.

Where, then, was Bere, Maurice's father and Itsyk's oldest son?

Nowhere. I searched in vain for information about his financial standing, but he didn't show up in any of the records as a property owner, nor as having had savings in the bank or as a taxpayer. On the other hand, he was not listed as having failed to pay his taxes. Perhaps the relevant records are missing from the archives, or he just didn't amount to much and remained invisible to the official eye as neither here nor there. Given where Bere ended up in his later life, it could well have been the latter. A son who stayed low, in a family that rose.

18 | Sitting and standing

Even in the smallest shtetl, writes historian Samuel Kassow, gradations of income and status mattered – a great deal, in fact. 'The social differences that divided shtetl Jews were felt everywhere, from the marketplace to the synagogue.'[28]

The synagogue? In the shtetl of the mind, the synagogue, the heart of the community, is a warm and welcoming place, bringing Jews together in the comfort and unity of prayer, all equally at home. Clearly, I had to look again.

The synagogue was first and foremost a community of men; women were relegated to the margins, either upstairs or behind a curtain, hidden from view. Here men were amongst men, but not all the same.

The seating said it all. For centuries already, seating in synagogues had been a contentious matter – not dissimilarly from some of the Christian churches in early Europe and North America.[29] Where you sat revealed much about where you stood outside the synagogue: how important and powerful you were, and how prosperous and successful. The seats were sold, with a sliding scale of cost, in accordance with the prestige of the seat's location. Records of the transactions were kept; these were matters of substance, worth recording for the future. Rabbis were brought in to pronounce upon, and help resolve, disputes about who was entitled to which seat.[30]

The most desirable seats were closest to what Jews call the Ark, which contained the sacred texts of the Torahs, located on the eastern wall of the synagogue. The *balebatim* – those who had worked to achieve social standing and commanded the admiration and respect of others – shared that proximity with the men of *yihus* (standing conferred by family lineage) and the *sheyne*

Yidn (the learned Jews), including the rabbi and others closely associated with the synagogue and its life of religious learning. The lowlier and humbler the worshipper, the further he sat from the Ark – a measure, literally, of his diminished status in the eyes of the congregation.[31]

The synagogue and its community of men was a hierarchical configuration, then. There was no pretence, no effacing the fact that members were of unequal standing. Including – perhaps especially – in the house of their Lord. Everyone knew who had status, and how they had acquired it; and who did not.

Itsyk must have had a seat on the eastern wall. The status of tavern-keepers varied, sometimes judged to be respectable and influential, sometimes a lot less so.[32] On the other hand, Itsyk was a man of substance in other ways. A reasonably prosperous property owner, he had also attained the status of a 'municipal deputy' in the later years of his life (either elected to represent Jewish interests in the (Russian) local government of the area, or an appointed representative of the local urban community in the provincial government in Vilnius).[33] According to Petrovsky-Shtern, attaining this position would have reflected Itsyk's standing in the shtetl as 'a VIP of good standing, respected by both Jews and Christians in Pumpian'[34] – a judgement of him that accreted over several years of his adult life as one of the *balebatim*.

It's likely, too, that flax-trading Chatzkel – Itsyk's 'well-to-do' second son – was sufficiently prosperous to have taken his place alongside his father in one of the prestigious seats on the eastern wall.

I wonder then, did Bere sit in a different part of the synagogue from his father and younger brother? Or could well-to-do

Itsyk prevail and secure Bere's seat next to him, to mitigate some of the shame of the not-well-to-do eldest son? Either way, in the Jewish world of the shtetl, where everyone knew everyone else and the goings-on in their lives, Bere's lack of status would not have escaped anyone's notice. Least of all Bere's.

19 | Taverning

Itsyk had made his money running a tavern: one of the most dynamic and fluid spaces in shtetl life, where local people and strangers mingled, Jews and non-Jews; eating, drinking, talking, ducking and diving, wheeling and dealing, fighting, reconciling.

Every shtetl in the Pale had its taverns and Jews were most likely to run them. From the late eighteenth century, Jews in the shtetls had a near monopoly on the production and sale of alcohol in their towns. They leased their taverns from local feudal landlords and sold the alcohol made from the grains grown on these estates. The lion's share of the profit went to the landlords (who made substantially more money from the taverns than the revenues they extracted from their serfs),[35] but the alcohol trade was brisk enough for the tavern owners, too, to make a reasonable living and sometimes much more so.

It was the landlords who had instituted this arrangement. Selling alcohol was a reliably profitable business and Jews were deemed the most appropriate to do it. Not only did they have reputations for being savvy with sales; only a sober tavern-keeper would run a profitable, orderly tavern and Jews, according to local Christian folklore, were misguided enough to sell alcohol without drinking it. As a Russian proverb put it, 'Jews are fools; they have the vodka and they sell it'.[36]

Beyond the landlords, however, Jewish ownership of the taverns grew controversial. Drunken binges among non-Jewish customers were common and blamed on the Jewish taverners determinedly plying their drinkers with as much alcohol as possible. 'The peasant drinks at the inn, and the Jew does him in' went the lore of the time. The profitable monopoly that the Jewish taverners enjoyed irked the non-Jews, who wanted their turn, while the Russian state too began to covet the profits for itself. In the early nineteenth century, an official ban was imposed on Jewish tavern-keeping, which has led many historians to assume that this brought the occupation to an end for Jews. Not so. Recent research has revealed that Jewish tavern-keeping persisted until late into the nineteenth century,[37] with the consistent support of the profiteering landlords, but out of the official eye.[38] It was only in 1894 that a full-fledged state monopoly on alcohol was enforced.[39]

Itsyk was a case in point. Records show that in 1892, 'well-to-do' Itsyk was still a tavern-keeper – his tavern presumably the source of his prosperity. By 1904, however, his designation had changed; he was then recorded as a 'well-to-do owner of a small store'.

Taverns provided many services, all in one small space. It was here that a passing traveller could take a room for the night, feed his horse, and eat a cooked meal before retiring. In the taverns, shtetl dwellers could revel in folk music and dance, play cards or sometimes billiards (tavern-keepers competed with each other in providing attractions for customers), smoke and drink, strike up conversations and launch into arguments, make business deals and arrange marriages, or hook up with a sex worker plying her trade.

Historian Glenn Dynner has challenged the conventional wisdom that Jews did not drink at all outside religious ceremonies.[40] Still, most of the taverns' drinking customers were non-Jews. Trade in alcohol was briskest, and the tavern at its liveliest, during the fairs that drew crowds to the shtetl from the surrounding countryside – sometimes annually or, in the larger shtetls, monthly or biweekly. The more regular weekly market days, when local peasants came to sell their produce to shtetl dwellers and then set out to spend their cash on shtetl merchandise, also gave the taverns a boost, as customers gathered to replenish their energies.

'Taverns provided relief for the repressed libido of the shtetl,' writes Petrovsky-Shtern. 'Jews found a reprieve from the prohibitions and restrictions of shtetl life.'[41] This is not to say that chaos reigned and all discipline was abandoned; there were rules, surely, but they were different from the rules outside the tavern. It was up to the tavern-keeper to keep the order, not the rabbi.

The mists of shtetl nostalgia have banished many aspects of real shtetl life to the recesses of popular and scholarly memory – including in relation to the taverns. Recent research has brought the story of alcohol into the foreground of shtetl histories, showing how central the making and selling of alcohol was to Jewish livelihoods throughout the eighteenth and nineteenth centuries.[42]

Seen through this revisionist lens, the tavern was as important in the making of shtetl communities as the synagogue, albeit communities of a different kind. In the synagogue, boundaries were tight: all were Jewish, and their shared faith glued them together. The tavern made for a far looser set of arrangements. Non-Jews were as likely to frequent a tavern as Jews. Travellers who stayed the night may have been Jewish, but maybe not; likewise those who came to strike deals, exchange news or share a meal. 'The Jewish-Christian interaction,' writes Dynner, 'was arguably played out more in taverns, open every day and at all hours, than even in market squares.'[43]

As Dynner points out, most historical writings on the shtetl zoom in on the tensions and conflicts between Jews and their Christian neighbours. Less has been written about the confluences and convergences, the centripetal energies of the shtetl alongside the centrifugal ones. A tavern's customers gathered across ethnic boundaries. These could be uncertain, sometimes risky, social interactions, but they brought people together in a shared social space despite their long-standing habits of mutual suspicion and scorn.

Forgetting how central the tavern was to shtetl life also forgets the ways in which Jewish and Christian lives were entangled there.

20 | Itsyk

It soon became clear to me that despite putting down roots and staying put in Pumpian his entire life, Itsyk did indeed live up to the meaning of his surname. In running his tavern, which he must have done successfully over many years to have become 'well-to-do', he created his own border zone, which he criss-crossed every day – brokering, or at least overseeing, interactions between Jews and Christians, rich and poor, dissolute and respectable, strangers and locals.

The sociality in a tavern was precarious: potentially explosive, ever on the brink of conflict. Over-enthusiastic vodka-drinking was a flame that could ignite latent tensions in a flash. It was up to the taverner to contain the aggression and chaos. In a competitive environment, with many shtetl taverns all wooing customers, a well-run tavern was good for business. Itsyk must have been a particular type of man in holding his tavern together, with appropriate order: both savvy and affable, assertive and flexible, a skilled interlocutor. This resonates too with his appointment later in life as a municipal deputy: a sign of communal respect and recognition.

Everything that Itsyk was, his grandson Maurice wasn't.

Perhaps if Maurice had grown up in Pumpian, his grandfather might have helped mould him into a more socially competent, confident individual. Perhaps it was the stresses of his dislocation from the shtetl and the strangeness of the new country he arrived in that sharpened his edges and churned his insides, from his formative childhood years onwards. But it may also have had a lot to do with the personality of his father Bere.

The bits and pieces I put together about Bere suggest that he was not much like his father. Abidingly marginal, he was likely a less-effective and less-motivated individual than Itsyk – a man with fewer social talents, less of a way with people. 'The shtetl could be a cruel place, especially to those lacking status,'[44] writes Samuel Kassow. Low on status, the contrast between him and his father might well have stung. Its reverberations through the small and judgemental social world of the shtetl likely deepened his insecurities and worsened his wounds, making any future successes ever more unlikely. I'm speculating, of course, because in truth I know almost nothing about Bere's personality – other than through his social standing and the sort of son he produced. Let me simply hypothesise then: there is a strong possibility that Bere left the shtetl a damaged man, and that his son was brought up to take on those injuries, in his own way.

21 | Singles

Itsyk and Chaia-Sora produced twelve children, eleven of whom survived to adulthood. This was a large family, even by shtetl standards. The first three were sons, the oldest of whom was Bere. Iosel, born second, died at the age of seven. Then came Chatzkel. After that, only daughters were born – no fewer than nine of them – at a relentless pace.

In the main, the birth of a daughter among shtetl Jews produced less of a celebration than a son – and sometimes worse. In her story about life in the shtetl of her childhood, Sarah Hamer-Jacklyn wrote about 'my father's grief and my mother's guilt' at the birth of their third daughter.[45] Weary Chaia-Sora was forty-three when she gave birth to her last child, yet another girl, in 1879. She and Itsyk must have finally given up hope of producing another son.

This was not a family for the faint-hearted, particularly as the threshold of adulthood approached for all those daughters. Stories of shtetl life depict parents as single-minded about marrying off their daughters in a good match, and in the hope of many grandsons in the future. Matchmakers were called in; various options were carefully considered, argued and pleaded. Disappointments flared and conflicts exploded: the matchmakers worked in a minefield.

By the late nineteenth century, age-old Jewish traditions were coming under fire, including the ways of marriage. The *maskilim* scorned the machinations of the matchmakers, which robbed young Jews of their freedom of choice. Marriage, they urged, should be forged through young love, not parental scheming. Under such pressure, the theatre of marital tradition and its attendant dramas teetered. But it did not collapse entirely.

Marriage – the seed of the family – was a serious business, at the core of how shtetl communities reproduced and regulated themselves: a private matter very much in the public eye. Some young people chafed at the parental bit and broke away, with or without their parents' reluctant consent.[46] But in the main, parents continued to take charge of when and how marriages were contracted, with their eyes on the prize of a strong alliance with a good family.[47]

Once a match was made, there were traditional expectations of what the bride's family would contribute. This included a dowry, the price of which fuelled much of the volatility of matchmaking. The higher the status of the groom's family, the greater the dowry expected for the marriage. Then there was the practice of *kest*: the newlyweds would live with the bride's parents until they found their own financial feet.

Itsyk might well have been financially stretched by having to produce nine dowries, and put up nine young couples, in rapid succession. But fortunately or not, that is not how things turned out. Marriage in this family took some unexpected turns. Much as Itsyk might have preferred to empty his well-to-do pockets altogether in settling his daughters into the right sort of unions and grumbling at the burden of it, he was spared a large chunk of that expense.

His first three children did what the shtetl expected of them. The eldest, Bere, was the first to marry; in fact, he married twice, the second time soon after his first wife died in around 1893.[48] Chatzkel was next, marrying in 1885 at the age of twenty-three, the same age as his bride. And Chave (the second-oldest daughter) dutifully married in 1890 at the age of twenty-four; her husband was also the same age. By then, the average age of marriage among Jews in the Pale had risen sharply from the trend earlier in the century, of marriages arranged between young teenagers.[49] Chave's marriage at twenty-four would not have raised any eyebrows.

But then came the oddities: a combination of late marriages and no marriages at all. Daughter number four, Dina, married in 1895. She was twenty-six: getting on. Her husband was a widower, aged thirty-three: a man in a hurry to remarry and likely unperturbed by an older than average bride. Then all was quiet on the marital front for many years, until 1913, when Gena – daughter number seven – took to the *chuppah*. The *Jewishgen* database records the marriage to a man aged thirty-one, with Gena supposedly aged thirty-two. This does not square with several other records, which would put Gena's age at thirty-eight, maybe forty, in 1913. A very unusual – even desperate – match, then; perhaps so much so that Gena felt the need to conceal her real age to the officials who recorded her marriage.

Perhaps she lied to her husband too; perhaps not. The most likely scenario, as I see it, was that Itsyk – approaching the end of his life and desperate to see his daughter married off – made a substantial financial contribution to the prospect of the union; so much so that Gena's husband – who had left marriage rather late himself – was not overly concerned about his wife's age.

That left six daughters who remained unmarried. Clearly Itsyk's prosperity did not do the trick of luring a trail of eager grooms who could be matched with his batch of available brides.

Two of these unmarried daughters – Freyde and Basha – were recorded as living with their parents in Pumpian in an official household survey in 1887, when they were twenty-three and sixteen years old respectively. But after this date, they disappear entirely from the record. There is no further information regarding any marriages, deaths, income earned, journeys taken – nothing.[50]

The remaining four daughters – Yudis, Khasse, Rokha and Mikla – do show up in subsequent official records, but with no evidence of ever having married. As with Freyde and Basha, their archival traces may be misleading or incomplete, making it impossible to draw firm conclusions. I put that question to Galina Baranova, who had been a senior archivist in the Lithuanian national archive: were there archival sources I had omitted to consult? She reassured me that I had found whatever was available,[51] but pointed out that the marriage records for Pumpian during the years 1915 to 1921 are missing. Maybe then, one or more of the daughters married in their later years, but by the first decade of the twentieth century, the records suggest that these four of Itsyk's daughters were alive and well, in Pumpian or nearby, and had remained single.

All four seemed to have been industrious and resourceful women. Yudis (the oldest daughter) left Pumpian for Seduva (about sixty kilometres away), working as a 'bakeress'. Rokha, Khasse and Mikla stayed in Pumpian. Rokha and Khasse worked as 'tradeswomen' and Mikla as a 'dressmaker'. Nor were they hiding behind the parental curtains, shying away from their spinsters' lot. Rokha had a house to her name, and Khasse and Mikla likely moved into it with her: three Posel women waking up and going to sleep with no men in their line of domestic vision.[52]

It was commonplace for shtetl women to work; their contribution to the household income was expected, often indispensable. Far more unusual was the prospect of a Jewish woman owning property in the Pale of Settlement, not least one who had remained single. According to historian Benjamin Nathans, 'in general, women (of any religion) could not own property in their own names – it was always in conjunction with their fathers or their husbands.'[53] I think this is exactly what happened in Rokha's case. By 1910, when Itsyk would have been around eighty years old, he and his wife bought a second house, leaving their three single daughters in the original family home. Perhaps because Rokha was the most enterprising of the three (although not the oldest), Itsyk elected to transfer (part) ownership to her.

Why Itsyk and Chaia-Sora chose to move is harder to fathom. Perhaps, in their dotage, they wanted finally to be free of their daughters, and clearly Itsyk could afford to buy another property. Or perhaps the daughters found the family home too crowded and urged their parents to leave them alone. Either way, Itsyk and his wife ensured that these three single daughters had a roof over their heads, none of them disowned or disavowed.

Women in the shtetl who failed to marry (singlehood was typically regarded as a failure on the woman's and her family's part) generally fell into three categories: women who had 'fallen' in one or other way (typically, sex outside of marriage); the handicapped or mentally ill; and those who were too independent, obnoxious or unattractive to secure a match. Which of these trajectories might explain the fate of the Posel daughters?

There is no way of knowing what happened to Freyde and Basha. Perhaps they did 'fall' and ran away in shame. Maybe Yudis did too, and that's why she ended up unmarried in Sekuva. Rokha, Mikla and Khasse were unlikely to have been handicapped; they were too resourceful and independent. It's also unlikely that they would have remained in Pumpian if they had fallen into disrepute, because they had the means to relocate elsewhere.

Unattractive and unappealing then? Historian Alice Nakhimovsky informs me that in these settings, beauty and charm were by no means prerequisites for marriage, particularly if it came with a suitable dowry; and a man could go far with an unappealing bride who had her own earning powers. 'Believe me, undesirable women married. To undesirable spouses. As everywhere,' she writes.[54]

Perhaps these Posel sisters just did not want to marry the men who were offered to them, preferred being single, and were sufficiently pushy and loud-mouthed to cajole their parents into accepting their wishes. In Alice's words, 'I can imagine a scenario in which the first sister, looking over the options (they did have the right of refusal, though there was a lot of social pressure), said "no way", and then her younger sister said, "I'm doing what she did."' And, between Itsyk's capital and his daughters' earnings, 'there was enough money to maintain them'.

In the face of their unmarried daughters' pressure, Itsyk and Chaia-Sora then likely gave up and let them be. Perhaps part of Itsyk's wisdom lay in his foresight, recognising which way the cultural winds were blowing.

22 | Pushy daughters

Why might these unmarried daughters have been so emboldened? Where could their independence have come from? And how unusual would such behaviour have been for its place and time?

The Posel sisters were outliers. The shtetl norm was for women to marry, and most did their parents' bidding. But the Posel daughters' will to decide their own fate – and their parents' beleaguered capitulation to that – was a sign of the times in the making. By the late nineteenth century, the position of women in shtetl society was in flux, as young women became more educated, and with that, more attuned to wider debates about if and how Jews should modernise.

The traditional system of Jewish education in the shtetl, controlled by local religious authorities, had prioritised the education of boys. It was almost entirely a religious education, devoted to reading and writing in Hebrew and studying the holy texts. Very few girls received this kind of schooling: entirely inward-looking, uninterested in the world outside. Girls' futures lay in the household and the marketplace, looking outward, beyond the limits of an insular Jewishness. Shtetl elders considered it perfectly appropriate, then, that girls should learn to speak Russian and gain the basics of a secular education.

In the better-off households, a private tutor might have been hired; poorer households likely did not bother or could not afford it. But then things changed substantially, thanks to the notoriously aggressive Tsar Nicholas I, at the helm from 1825 to 1855. His efforts to 'Russify' the Jewish population of the Pale extended to the education of their daughters. Government-sponsored schools for Jewish girls popped up all over, with principals instructed that their pupils should become fluent in Russian. 'In addition to religion and Russian,' writes historian Eliyana Adler, 'almost all Jewish girls' schools offered German, penmanship and arithmetic', and sometimes French, science, history or geography.[55]

Here was an unexpectedly worldly education and, ironically, on offer to shtetl girls rather than boys – at least to those whose families could spare their daughters from the work of the household. And it opened the girls' eyes to life beyond the shtetl.

This development intertwined with debates among more secular Jews of the *maskilim* about reshaping the future for women, which picked up steam with the advent of the Yiddish press in 1862. Literate women took part in their own right, contributing to various newspapers, mostly writing letters to the editors, but also articles and stories. They took aim – often vitriolically – at their mothers and grandmothers: the so-called *kleyn-shtetl-vayber* (small-town women).

In his brief reflections on his childhood in Pumpian, Yiddish poet and essayist Benjamin Bialostotzky offered a song of praise to these traditional women of the shtetl, who 'kept the stores, went to market, stood at fairs, bought and sold, planted gardens, washed and sewed and spun and wove, and simply sacrificed their lives for the Torah of their husbands'. And they were key players in keeping Jews on good terms with their Christian neighbours. 'Thinking about my *bobeh* [grandmother] Chana,' he continues, 'I remember something else that was very characteristic of her and other such Jewish Lithuanian women. She brought together the Jews and the village, the gentile world. She spoke Lithuanian fluently and would go to the village a *verst* [two thirds of a mile] or two from Pumpian to purchase wheat from the peasants and would also sell them goods from the *shtetl*. She established a strong connection with many gentile women.

When the gentile women came to the *shtetl* on market days or holidays, before doing anything else they would always come to greet my grandmother.'[56]

For Bialostotzky, these women were the salt of the earth. For the daughters of the *maskilim*, they were 'uneducated, superstitious, narrow-minded, resisting any sign of progress, with no insight into their children's needs and at times simply cruel'.[57] Rather than being applauded for her stoicism and versatility, the bossy, outspoken shtetl wife, running her household and her husband, was now depicted as the instrument of his emasculation, and as a derelict mother.

The *kleyn-shtetl-vayber* had grown pushy and shrill in deference to the patriarchy of their traditional husbands: to give them their space in the *yeshivah*, freed from much of the business of daily life, and to venerate them as the spiritual heads of the household. But the *maskilim* had a different, more bourgeois, version of patriarchy in mind, in which a husband accepted the dominant role in securing the family's livelihood, and the wife paid greater attention to the needs of her children and running her home.

The critiques of mothers and grandmothers cut to the core of the shtetl, its umbilical cord. So it's unsurprising that there are strains of emotional pain, along with the sense of liberation, that ring through in some of the writings of *maskilim* women: daughters who felt bound to their mothers and grandmothers even as they strove to break free. Yiddish poet Kadia Molodowsky put her finger on it in her famous poem *Froyen Lider*:

> I will go meet the grandmothers, saying:
> Your sighs were the whips that lashed me
> and drove my young life to the threshold
> to escape from your kosher beds.

But wherever the street grows dark you pursue me –
wherever a shadow falls.[58]

The pull was often – perhaps mostly – too strong to break entirely. Yet we should not understate the stirrings of dissent either.

Even among the daughters of the shtetl who were not tempted by the *maskilim* but had been educated with an eye to a different sort of future, the yearning for change – for a more flexible version of the old ways, that gave more freedom to choose, more scope to be different – was often strong.[59] The lives of their communities would not stay unchanged.

Itsyk's and Chaia-Sora's independent unmarried daughters – whose trajectories don't suggest that they became *maskilim* – likely fell into this last category. Daughters who did not want to leave the shtetl but wanted – and received – a loud, pushy say on the terms on which they stayed.

23 | *Stille chuppah*

What might have happened to Freyde and Basha, the two daughters who disappeared from the record? Might they have stayed in Pumpian, their lives erased from history by large gaps in the existing archives?[60] The official record is incomplete and flawed, it is true, but I think it unlikely that there would be no traces of them at all when reasonably regular information is available about Itsyk's other daughters in Pumpian. One possibility, then, is that these daughters left Pumpian, or Lithuania at large, never to return.

It was not uncommon for young women to leave their shtetls and disappear from the records forever, and this was most likely if they were tempted – alas – by the exotic prospect of a married life far away.

Not all shtetl marriages were recorded; some were informal or clandestine, deliberately to avoid any official documentation. *Stille chuppah*, they were called: silent marriages, marriages that would escape the purview of history. Could Freyde and her sister have ended up in one of these? By the late nineteenth century, there were many – most, for all the wrong reasons. *Stille chuppahs* became a driving force in Jewish involvement in the so-called White slave trade.[61]

By the late nineteenth century, many parts of Western and Eastern Europe had woken up with alarm to what became known, somewhat sensationally, as the White slave trade. Young vulnerable White girls were being tricked into liaisons with duplicitous pimps, who sold them into sexual servitude in far-off places. Their Whiteness was central to the outrage: signifier of their youthful innocence. Apparently, the darker the woman, the more carnal her instincts. Moral panics likely exaggerated the numbers involved, but there was no denying that this was a global operation. Argentina was one of its headquarters. South Africa would be another.[62]

The market made space for all the unscrupulous. Among them, Jewish pimps featured prominently. Most of their prey were Jewish women in Eastern Europe. Some of these women were entirely unsuspecting of the fate that would befall them, while others were more worldly and willing to take their chances in a land of greater opportunity. 'East European Jewry', writes historian Lloyd Gartner, 'was the main reservoir out of which thousands of Jewish girls were drawn into prostitution in foreign lands, and of which Jewish men, as well as women accomplices, emerged as procurers and transporters of prostitutes and keepers of brothels.'[63]

Polish and Galician cities were hotspots, but the tentacles of the trade spread throughout the Pale of Settlement. Even the marginal shtetls, remote from city life, could become links in this modern global sex chain.

Jewish pimps understood the ways and means of marriage in the shtetl, including the possibility of a *stille chuppah*. It suited their purpose perfectly: a low-key, sometimes entirely private, Jewish marriage, without any basis in civil law. The bride would have no legal protection, therefore, but she and her family would consider the marriage to be binding nevertheless. It became a tempting prospect for various groups of women: the restless young daughters of impoverished families yearning for a way out of the bleakness, young widows and deserted wives without support, as well as women with poor marital prospects desperate for a catch, including those who had in one or other way disgraced themselves and their families, then happy to send them away. When an apparently fine young man appeared in the shtetl looking for a bride and made her or her family an offer they could not refuse, a *stille chuppah* was all it took for the marriage to be confirmed, in haste.

It was no secret, however. There were public warnings against these dubious bridegrooms, whose real purpose was not unknown. Newspapers published letters, many from shtetls, exposing the scams. In 1903, a conference on White slavery held in Ukraine was attended by rabbis from across Eastern Europe.[64] To little avail, it seems. Many an amorous 'husband' would gather his many conquests (for he did not restrict his beneficence to only one woman) and take to the seas, set to deliver the booty to brothels ready and waiting for new talent. The global market was pumping.

Itsyk and his wife were not too poor to afford a desirable husband for their daughters, nor did they seem to have been overly unsettled by having a houseful of spinster daughters. But it is not impossible that one or both of their daughters Freyde and Basha – longing for new horizons and more breathing space – decided to take a chance and head off into the unknown, hoping that a quick marriage would take them there.

24 | Conversion to Christianity

In *Fiddler on the Roof* – the popular musical about life in the fictional shtetl Anatevka – the milkman Tevya's troubles pile up around the marriage of his daughters. All three break with shtetl tradition. Most catastrophically for him, one daughter decides to marry a young non-Jewish man who courts her with books and ideas. Tevya is distraught; it is as if she is dead, a daughter who is no longer.

It could have happened to a real Tevya too. Women of the shtetl were not fleeing their faith in droves, but some did, and with increasing frequency by the end of the nineteenth century.

Converts were more likely to be female than male, and many – although not all – conversion decisions involved marriage. As with Tevya's daughter, it might have started with a passionate love affair across the highly fortified religious border, with a Jewish woman more likely to convert than a Christian man (I haven't come across any shtetl conversions from Christianity to Judaism). A conversion might also have been tempting as a refuge from a dreadful husband delivered by an unwanted arranged marriage,[65] or because it resolved the impossible plight of an *agunah* – a Jewish wife whose husband had deserted her but refused to give her a divorce, leaving her languishing in a painful limbo, unable to marry again and shamed by her desertion. Converting to Christianity released her from the marriage in the eyes of Russian officialdom, as well as the church; she could begin her life again but as an exile from her shtetl community.

Other younger converts were not in pursuit of a marriage, nor of a romance outside the faith. Theirs was a form of cultural or spiritual emigration, a decision to leave one social homeland in search of another. The Catholic church was ready to welcome them. Historian Elena Keidošiūtė writes of the Catholic convents that geared themselves to receive young female converts, providing accommodation and financial support while preparations for the conversion began. The Russian state also paved the way. As has been mentioned, from the mid- to late-nineteenth century, a policy of 'Russification' was introduced, with the intention of weakening Jewish institutions and traditions. The goal was to absorb Jews who had detached significantly from their faith and culture into Russian-speaking society. Enabling young Jewish women to convert to Christianity was a step in the right direction. Some financial support was on offer to sweeten the prospect.[66]

In Elena Keidošiūtė's study, a small-scale analysis of Jewish conversion to Catholicism in a district in northern Lithuania, she discovered that many of the converts were the daughters of tavern-keepers. It makes sense. Tavern-keepers' families were helping hands in the tavern: keeping the food and drink circulating, cleaning up the mess, ensuring that rooms were ready for overnight travellers. That made for encounters with visiting strangers with different ways and ideas, and for conversations about a wider world. The churches were as aware of that as the tavern-keeper and his family. As the drive to convert Jews picked up speed, Dynner writes, taverns became 'the hunting grounds of Christian missionaries'.[67]

A tavern opened a door to the outside, as much as it welcomed strangers to the inside. Clearly, some daughters made the break. Perhaps Freyde or Basha were among them.

25 | Margin of margins

A woman's erasure from the historical record could have had at least one further explanation. Had Freyde or Basha revealed any inclinations to prefer women to men, the small Pumpian community would surely have pushed them out – the Posels included.

Homosexuality could not have been unknown in the world of the shtetl. But the topic was publicly taboo, and its practice was shunned. Traces in the art and literature of the time were also scant and feint. All of this makes celebrated Yiddish writer Sholem Asch's play *Got fun Nekome* (God of Vengeance), published in 1906, an extraordinary creation for its time – and confirmation, surely, that same-sex relationships were making their presence felt.

Set in a shtetl, the play tells of the desperate desire of Yankl and his wife, owners of a brothel operating below the stairs of their more respectable house, to change their ways in the eyes of their God. Their only child, a daughter, Rivkele, is rapidly approaching the age of marriage, and Yankl is determined to find her a good match, to remedy his morally dubious past. He goes to great lengths and expense to secure a Torah scroll to present to her future husband, as if to sanctify the house and redeem Yankl. But neither Rivkele's future, nor God's mercy, is so easily bought. Rivkele falls in love with Manke, one of the sex workers in the basement, the place where Rivkele prefers to spend her time.

Life above ground is hardened by habits of snobbery, social climbing, and *faux* responsibility; it's the supposedly disreputable basement that offers love and affection. In Act Two, Manke draws Rivkele close to her, speaking with 'a concealed passion, and love, softly but deep and ringing'. 'Do you feel cold, Rivkele?

Snuggle up close to me. Let me keep you warm, nice and warm. That's right, press your face against my breast. Like that, that's the way. And let your body caress me. So cool, like water running between us.'[68]

The script is in line with Asch's oeuvre: showing the realities of shtetl life beyond the strenuous moralising of its traditional patriarchs. Yet it is the most courageous of his works, and its staging showed one of the first explicitly lesbian scenes ever dramatised publicly.[69]

Sixty years later, Nobel laureate Isaac Bashevis Singer revisited the topic. His story 'Tsetyl un Rikl' tells of two orphaned women in a shtetl, who found each other, fell in love, and lived together. In describing their fate, Singer did not mince his words. The text is a reminder that the shtetl pulsed with gossip and superstition, and spewed malice towards those who breached the communal norms; this was not a tolerant, open-minded space. To make the point, Singer's narrator is cantankerous, prurient and intolerant, an unreliable captive of all sorts of local conspiracies and gossip. The story's ending is desperate: both young women commit suicide, unable to bear the pain of their social rejection.[70]

There must have been some women who would have identified with Asch's and Singer's sagas. It's not impossible that Freyde or her sister was among them.

26 | A boy child

According to Russian records, Maurice was born in 1895, the youngest of Bere's five surviving children (two daughters had died during childhood). The first four were the fruits of his first marriage, to Beyla Sudak: two sons, two daughters. But Beyla died young – perhaps during or soon after giving birth to her youngest daughter, Leah, in 1893. Bere married again very soon after that. Shtetl custom allowed a widower to remarry after thirty days' mourning; in fact, remarriage was actively encouraged.[71] Coincidentally, his second wife had the same first name as the first one: Beila Rabinovich. Maurice would be her only child. A son! Bere and Beila must have been delighted.

Maurice spent the formative first seven years of his life in Pumpian.[72] Like all young Jewish boys of the shtetl, from age three or four his upbringing would centre around institutions of the faith, preparing him to join the synagogue's community of men.

Each step was ritualised, rich in meaning: early milestones in the boy's journey into Jewish manhood. The first was his circumcision eight days after birth – symbol of the Jewish covenant with God and enduring physical mark of male community. Then came the boy's first haircut, at age three or four, often undertaken by his father or grandfather. It was an important occasion for the family, rich in ritual and celebration.

As told to historian Simon Dubnow, 'at home, a festive table was laid with pastries and drinks. I had a place of honour and a toast was drunk to me ... Someone passed me a prayer book, two pages of which were smeared with honey, which I was supposed to lick off. When I bowed my head in compliance, a shower of silver and copper coins fell upon me. They had been tipped onto me – according to my grandfather – by the angels. Because the angels, he said, had faith in me and they knew in advance I would be a good student and because they were willing to give me an advance. When the celebration was at an end, my father lifted me up, covered me from head to foot in a *tallit* [prayer shawl] and took me the whole way to the *kheyder* [school] in his arms. My mother could not go with us; that was a matter for men.'[73]

Dubnow then adds his own postscript: 'The parents had a dim perception of the sombre idea that the child was a sacrifice which they were presenting to the *kheyder*.'[74] Indeed. The *kheyder* would then dominate the boy's life from morning to night every day except for Saturday, the sabbath.

From then on, the boy would learn with other boys and play with other boys. And he would learn to recite the prayer that the shtetl's menfolk would chant every day too. 'Blessed art thou, Lord our God, Ruler of the Universe, who has not made me a woman.'

During these years, the man who loomed largest in a boy's daily life would likely have been his *melamed* – or teacher – in whose home the *kheyder* was usually set up. Typically, the *melameds* eked out a living from the fees paid by the boys' parents, many of whom were themselves poor and expected their sons to learn as quickly as possible, to maximise the return on their payments. The parents put pressure on the *melamed*, who put pressure on his pupils. 'Corporal punishment was by no means infrequent ... Attendance at the *kheyder* was often a torment for children.'[75]

How much of a torment was revealed in most detail by an exercise in local anthropology, undertaken by a group of secular Jewish intellectuals based in St Petersburg and their team of young fieldworkers, in 1912. It was called The Jewish Ethnographic Expedition, and its purpose was to document 'the naked pulse' of traditional life among Jews in the Pale, capturing as much of the detail as possible.[76] Close to ten thousand questions were compiled, far too many to have been administered, so the researchers settled on a mere two thousand and thirty-seven. These included a series of questions about discipline and punishment at the *kheyders*. By the turn of the century, these institutions had become notorious for their 'poor pedagogy, horribly overcrowded conditions, and frequently violent instructors'.[77] The Jewish Ethnographic Expedition wanted to know more:

> For what does one most often strike the children: for mischief, for poor comprehension, or for bad habits?
> Where do teachers lay the child, over a stool or a knee?
> Are there still teachers who soak the rods in salt water?
> Do teachers always strike the bare flesh?
> What does the teacher say while he is beating the child?
> Does the teacher ever command one child to beat another?
> Does the teacher ever command the children to spit on the place which has been beaten?
> Does the teacher ever command the children to taunt the beaten child?
> Must the child kiss the rod after the beating?
> Does it often happen that the teacher beats a child on the parents' order?
> What derisive jokes and songs are there about a beaten child?
> Do you know of a phenomenon from the past in which every Thursday the entire *kheyder* was beaten, guilty and innocent alike? What is the reason for this?
> How else does the teacher shame the children?

As it turns out, the questionnaire was never administered.[78] But Nathaniel Deutsch, who translated the questions from Yiddish into English, points out that the questions themselves are rich sources of information. The detail of their wording and very specific foci of interest suggest that the researchers had prior knowledge of the goings-on in *kheyders*, which they intended to put to a more systematic test through the survey.

Not all *kheyders* were the same and not all *melameds* were equally violent; we should treat the questions as pointing to norms and tendencies, allowing for some variation. Even so, I come away with a picture of an education system that could inflict deep psychological as well as physical wounds on the young boys. The *kheyder* went in for more than just corporal punishment; it embraced rituals of humiliation and degradation. Boys who misbehaved, or performed badly, could expect to be mocked and diminished by their peers, with the active encouragement of the *melamed* and support of the parents. And this would be a life lesson: the shtetl would be quick to judge, and harsh in its verdicts. Boys to boys; soon, men to men. Shaming would be part of that journey.

By the time his mother was packing up to leave for South Africa in 1902, Maurice would have spent between three and four years in his *kheyder*. Did he once breach a rule and have to kiss the rod that beat him? Or was he one of the meeker, more obedient ones, who mocked the boys who took a beating, as fearful as he was snide? Either way, he – like all the boys who endured the *kheyder* – surely imbibed the cultural messages the institution was transmitting on how to become a man, the shtetl's way. Here was one version of the mix of superiority and insecurity, arrogance and fear, that patriarchies all over instil in their growing men, each in its own way. And it would resonate with the version of manhood Maurice would later inhabit as he entered adulthood in the White colonial mould, then thousands of miles away in the city of Cape Town.

27 | Veins of violence

The heart of the shtetl pumped violently.[79] Jews and Christians alike understood a language of violence, which communicated ways of dealing with conflict in the marketplace, in the tavern, and on the street. This is yet another aspect of the real shtetl that has been omitted from many histories:[80] the weak, meek Jew who inhabited the mythic shtetl, succumbing passively to the mockery and abuse of his Christian neighbours, is a figure of the imagination. Sholem Asch made the point in his novels of the time: his Jewish characters 'resorted to violence when defending their competitive economic territory, their dignity, their independence and their small modicum of power'.[81]

Russian courts were slow and cumbersome, so conflicts over a business deal that went sour, or accusations of the sale of poor-quality vodka, or arguments about money mishandled, were seldom resolved legally: more likely a fistfight, or worse.[82] Christians might land a punch on Jews who had offended them; and vice versa. Cases of pre-arranged hits by gangs (on either side) were not uncommon, sometimes in dealing with the menace of Christian criminals but within Jewish circles too. And if not physical violence, verbal abuse was prolific. Jews and Christians denigrated each other in comparably vile language, often.[83] For Jews, writes Petrovsky-Shtern, it was a repertoire of 'violent dignity': resorting to whatever means necessary to try to get even.[84]

Aside from the routine violence of everyday life, more explosive spectacles of brutality might erupt, usually as a pogrom against a local Jewish population. In the northern parts of Lithuania, this more cataclysmic violence was rare; it was more common in the south, and most dramatically after 1880. It turns out, however, that Pumpian was once an exception.

Writing at the turn of the twentieth century, Pumpian's most famous son, the poet Benjamin Bialostotzky, told a story of terrible bloodletting in this little town. 'Generations ago, at the beginning of the nineteenth century, a "blood-accusation" [blood libel] took place in Pumpian. The Jews were put into jail and told: "Either give up the guilty Jew who killed a Christian child for Passover, or all the Jews will die". At that time there was a Pumpian householder, Yisrael Pumpiansky, who chose *kiddush-hashem* [martyrdom in sanctification of G-d's name] when he took upon himself alone the despicable calumny. He told the priest and landowner: "I alone killed this child. The other Jews are not guilty". And so the martyr was burned alive beside the synagogue. Afterward a stone was set at this holy place with a fence around it. But over time everything was forgotten. This was told to me later, in 1901, by my rabbi, Rabbi Hertzl, in the *musar* yeshiva of Ponevezh.'[85]

Not much has been written about the history of Pumpian, but the few websites I find reproduce Bialostotzky's story (some with slight variations) as if a factual record of what happened there. For example, 'at the beginning of the 19th century, the Jewish Community of "Pumpenai" was falsely accused of blood libel. The rabbi was burnt to death near the Church and saved the entire community.'[86]

It's highly unlikely, however, that this is what happened.

The historian Darius Staliunas is an authority on blood libels in Eastern Europe – that is, murderous accusations against Jews, stemming from the belief that they needed the blood of Christian children for their religious rituals, especially to make *matzah* for Passover. Blood libels against Jews had a long history in Western Europe, going back to the eleventh century. By the nineteenth century, they had receded in the West but remained prominent – on the rise, in fact – in Eastern Europe. This included Lithuania.

As Staliunas explains, during the nineteenth century, Lithuania was industrialising (albeit more slowly than elsewhere in the Russian Empire). The social fabric was being pulled and stretched, making way for new patterns of class. The better-educated and aspiringly modern Russians drew away from the peasants still anchored in their villages of old. Antisemitic prejudices were common in Lithuania at large, but they manifested in different ways across this changing society. By the nineteenth century, accusations of Jewish bloodletting were most likely to erupt in the villages. And prolifically so: I read, with shocked surprise, that between 1881 and 1890, one hundred and twenty-eight blood libel cases were recorded.[87]

It wasn't just the lower ranks of Russian society who saw Jews as faithfully murderous. No less a person than Tsar Nicholas I – at the very apex of the Russian Empire in the first half of the nineteenth century – was of like mind; he too insisted that Jews sought out Christian blood for their religious rituals. But he did require that in the event of an accusation, the case should be investigated, and guilt proven on the strength of available evidence.[88] A modern advance.

Staliunas selects some of these blood libel cases for detailed commentary. The local dynamics varied, and conditions changed over time, but some patterns emerged. A child disappeared or died, sparking vehement accusations against one or more Jews. Sometimes a mob went on the rampage, attacking Jews and ransacking their homes. Tensions ran high; usually, local authorities became involved. Investigations and interrogations of Jews – sometimes brutal and humiliating – began. Evidence was sought, which could include local police searching for jugs of blood in a synagogue or a rabbi's house. Usually, a court case ensued – in some cases, escalating to the Lithuanian Supreme Court. Judgments might have taken a long time to emerge, as evidence wavered, and witnesses gave contradictory accounts. Some convictions resulted, but not invariably. The local and national newspapers covered the case, particularly if the details were violent and dramatic.

Bialostotzky's account does not fit this mould at all. There were no local authorities, no investigations, no courts, no bureaucratic mediations of the murderous rage; just a threat of unmitigated destruction – 'all Jews will die' – and a martyr who was burned alive to assuage the rage.

Confused and intrigued, I wrote to Staliunas to ask if he was familiar with Bialostotzky's account and what he made of it. Generously, he replied: 'blood libel accusations were so widespread in the Lithuanian countryside that something might have happened in Pumpian as well.' But he had not found any trace of this case in the course of his archival research, nor in the press coverage of blood libels. Bialostotzky's story was especially dramatic; for a case such as this to have been undocumented would have been highly unlikely, he thought. All the more so since there are no known cases of Jewish martyrdom – let alone of the accused being set alight and burned to death – in Eastern Europe at that time.[89]

How then do we make sense of this tale? I turned to the recent work of some Jewish historians who have revisited various histories of antisemitic depredation in the Pale.[90] They don't deny the horrors of violence and brutalisation inflicted on Jews at various times; on the contrary, they put these centre-stage but look at them anew. At most times, they stress, Jewish and Christian lives were entangled and interdependent, rather than entirely segregated and distant. Conditions and contexts varied, of course, but Jews and Christians were often neighbours rather than disengaged strangers; they interacted and transacted, even amidst simmering tension and episodes of horrific violence.

This was quintessentially so in the shtetls: always spaces of Jewish and Christian cohabitation and communication. The traffic of ordinary, everyday life – from hour to hour, day to day, week to week, the time between bouts of conflagration – moved through a landscape of hostile neighbourliness, with spaces for civility amidst the suspicion. On the other hand, prejudice and provocation could erupt violently and disruptively, for both sides. With communities of Jews and Christians in the habit of tense engagement, it would be unsurprising that Jews found ways of retaliating against such predations, even if just talking back in the ways available to them, rather than slumping into inert victimisation.

Holding this prism to Bialostotzky's story helps make mythical rather than literal sense of Yisrael Pumpiansky's murder. As Staliunas suggests, there likely was real horror at the root of the story: a terrible event in Pumpian, that may well have been triggered by an accusation that a Jew had murdered a Christian child. But we can now see the tale of Pumpiansky's martyrdom in symbolic terms, as a Jewish retort to their Christian aggressors.

The very name of the hero of the tale – Yisrael Pumpiansky, Pumpian's Jewish everyman – points us in this direction. In response to a fantastical accusation, Jews likely produced a fantastical rejoinder, to claim the moral high ground. And to do that, they drew on a symbol of martyrdom that Christians could well understand. In the story, Pumpiansky was Christ-like: a man who gave his life under horrific circumstances, to save his people, sanctified in the eyes of God. His story, like that of Jesus, elevated him – and by symbolic association, his fellow Jews – high above the moral morass of his accusers.

Russian Jews would arrive in South Africa to jibes and diatribes, diminished and dismissed as unwanted aliens. Here too their lives would become entangled with their accusers, about whom stories would be told. But the terms of engagement would change. There would be no accusations of murderous blood lust, no raids on synagogues in search of jugs of blood.

The sons of Pumpian who thrived in their new homeland, far from the shtetl, would have taken the mythical lesson of the blood libel to heart: find ways of engaging with unappealing others, even in the midst of their disdain and outright menace. Learn the social language of the other, otherwise there is no way of speaking back.

Part Three

28 | Leaving Pumpian

There's no point in leaving if you don't hope that there is something better that lies ahead. Hope pulses with the anticipation of a better future. Yet even the most fervently hopeful immigrant may also confront a horizon of dread. Things might go badly wrong; that has happened before. Not least for Jews. The dread makes hope more urgent; but the more intense the hope, the more difficult to banish the dread.

I imagine immigrants move ahead charged with hope, accompanied by a dread of what might yet come to be. Two pieces of emotional luggage, one in each hand.

Bere was somewhere between forty-three and forty-seven years old[91] when he stood up to take his place in the throngs of people on the move across the globe at the turn of the twentieth century. A man beyond the cusp of middle age. In the Jewish migrations of the time, this was relatively unusual. I've looked through many passenger lists of those who arrived in South Africa by ship from Eastern Europe. Most were in their twenties or thirties, only a handful in their forties or older.

For the young ones, the prospect of an adventure, even if to dauntingly unknown parts, might have seemed exciting, the departure from familiar climes a youthful liberation – if also an enormous emotional wrench. For the older ones, there must have been especially compelling reasons to up and go, leaving an established world of adulthood behind. The upheaval of uprooting must have been more exhausting and the ruptures more painful than for the younger émigres; and yet even more hopeful, surely, because time had started to run out on their lives. Exactly that notched up the dread too. This would not be easy.

Some fled the Pale in the face of violent pogroms; young men who faced the dreaded prospect of conscription into the Russian army (introduced by Tsar Nicholas I) were also among those on the way out. For many – in some parts of the Pale, for most – the overriding pressures to emigrate were economic. The poorest and the richest were unlikely to leave: the poorest because they could not have afforded the fare, and the richest because their heads were still comfortably above the economic floodwaters. It was typically those in the middle – with some means but diminishing prospects – who journeyed away. Many looked first for better options closer to home, but if that failed, more distant shores beckoned.

Modern lines of communication brought South Africa into the consciousness of Jews in the Pale. There were articles in Yiddish newspapers about this otherwise invisible destination, written by those who had already arrived. Some were stories of hope; others did little to banish the dread of departure, with stern warnings that life over there could be tough and unappealing.

The most persuasive and tempting accounts of South African opportunities likely came from the letters of people who had already settled and who kept their families informed about the details of their everyday lives. It so happened that Jews in Pumpian had a hot-line to one of their own, Wulf Cohen, who had left the shtetl in around 1895. After a few weeks in Johannesburg, he wrote home declaring his unusually good fortune in earning five pounds (the equivalent of about fifty rubles) in a single day. 'In Johannesburg for only a few weeks and he can already send his family his earning of five pounds. It must really be a golden land!'[92]

The prospect of a new life on the unknown and distant African continent became more tangible thanks to the entrepreneurial zeal and strategic savvy of the British shipping entrepreneur Donald Currie.[93] He invested in creating a travel infrastructure for Jews from the Pale heading to South Africa, which yielded handsome returns for him and eased the way for Jewish passengers unaccustomed to the ways of global travel.

A rags-to-riches figure, Currie worked his way up from lowly 'office boy' to 'head of one of the greatest shipping companies in the world'.[94] Assiduously cultivating political connections in the Cape that powered his business ventures, Currie established the Castle shipping company (later enlarged as the Union Castle company), moving people and cargo between Great Britain and the Cape.

Winning the contract for the royal mail in 1876 and vigorously courting the British elites to enjoy the luxuries of first class sea travel, business was good for Currie. But then, with periods of economic depression and diminishing international trade, his fortunes began to fluctuate. His ships had been transporting Cornish miners to the tip of Africa in profitable droves, huddled in steerage in the bowels of these vessels. But then the miners' journeying ended, leaving a costly hole in the hold.

Currie spotted a lucrative opportunity among a similarly insalubrious category of passengers.

He realised he could replace the miners with Russian Jews, by creating the opportunity for them to follow a trail from the cramped confines of the Pale of Settlement, first to the Latvian port of Libau on the Baltic Sea, then to the ports of London or Southampton, and from there, to the Cape. Setting up contacts and networks in the Pale, Currie offered Jews a no-frills, all-in ticket in steerage class on his steamships. It included a night's stop-over in London, at the Poor Jews Temporary Shelter.

I wince at that name: a reassurance to those watching queasily from the outside that while these people were pitifully, distastefully, precarious, they would be on their way somewhere else, soon. In fact, those who passed through the shelter were more alien than poor, cultural strangers who were ill-mannered and uncouth in British eyes. The name was penned by the wealthy British Jews who funded the shelter, anxious that a deluge of unappealing foreign Jews would harm the reputation of their more respectable brethren in the city of London.[95] Donald Currie made his contribution to the costs of the Temporary Shelter too; it was good for business. Staff met the passengers as they arrived and escorted them to the shelter, ensuring that none escaped into the recesses of the city. It made for an orderly transition from the first leg of the journey to the next, which served Currie's interests well.[96]

The first of the Pumpian Posels to travel was Chatzkel – Bere's younger brother – who sailed south in 1895 on his own, leaving his wife and three daughters behind. He had already done well for himself, but with shtetl economies in decline by the late 1800s, Jewish participation in the flax trade was waning.

Chatzkel likely chose South Africa as a place to rejuvenate his prospects on the advice of his brother-in-law, Harris Plein, who had left for South Africa even earlier, between 1890 and 1893.[97] Aged around thirty-eight, Harris had headed to the Witwatersrand goldfields, where he and a business partner had bought a stand and set up as traders. Chatzkel would do much the same. Within two years of having arrived in South Africa, he was co-owner of a stand near the Driefontein mine on the Witwatersrand, where he set up shop – clearly Itsyk's enterprising and energetic son.

Chatzkel then returned to Pumpian for a few months in 1901. He must have told his family – and his brother Bere in particular – about conditions down south, and the opportunities on the goldfields of the Witwatersrand.

LEAVING PUMPIAN

Bere, surely the black sheep of the family, had been contemplating a move before that. He first applied for a passport, which he received, in 1900. It was valid for three months. He did not travel to South Africa then. Perhaps he went elsewhere, closer by, took one look and decided to come back home. Or his nerve failed him, and that passport expired, entirely unused. The second passport, which he received in 1901, was valid for a year. Did Chatzkel give Bere a brotherly push to take a leap into the southern unknown and try to make something better of his life; to become a colonial 'well-to-do'?

Itsyk and Chaia-Sora tried nine times for another son. That's surely an indication of the premium they placed on having sons as assets to the family, and therefore of some of the pressure on the shoulders of Bere, their first-born and oldest son. Make something of your life in that faraway place, dear son; make us proud! The passenger list that recorded Bere's journey to South Africa listed his occupation as 'miner'.[98] There was no mining to be done in Pumpian. 'Miner', then, must have been Bere's rather desperate, if inchoate, hope for the future. As if there was gold to be had by the likes of him in the dust of the Witwatersrand and in the heat of the sun. For Jews in the cold of the Pale whose prospects had withered, it must have been a gloriously hopeful thought. Not only gold, but sun! Dread, too, that dirt and cold were more likely.

It was not to be, however. Bere arrived in Cape Town in 1901, during the South African War. It was not possible at that time for him to leave Cape Town for the Witwatersrand to try his luck in the dust. Beila and her four children would arrive a little under a year later, soon after the war had ended. Perhaps by then Bere's energy to move had been used up. Cape Town would be good enough. He stayed there until he died in 1928 at the age of seventy-five.

29 | At sea

More than merely liminal, on-the-way to somewhere else, the ocean is a place, and the ship is a dwelling. Journeys took time; the ship was where people lived, with the rhythm of the sea, as storms broke, and waves swelled. Connections were formed, love arrived, conflicts erupted, violence was inflicted.

In Yiddish writings of the period, the ocean journey was a time for Jewish emigrants to grapple with their 'massive dislocation'.[99] already 'at sea', and about to become more so. As the narrator of Lamed Shapiro's novella *Oyfn Yam* (On the Sea) put it, 'little man, what are you creeping toward? Toward what are you moving yourself?'[100]

Most Jews travelled steerage class, the cheapest option. Currie's large steamships that travelled to Cape Town could stuff a few hundred passengers into steerage, situated below the first and second class cabins, in the bowels of the vessel. Their quarters were dark and cramped, but not unmanageable; the crush of bodies in pinched spaces was not unfamiliar.

Typically, the men had separate sleeping quarters from the women and children. In each case, 'on both sides of the cabin, stood rows of beds upon beds. And over each bed hung yet another bed. The passengers in the upper bunks almost touched the passengers below with the weight of their bodies.'[101] Recounting her journey in the 'underground abyss' of a ship's steerage, Malka Lee – sailing from Libau to the USA – recalls that the living quarters 'had no windows to look out at the sea. Huge fans produced a constant deafening noise, providing the only ventilation. People felt sick from the smell of rotting meat.'[102]

The ticket covered daily meals. On some ships with Jewish passengers, kosher food was on offer, but perhaps not every meal. Currie offered this, unreliable as it initially was, as one of his selling points. Maybe it was more appealing in theory than in practice. At sea, the nausea and vomiting were overwhelming; shtetl Jews were unaccustomed to ocean travel. 'In every nook and cranny, people were lying, moaning heavily, dirty with vomit, and very deep groans were coming out of everybody's heart.'[103]

For the religiously observant, the space was distressing, as strange men and women jostled in the throngs, uneasily close. Bere's ship sailed from London on a Saturday,[104] a transgression of the rules of the sabbath, if such things mattered to him. The ship was a taste of a secular world to come, where the rules of the sabbath would bend when necessary; a world in which the dominant rhythms of daily life were not the Jewish ones. Exactly this would be liberating for some of those who sailed away; 'seaborne travel helped define the Jewish drive to modernity,' writes historian Nick Evans.[105] For those of more traditional bent, life on the ship was a portent of dread.

Jews were not the only ones stuck in steerage. 'A steerage passenger' – not Jewish – travelling from London to the Cape in 1895 documented his journey for the Johannesburg newspaper *Standard and Diggers News*. It was a rough ride; many fights broke out. 'Pillows, hairbrushes, boots, shoes, blankets, hats – anything and everything that lay handy' were thrown around. 'Occasionally, there were scuffles during the meal hours; one day in particular, when a Cornish miner and a German attempted to settle a small affair, the German was knocked clean over, smashing into butter, beef and dishes.' On this voyage, the Jewish men had an especially bad time: 'the poor persecuted Jews, I am sorry to relate, were knocked about most unmercifully for the first week.'[106] These kinds of violations happened frequently. The Cape Town Jewish Philanthropic Society wrote to Currie's establishment more than once, complaining of the 'harsh treatment' meted out to Jewish passengers.[107]

Sexual breaches, like the buffeting waves, were not uncommon. Some were consensual, others forceful, even violent. Awake in her bunk one night, Malka Lee heard the ship's watchman enter the cabin and slip into the bunk of a mother and her daughter. 'I heard laughter and whispering in the dark cabin. I pulled the covers over my eyes so as not witness the shame of the mother and the daughter with the brazen watchman.'[108] Interviewed about her journey by ship to South Africa as a child, Tilly Whiteman remembers 'I used to see these girls carrying on with the sailors, and I remember my brother and I used to hide behind the screen and watch them make love.'[109]

Steerage passengers were not permitted to enter the first or second class decks, but anyone could go down to the people in steerage. Among the Jewish women who ended up in the Valkenberg mental asylum in Cape Town were some who had been violated on board ship; the thick human presence down in the hold could not guarantee their protection.[110] The lucky ones found solidarity in groups of people they already knew, travelling from the same shtetl, or meeting up and sticking together as they journeyed.

It seems Bere's wife Beila was lucky. She and her children stayed in the company of a group of other Jewish passengers, all leaving Libau together for London and then onward from Southampton to South Africa.[111] I hope there were other children among them, fellow sufferers in their sea-sickness, as the ship heaved and slumped, and they cried for home.

After their night in the Poor Jews Temporary Shelter, they endured the second leg of their journey in the bowels of *The Briton* – the largest and smartest steamship in Donald Currie's fleet at the time. It would have been a fabulously luxurious experience had the Posels travelled first class. 'The accommodation was the finest yet seen on the mail route ... in roomy and spacious apartments fitted in rich mahogany.' The first class dining saloon, 'furnished in solid oak, with handsome carved work', held a 'splendid piano and a very fine organ'; the first class smoking room, with a central 'dome of stained glass', offered chairs 'figured in Morocco leather'.[112] Alas, this was all upstairs and entirely out of sight, let alone reach.

The Briton was carrying the arrangements of class from the imperial metropole to the Cape Colony. As they docked, most of the Jews from the Pale would start out exactly as they had travelled: at the bottom of the heap.

The ship took seventeen days to sail from Southampton, delivering Beila and her children to the port of Cape Town. Seventeen days and counting. In your small bed, even among the stink of bodies too closely ensconced, you could keep a piece of hope in your pocket, checking occasionally that it was still there. The journey would soon be over.

30 | 'They came with nothing'

In the story of the mythical shtetl, which tells of the journey from the abject East to the promise of prosperity in the West, its travellers 'came with nothing'. Immigration redeemed the pain of poverty by awarding a new beginning: a move onwards and upwards, from nothing to degrees of plenty.

In fact, we have no way of knowing how many left and arrived with nothing, a little, or a lot. At the very minimum, new immigrants to South Africa had to have brought the fees payable for admission to the country. Five pounds sterling per adult. For some, that money plus the costs of the voyage might have diminished their funds to nearly nothing. Knowing the speed with which Chatzkel bought property in Johannesburg after arriving, I think it's likely that he had left Pumpian with reasonably full pockets. Bere, on the other hand, who never acquired any property in Pumpian, must have had far less. Just like these two brothers, immigration would have been a mixed bag, money-wise.

Even if immigrants' coffers were empty, their heads were not. The older they were, the greater their previous experience in making a living, which came with an acquired bundle of strategies and tactics, skills and work habits, prior successes and failures. They would all travel with their working pasts, even if their working futures would look very different. Their cultural norms, values and prejudices, hopes and aspirations, varied as they were, journeyed too. The fault-lines and breaches of Russian Jewish communities, their ways of judging and withholding, forms of respect and modes of disdain, would migrate, arriving in new destinations and under new rubrics.

In the case of those who left the shtetl, however, there was one feature of everyday life that would be lost forever. In the shtetls, Jews and Christians lived alongside each other, dealing and trading; transactions with Christian neighbours in the local marketplace were essential to the Jews' survival. Jews were subject to Russian local authority, governed according to the rules of the town at large. Yet in the shtetls, Jews were usually in the majority.[113] It was the coercive contrivance of the Russian Empire: concentrate almost all the Jews in one place, limit their movement and stifle their prospects. But there was an irony in it too. Exactly that created the conditions for Jewish life where Jewishness – however divided and argumentative – was confident and secure. The exodus from the shtetl would leave this behind.

For the Jews who journeyed away, this would be the abiding challenge: living on the defensive, moving forward on the back foot, and all the while carrying the baggage they had brought with them.

31 | Those who stayed

Throughout the nineteenth century, Jewish life was centred in the Russian Empire: around half of the world's Jews lived there. The mass migrations of the late nineteenth/early twentieth centuries – momentous as they were – did not immediately change that.

By the start of World War I, around two and a half million Jews had left for various parts of the West, and particularly the USA. It was an unprecedented haemorrhage with profound effects on the future of Jewry in the West. Yet focusing too much on the enormity of the departures deflects attention from 'the most crucial, if little noted, element of the story of Russian Jewish mass migration, that it only accounted for one third of the Jewish population of the Empire. Two thirds of the Russian Jews stayed home.'[114]

In Western collective memory, most stories are told about those who left; there has been much less interest in the far greater numbers of those who stayed behind.

Overall, their lot was not a happy one. The Russian Empire fell, finally, with the Russian Revolution of 1917. Initially, this offered hope and promise for the Jews, who gained new opportunities and freedoms, as citizens of the new Soviet Union on the same terms as others. The Pale of Settlement was dissolved. Jews could move anywhere in the Soviet Union, enter universities in far greater numbers than ever before, and take up jobs from which they had been excluded in the past. Many Jews supported the Bolsheviks; some entered their government. Still, there were tumultuous and insecure times ahead, which saw Jews caught in the crossfire, once again, of virulent pogroms. Ukraine was the epicentre. The years from 1917 to 1921 saw the 'largest and bloodiest anti-Jewish massacres before the Holocaust'.[115] On one account, over one and a half million Jews were murdered, raped or uprooted.

World War I created other upheavals. Many Jews living on the so-called eastern front of the war had to flee their homes, as Russians accused them of loyalty to the enemy. In 1915, about six months after the outbreak of the war, the Russian military authorities exiled all Pumpian Jews to central parts of Russia.[116]

I don't know how many Posels were among them, but JewishGen records show that Bere and his oldest son, Leyzer, who had not accompanied his father or step-mother to South Africa, were in Simbirsk, in central Russia, in 1915. Itsyk likely died during 1913/4. Bere had not seen his parents for over a decade. Perhaps before the outbreak of the war, Bere, the eldest child, went back to Pumpian to say his farewell to his dying father, or went for the funeral and to pay his respects to his widowed mother – only to find himself stuck there, in the middle of a world war, and then dragooned, along with the rest of his Pumpian family, to Simbirsk. He returned to Cape Town after the war had ended, when Jews were free to leave.

After the war, Lithuania was declared a separate state, and Jews began to return. One was a Posel offspring, born on the cusp of the new century in 1899. She and her husband are recorded as having returned to Pumpian from Simbirsk in 1921. According to a government census of 1923,[117] there were then a little over one thousand one hundred people living in Pumpian, of whom only three hundred and seventy-two were Jewish. The vestiges of a community that had been shredded.

After a pause during the war years, Jewish migration from the Pale picked up again, which saved those who left from the dreadful fate of those who stayed. During World War II, Nazi troops cut a swathe across Eastern Europe, eliminating almost all the Jews still living there.

In Pumpian, on 15 July 1941, all its Jewish inhabitants were forced to leave their houses and crowded into a ghetto surrounded by a barbed-wire fence. Five weeks later, on 26 August, they were led into a nearby forest, forced to dig their own graves, and 'there, beside the long pits, all were shot to death.'[118]

The Jews who left the Pale as the twentieth century arrived had no way of knowing that they were journeying to save themselves.

32 | The 'East' of the 'West'

The journeying from the Pale was not merely a geographical migration; the Jews were relocating from one symbolic universe to another. Somewhere along the line, sooner or later, they would discover that they were from 'the East' in ways that were understood from standpoints of 'the West'. They would realise that from these standpoints, they did not necessarily know themselves and that unknown others considered them ripe for rescue.

They would become a battleground, in fact – for the Western Jews who had already been saved, or who had saved themselves, and for the non-Jews who sat in judgement of their successes or failures along the way. There would be various campaigns and strategic interventions, along with attacks and counter-offensives. It was a different scenario from the variety of challenges that marked the skirmishes of life in the Pale.

Edward Said reminds us that the imperial project in the West was very much a matter of meanings – and the power to impose them on subject peoples. The Jews from 'the East' were among those who did not fit neatly into the British colonial grid of racial difference and its civilising mission.[119] Ambiguous and unsettling, their place in the symbolic optics of the British empire would be defined by a racial oxymoron, as what some referred to as 'White Negroes'.[120] As if 'Eastern' Jews were not entirely Black, and therefore not wholly uncivilised. Yet they were not considered entirely White, and therefore not fully or appropriately civilised either. As low-grade, dark, Whites, they would be judged as lesser in particular ways, and targets of a civilising mission of a special type.

Part Four

33 | Rats

The *Cape Times* had nothing much to say on 25 September 1901, the day Bere's ship docked in Cape Town. There were a few pieces of good news. 'The Duke and Duchess of Cornwall spent yesterday at Ottawa. Their Royal Highnesses shot the rapids of the Ottawa River on a raft.' No injuries, thankfully. Closer to home, even better, the daily twenty-four-hour plague report, 'ending midnight last night, states that there were no cases in the Cape Peninsula'.[121]

Cape Town had been in the grip of a bubonic plague since the beginning of February that year. By May, there were about thirty-three deaths a week. The last plague victim was discharged from hospital in late November. Bere arrived as the contagion was ending. But that was not how it seemed.

From mid-February, the local authorities had taken the matter in hand. A handbill was circulated to all householders: 'For cleanly people in cleanly homes which are free from rats, there is practically no danger of getting the plague. DIRT, OVERCROWDING, WANT OF VENTILATION AND THE PRESENCE OF RATS encourage the presence of Plague in any home or locality.'[122]

'Uncleanly' people attracted the rats; but in the popular mind, it would not take long for uncleanly people to become the rats. Contagious in their dirt, contaminating in their stifling overcrowding. 'Raw kaffirs and filthy Asiatics', for starters.[123] Also, 'Europeans ... seldom of British origin, foreigners from every part of the Continent, consisting largely of Portuguese, Italians, Levantine and Polish Jews'.[124] And among that lot, the Jews in particular.[125] 'Cape Town is full of those Polish[126] Jews who live in dirtier style than the Kaffirs.'[127]

Encountering people named as 'Black'[128] would have been a new experience for Bere. Perhaps when Chatzkel returned to Pumpian in 1901, he had spoken to Bere about the 'Black' people he had already encountered in Johannesburg. Maybe Bere had read Yiddish newspapers publishing articles about Jewish prospects in South Africa, in which case he would have caught glimpses of the 'Blackness' of life in these parts. Writing from Johannesburg at the turn of the century for Jewish readers in the Pale, Meyer Dovid Hersch depicted Black people and Jews as bonded together in a life-giving commercial pact. 'Many of the businesses rely mostly on the purchasing power of the Blacks, as a spring of fresh and never-ending water,' he wrote.[129] Clean and cleansing. Hersch understood it perfectly: be grateful for these people, they will make your garden grow. Many of the first generation who came from Eastern Europe would go into some form of commerce; for most, their most profitable markets would be 'Black'.

There were fewer Black people in Cape Town than in Johannesburg. Many had arrived in that port town from more rural parts, in search of work; others, originally from elsewhere in Africa, had been slaves in the colony, and then freed after 1834. At the turn of the century, some had taken cover in District Six, an area named by the colonial authority, occupying about one and a half square kilometres close to the Castle (built in the seventeenth century as the colony's fort) and the foreshore. Earlier in the century, it had been a more middle-class space; by the late nineteenth century, District Six – with its convenient proximity to the harbour – had grown poorer, having become a destination for many of the insalubrious arrivals into Cape Town from other parts of the globe.

Bere would head there too. He would find himself amidst a human variety beyond anything he would have likely imagined: Cape Malays; Bantu-language speakers referred to as 'Natives' or 'Blacks'; Syrians, Lebanese, Italians, Greeks, Portuguese, and others from elsewhere in Europe; English, Scottish and Irish from the lower reaches of British society; Africans from various parts of the continent; Indians; Chinese; and Jews who had already arrived from the Pale and elsewhere in Eastern Europe. This was the most cosmopolitan area in Cape Town by far, where people of different nationalities and races, as they were then understood, lived precariously, pushing for space in these overcrowded parts, sometimes at odds, but mixing freely, should they have wanted to.

Did Bere recognise a fellow rat? Could he feel some empathy, a human recognition, for his Black and Asian neighbours, co-accused of being dirt and contagion? What is it that leads some to reach out, and others to pull back?

The ranks of Jews entering South Africa from the East would include those who did reach out. Some were neighbours, friends, lovers, teachers or caring shopkeepers, who extended a hand to those beyond their own. Others became more articulate about their stance, speaking a language of shared suffering among the poor and downtrodden. The first non-racial socialist organisation in South Africa (the Social Democratic Federation) was founded in Cape Town in 1904;[130] after 1915, District Six had its own branch of the anarcho-syndicalist International Socialist League, anti-racist in its cause, with several Jews as prominent members.[131]

Many, if not most, Jews arriving in their new homeland would choose a different path. As they crossed the South African threshold, they would have felt the force that pushed these various clusters of the victimised and vulnerable apart. In this new land of viciously skewed hope, becoming 'White' would make all the difference. Whether Bere comprehended it from the moment he arrived or not, he would soon have realised that he had landed on the lighter side of hope. By the end of that very year, most of the Black residents of District Six were removed to a location further out of town. 'Cleansing' the place of the plague provided the pretext. Racial prejudice was hardening. Cape Town was already on the path of racial segregation; the governing authorities were accelerating their pace. Jews would be spared, permitted to stay in District Six, 'dark' and 'dirty' as they were.

34 | 24 June 1902

The Briton, carrying Beila and her children down in the hold, sailed into Cape Town harbour on the morning of 24 June 1902. It was a Wednesday, an ordinary day, inserted between two other days of far greater significance. On the day before, Lord Horatio Herbert Kitchener – victorious Commander in Chief of the British armed forces and hero of the South African War – had received a rapturous send-off in Cape Town before sailing back to Britain. On the day after, Edward VII was scheduled to be crowned king of the United Kingdom and the British Dominions, in a ceremony set to bring these territories to a unified standstill, with all singing *God Save the King* at exactly the same time. The Wednesday could be nothing other than an interlude between one day of imperial hubris and another.

Kitchener left for Britain with the reputation of the British army restored. The war had taken much longer to conclude than initially anticipated, the Boers having won some unexpected victories at the outset. Then Kitchener, along with legions more troops, had arrived in South Africa and turned the tide of the war. Boer farms were destroyed, and women and children were imprisoned in concentration camps, where tens of thousands perished. Boer guerrilla forces were finally subjugated, and the war ended in May 1902.

On 23 June, Cape Town was ready to receive him. According to the *Cape Times*, 'every building in the city was gaily decked out in honour of the Great Commander' – all festooned with Union Jack flags and red bunting. The harbour too: 'the shipping at the Docks presented a remarkably gay appearance, nearly every vessel – from stately liner to humble tramp – being plentifully dressed with flags from bow to stern.' The large glass shop windows of the imposing department stores in the town centre were also clad for celebration. The two largest of these proud establishments were especially lavishly decked out. Stuttafords' windows boasted a 'special display of Table and Bed Linen'; not to be outdone, Garlicks mounted a 'special show of exquisite creations'.[132]

All these decorations would double up, just as appropriate for the celebration of the coronation on the Thursday as for the Kitchener reception, and so they remained in place on the Wednesday, just as they had been on the Tuesday. As it turned out, Edward VII would take ill on the Wednesday and his coronation would be postponed until August. But this news would take a day to reach the Cape, and so it was not until the Thursday that the removal of the decorations would begin.

Consider, then, how Cape Town presented itself to Beila and her brood as they arrived. As the ship headed towards the harbour, they surely gasped at the sight of Table Mountain: arrestingly grand, bewilderingly huge. The landscape of Pumpian was low-slung, not a mountain or even a swollen hill anywhere in sight. Life in the shtetl trained the eyes for flat fields and open grasslands: a modest geography lacking any wonders of nature, let alone a hunk of rock as monumental as confronted them now. They must have been astonished too at the imposing buildings that stood astride the edge of the foreshore, visible from the ship. Garlicks, Cape Town's newest department store, pushed five storeys up into the sky – an unthinkably bold and futuristic construction for a child of the shtetl. Its premises commanded an entire block with all manner of architectural ornamentation to exaggerate the statement: 'ornamental ironwork, mock Renaissance turrets, porticos, and other trimmings'.[133] And on that Wednesday, just like the other imperious colonial structures at their proudest, Garlicks was overlaid with all the victorious puffery of the moment.

Coincidentally, Beila and her children crossed the colonial threshold at the peak of its grandiosity, with the town at its most visually jubilant: a statement of the cultural and social distance they had travelled in the most strident of terms. Was it intimidating or exhilarating? Or both, in heart-thumping vacillation? What would it take to feel at home within such bombastic strangeness?

I imagine the seven-year-old Maurice wide-eyed and overawed in the presence of a spectacle of power and glory entirely unlike anything he had ever seen before. Would he remember it from then on as a promise and a temptation; what the colony had to offer its people, if only they wished to partake?

35 | Towards District Six

Bere would have been there as the ship docked, standing modestly and inconspicuously to the side of the pier, in the shadow of Table Mountain, waiting to escort his family to his lodgings in Longmarket Street, not far from the harbour. Beila surely heaved a sigh of relief to see him come into view; Bere had not let her down. There must have been agonising moments of doubt for many a wife arriving alone or with her children and wondering whether her husband had taken ill and died or abandoned her after a sudden change of heart. I hope it was a joyful reunion, for the young children too, otherwise bewildered by all that was new and foreign.

Bere would have made it a lot easier; he would have known where to take them: first to the Customs House to have their luggage checked and then to get their paperwork stamped. Beila had the flimsy permit, carefully stowed. All was in order. Perhaps a crusty official even grunted a greeting, or mustered a hint of a smile, given the festive mood of the moment; I'm imagining a promising start. Off they then went, their goods loaded onto a horse-drawn wagon, heading along Adderley Street, the wide main street of the town paved with wooden blocks to muffle the din of horses' hooves and clanking carts.

Turning left into Longmarket Street, past the well-dressed City Hall, the Posels would then leave the town's architectural finery and its immaculate wardrobe of red and blue behind. As they headed into District Six, the buildings took a dive from the lofty elevation of the town centre. Apart from a few vestiges of solid decorum, most houses were shabby and dishevelled, several on the cusp of dereliction, dressed only in their dirty underwear. Beila and her children would take their first steps into the colonial underbelly, rough and tough, a place of many colours, where the sound of the King's English was scant amidst the noises of more ebullient life.

Longmarket Street was the longest in the town, starting high up in the Malay quarters of the Bo Kaap and then descending through the town centre into District Six at its western edge. The Posel family made their way to the house at number 28.

At least, that's how I have put two and two together. Beila's permit for entry to the Cape stated that she was joining her husband who was living in Longmarket Street. I know that in 1901, when Bere arrived in Cape Town, Chatzkel's brother-in-law Harris Plein was there too – one of the many Jewish refugees fleeing the war in the Transvaal. (Chatzkel had gone back to Pumpian briefly during this time.) By 1902, the Cape Town Voters' Roll included Harris, listed as a 'general dealer' living at 28 Longmarket Street. The municipal vote was restricted to property owners, so Harris had done well enough to buy the house he was living in. It was the norm at that time for Jewish home owners to rent out rooms to paying tenants. Given the family connection, I'm surmising that Bere would have been one such tenant in Harris's home, bringing his family there too when he collected them from the harbour a little under a year after he himself had arrived.

The Posels would spend their first night in Cape Town in a small house, dusty and cramped. At least that much would be familiar.

36 | A shtetl that wasn't

The Posels joined the ranks of the many hundreds of Russian Jews who had unpacked their bags and settled in District Six. In some respects, they had left one shtetl and would now take refuge in another. Here was another sizeable and conspicuous concentration of Jews, most of whom were working hard to establish themselves in one or other form of trade, or plying their artisanal skills in the textile, leather, tobacco or construction businesses that sprang up. They were setting up synagogues too, determined to keep up their rituals of regular prayer.

The streets of District Six were already bustling with raucous commerce: butchers, bakers, drapers, shoemakers, cabinet makers, booksellers, tailors, greengrocers, liquor stores – many of them already Jewish-owned. And many of the new arrivals would set up more. There was more noise, in more languages, than they had been accustomed to back home. But the Jews could make themselves heard and their presence felt, even so. As Beila began exploring the neighbourhood, she would have taken some comfort from the Yiddish signage on several shop fronts and the high volumes of garrulous Yiddish ringing out in the noisy outdoors: a thread of connection winding through these strange spaces. For most of the Jews, Yiddish was still their lingua franca, despite the scorn for the language from the English and German Jews already settled in Cape Town: a mere 'jargon', they spat. Some of the families with a bit more cash employed domestic servants, usually Cape Malay men or women. Many of them too learned to speak Yiddish.[134]

Most of the Jewish children in District Six would go to Jewish schools, in or nearby the area. There was kosher meat, bread and various home-spun delicacies for sale, and a Jewish-owned hotel or two offering kosher food to their customers. There were Yiddish plays to watch. Bookshops, like the renowned Beinkinstadt's, provided Jewish meeting places and the prickly comfort of a heated argument on common ground. One shilling could buy a dip in the local *mikvah* (ritual bath), with a small bar of soap, clean towel, and hot and cold water.[135]

There were the predictably Jewish rifts too, not least in a proliferation of 'little shuls' alongside the grander synagogues already there. Equally familiar were the arguments and skirmishes that erupted between the various congregations: 'the people of the one did not like the people in the other'.[136] And associations were emerging in District Six that mirrored some of the ideological divides that had marked life in the Pale, between varying types of socialists, Zionists and orthodox Jews, all grappling with their transitions from one world of Empire to another.[137]

The push up the social ladder was making itself felt too. Many were preoccupied with moving up and out to more genteel parts of the city. Louis Fiddel, who spent his early childhood in District Six, recalled one of the 'little shuls' as a place to start, and from which to move on, as prospects improved. 'The people that came here [from Russia] started here and they made money and they became a better class, [then] they went to the Gardens shul. Or they went to the Roeland Street Synagogue ... and if you were well off you belonged to two shuls. You paid your way in Roeland Street shul or Gardens shul, but you also became a member of the smaller shuls.'[138] For many of the Russians in District Six, in those early years, the synagogues were a focal point of Jewish life; routines of worship and celebrations of Jewish festivals and the sabbath continued to punctuate the rhythms of the everyday.

Yet District Six was not a shtetl after all. Here, Jews were in a minority, taking their place alongside many others with their own faiths, ways of life, styles of dress, walking and talking: a concatenation of cultures, and a range of phenotypes in a wider variety of body shapes, sizes, skin shades and claddings than these Jews had ever encountered before.

Ruth Schechter arrived in Cape Town in 1908, married to the eminent Jewish lawyer Morris Alexander. She did not come from a shtetl, but she spent time visiting people in District Six and made the point with a keen eye. For 'the stranger who lands in Cape Town,' she wrote, 'the coloured people will be of a variety of dress, complexion and general appearance that will be a new spectacle for him': 'women with tight fitting bodices and wide gathered skirts, touching the ground, their skins all the shades from the olive ivory that would be white in a Latin town, to the blue-black-black that seems to have a bloom on it like a black grape'; 'a lad with a fez on his head [who has] a pale brown skin but negroid lips'; young sisters, one of whom is 'nearly white' and the other one 'many shades darker'; slim women with 'dark brown skins and Chinese slanted almond eyes'.[139]

Exploding the narrow horizons of shtetl life, District Six would open its Jewish inhabitants up to a far wider world, concentrated into one small, heaving space, blaring sounds and flashing colours that were entirely unfamiliar. Did the new arrivals find it frightening or invigorating? Full of possibility or replete with menace? Or all of the above, in confusing combinations, one day different from the next?

To be sure, getting by in District Six would not be easy. Most accommodation was near derelict. Many landlords renting space to eager tenants refused to spend anything on repairs, and the colonial authorities were lethargic and disinterested in local improvements except in emergencies, when they were urgently called upon to investigate dangerous conditions: walls collapsing, cracked balconies teetering precariously, burst pipes. Standards of sanitation were low. Brawls erupted on the streets, sometimes with a racial spark. Indignant residents would complain about 'disgraceful rowdyism', amidst the many 'gambling dens' and 'public houses'.[140] 'By the 1890s,' writes historian Vivian Bickford-Smith, 'gangs were common: one terrorized the Harrington Street neighbourhood on Saturday nights, [while] a "Malay mob" was "at work" in Buitenkant Street hijacking vans.'[141] District Six was a criminal home ground, with police in cahoots with local and international syndicates and their lackeys.[142]

As I see it – looking back – life in District Six was remarkable nevertheless, even unique. Bere's bad timing – arriving in Cape Town during the South African War, making a move to the Witwatersrand impossible – meant that he, like his neighbours in District Six, had accidentally arrived in that part of South Africa with a less brutal, more fluid record on racial mixing than elsewhere in this territory. As the nineteenth century reached its end, what some saw as this 'special tradition' of Cape liberalism was under siege; but it had not been erased entirely.[143] Its residues were still in evidence, and especially noticeable in the cosmopolitan, poorer areas of town like District Six. Neighbours from who knows where lived cheek by jowl. Political associations and their meetings – and protests – were mixed. Any of the locals might sit next to each in the same bioscopes and theatres or strike up conversations in the same shops or bars or on the narrow streets.

For new immigrants, here was a real live education in what this new country of theirs was made of, bottom up: hands-on lessons in how to get along and make good – or bad – in new ways. For most, it would be an experience they would not have again, the closest they would come to such motley lives.

37 | 'Squat-bodied'

The official permit enabling Beila Posel and her four children to sail to Cape Town in 1902 recorded details of her bodily appearance.

Age about	44	Complexion	Dark
Height	4½	Hair	Black
Build	Med	Eyes	Black

Beila was only four and a half feet tall – as officially measured. That's a mere one hundred and thirty-seven centimetres.

I struggle to imagine a woman so short, stepping off the ship into bustling crowds of higher types. How could she have made her way in the alien colony without being invisible, an absent presence? Or worse: visibly overlooked, looked down on?

Human height has varied significantly over time. It's largely an environmental matter, height being one index of overall health and welfare. 'Human stature,' say Joerg Baten and Mathias Blum, who have studied the phenomenon historically, 'is a well-established indicator for the biological standard of living, positively correlated with a nutritious diet.' Collating disparate sources of data, they discovered that in the late nineteenth century, average height declined in Africa and Asia, while Western and Eastern Europe saw 'dramatic height increases after the 1870s'. By 1900, the average stature of males in Europe was 168 centimetres, compared to 163 centimetres in Asia.[144]

In the case of Jews, the measure of height was different.

In the mid- to late-nineteenth century, in line with the burgeoning interest in racial 'science', 'the Jewish body' became an object of what was purported to be scientific knowledge.

'SQUAT-BODIED'

Various body parts – too large or too small, ill-shaped or misaligned – were copiously measured and compared. Height, for example. According to a study of the population in Galicia published in 1876, Jews were much shorter than Poles and Ukrainians. Another author reported in an article in 1906 that the average Polish Jew was as short as 160 centimetres, which was 'far below the average height of the Poles'. It was sign, supposedly, of 'the effeminacy of the male Jewish body'.[145]

Standing shorter, lower standing.

When Jews from Russia journeyed to the Cape, they took 'the Jewish body' with them. It did not escape colonial attention. I'm thinking of Sir Patrick Duncan, for example. British born and Oxford educated, he came to South Africa in 1901, appointed by Lord Milner to his government to assist in anglicising the Transvaal, recently elevated in Britain's imperial project by the discovery of gold. A successful legal career followed for Duncan, together with a succession of cabinet positions. His was a life of worthy and illustrious colonial service, culminating in his appointment as governor general, the first South African resident to occupy that position. More accolades followed, including from the University of Cape Town. The institution saw fit to celebrate the achievements of Sir Patrick Duncan with its highest award of an Honorary LLD degree at a graduation ceremony in 1939.

The colonially impeccable Sir Patrick Duncan had this to say about Jews. 'I have many Jewish friends whom I like and admire. But something in me revolts against our country being peopled by the squat-bodied, furtive-eyed, loud-voiced race which crowds Muizenberg ... We have too many of them.'[146]

38 | Shapeshifting

Squat-bodied – or what the medical officer of Cape Town called 'inferior physique'[147] – was the least of it. By the early twentieth century, Jews had to contend with newly toxic versions of antisemitism that drew every which way from the supposed science of race. Jews, now defined as a distinct race, found themselves judged biologically – and therefore ineradicably – deficient. For any number of reasons, this was an imprecise 'science'.

Their bodily blights and blemishes were many, albeit changeably so. Sometimes it was their noses, judged to be offensively large; almost all the antisemitic postcards in circulation around the turn of the twentieth century depicted Jews with exaggeratedly bulging protuberances. But when small-nosed Jews came into view, it could be their shrunken stature or unpleasantly swarthy complexion – until a tall, pale Jew came along, whose deficit was then something else.

A demeaning physical trait could also be seized as a marker of a deeper, more menacing blemish – such as the alleged look of the Jewish eye that opened a window onto the deficits of the Jewish psyche. So said Francis Galton, for example (who coined the term 'eugenics' while pursuing his racial research), when visiting a Jewish school in London's East End where he did some of this work. 'As I drove to the school through the adjacent Jewish quarter, the expression of the people that struck me was their cold, scanning gaze, and this was equally characteristic of the boys. I felt, rightly or wrongly, that every one of them was coolly appraising me at market value, without the slightest interest of any other kind.'[148] A lively prejudicial mind could make a variety of links and connections. Here, the long-standing stereotype of the Jewish Shylock – mean, scheming, greedy – found its way into and onto the Jewish body.

Typically, it was the poorer Jews – dishevelled and unkempt – whose bodies offered themselves up for classification as recognisably different from non-Jews. In the case of more affluent, well-groomed Jews who blended well into Western bourgeois society, a different challenge arose. If distinguishing Jewish bodily features could chop and change, the differences might sometimes disappear altogether, when Jews and non-Jews looked all too similar. 'One does not recognize him; unnoticed, he invades all circles.'[149]

This made another sort of case for a science of race: one that looked beyond bodily appearances altogether to an inner essence that differentiated a Jew from a non-Jew after all. As Deborah Cohen puts it, writing about Jews in late nineteenth century Britain, 'racial categories could arise as a response to apparent similarities, as well as the perceived differences, between Jews and Britons. Put differently, Jews came increasingly to be identified as a race precisely because they were difficult to differentiate from their fellow citizens.'[150] Which is what then defined them racially: Jewishness was distinguished by its duplicity, as it sought to conceal itself, masquerading as something else: 'he slips through the fingers like eels.'[151] The Jewish race comprised those who dissembled and disguised, which therefore also made them untrustworthy, scheming and dishonest. Especially – it was claimed – in relation to money; another one of those lateral connections. In these instances, writes Alain Finkellerant, 'racial hatred and its blind rage were essentially the Jews' punishment for no longer placing their differences on display.'[152]

Yet another dimension of this mobile antisemitic sentiment came into play once the Eastern Jews made their presence felt en masse in the West. The diminished body of the poor Jew now carried the additional stain of the Orient: the despised East of the West, culturally strange, less civilised, darkened by its difference. The lesser Russian Jews – and the evocation of the Russian Empire more generally – became a foil, a benchmark against which to measure how much more the West had advanced. Historian David Feldman writes that 'the notion of a backward and medieval Russia was arguably as significant as that of Darkest Africa in validating Britons' sense of their modernity at the start of the twentieth century.'[153] In the eyes of the Western Europeans receiving them, the migrating Russian Jews arrived wearing the mantle of that backwardness. Many antisemitic cartoons of the day depicted the smart bourgeois Western Jew as a dirty Oriental in disguise: the 'real' Jew exposed.

But this was a cartoonist's fantasy: as if modern Jews in the West could be visually undressed in this way. As Jonathan Judaken puts it, 'the ambiguity, ambivalence and heterogeneity of Jewish identity – the obsession but ultimate failure with categorizing or compartmentalizing "the Jew" – was one of the defining markers of "the Jewish question" in the twentieth century.'[154]

39 | At risk

As Bere and Beila tried to accustom themselves to their new surroundings, a haughty distaste at the stream of 'dirty' Easterners infiltrating the Cape Colony was making itself felt in polite White society. The stereotypes of the time – 'hordes of hook-nosed Polish and Lithuanian Jews whose evil countenances now peer from every little shanty'[155] – popped up in the pronouncements of magistrates and other officials, in various periodicals and papers, even in novels of the day. 'Look at the hang-dog faces, the bowed shoulders, and the shambling walk of specimens of the race who are landing here and ask whether they are "men". Of course they are not.'[156]

District Six became notorious as the geographical core of the problem, with its concentrations of this 'lowest class of Russian and Polish Jews, filthy and evil smelling',[157] with 'that hunted crafty look'.[158] A journalist for a Cape Town paper recoiled at the 'hard white faces of the wives and daughters of the hunted Russians, sitting on shabby balconies or lounging against the shop doors'.[159]

This was bad news for the established Jewish community of Cape Town. For one thing, these Jews – of British and German origin – shared some of the distaste. Much like their counterparts in the UK and the USA, Cape Town's settled Jews felt entirely estranged from this 'piece of Oriental antiquity in the midst of an ever-progressive Occidental civilisation'.[160] For another, these undesirable arrivals threatened to upset the delicate equilibrium that the Anglo-German Jewish establishment had worked very hard to create.

The first Jewish community in Cape Town had developed around mid-century. By the end of the nineteenth century, most of them had assimilated rather smoothly into the Cape Town colonial elite. They sang *God Save the Queen* (or *King*) whenever appropriate; the local congregation sent messages of congratulations and support to the British sovereign whenever timely. In the main, life in the colony had been good to these Jews. Religious freedom came with the British takeover from the Dutch in 1806, and there was little overt discrimination on the grounds of their religious difference.

Culturally, too, these Jews had found ways to adapt and fit in with relative comfort – as observed by one Lady Duff Gordon, for example, who visited the Cape in 1861/1862. 'These colonial Jews are a new phenomenon to me. They have the features of their race but many of their peculiarities are gone. Mr L, who is very handsome and gentlemanly, eats ham and patronises a good breed of pigs on the "model farm" on which he spends his money. He is (he says) a thorough Jew in faith, and evidently in charitable works; but he wants to say his prayers in English and not "dress himself up" in a veil and phylacteries for the purpose; and he and his wife talk of England as "home", and care as much for Jerusalem as their neighbours.'[161]

On the other hand, the experience of Benjamin Norden mid-century had sounded a cautionary note, not to be forgotten. A leader and spokesperson for his fellow Jews, on excellent terms with the local British, Norden – a merchant – had made the mistake of reneging on an undertaking not to supply a convict ship with provisions. Other Jews, appalled by his disobedience, rallied to defend their community against the ensuing colonial outrage. 'Norden was ostracized and boycotted by Cape Town merchants ... [and] he became the victim of riotous behaviour, stoned [on the street] by angry mobs.'[162] Fortunately, the hostility eased, and equanimity returned. But for the Jews, the message was clear, confirming lessons learned many times before in

Europe and the United Kingdom: when the going is good, don't rock the boat. Keep it afloat because no one else will do it for you.

To this end, the Anglo-German establishment committed itself zealously to proving and publicising its colonial loyalty. Remarkably, in 1904, Cape Town would appoint its first Jewish mayor. Hyman Liberman, arriving in South Africa from Birmingham as a child, would occupy the position for three years – a demonstration, it was said, of the Jewish community's commitment to civic engagement. As their numbers expanded, the respectable Jews oversaw the building of an impressively large and well-appointed new synagogue – the Great Synagogue, as it was known – in the heartland of the colonial polis, near parliament. Its overseers made sure that its consecration was a visibly colonial ritual. The cornerstone was laid, in 1904, by His Excellency the Governor, the Honourable Sir Walter Hely-Hutchinson, in a ceremony that included a prayer for the King. Consecrated in 1905, the service in the synagogue would be led by the town's most prominent religious leader, Reverend Alfred Bender, a Cambridge graduate, who also took up a chair in Hebrew at the South African College (precursor to the University of Cape Town) and joined the institution's governing council. An influential and popular figure in the town, his pockets full of sweets for the colony's children, Bender had friends in some high places, well beyond the confines of Jewish circles.

Bender was set on nurturing and demonstrating what he called 'the Jew's capacity for citizenship'.[163] Religious gatherings provided one such opportunity. In 1901, for example, a special service, held in the Gardens synagogue, was reported in the *Cape Times*. It illustrated Bender's approach perfectly – including the fact of its coverage in that venerable paper. 'The synagogue was crowded, amongst those present being a number of regulars and Town Guardsmen dressed in uniform, a fact which lent an appropriate significance to the service. The minister for the evening was the Reverend Professor A.P. Bender, M.A., who preached a most stirring and eloquent sermon which could not possibly do otherwise than rouse his congregants to a feeling of deep and patriotic responsibility which they owe to this country, and to their creed.'[164] A country, in Bender's words, 'illumined by the sunshine of British rule'.[165]

How, then, to transform the shuffling Oriental throngs into upstanding Occidental colonial subjects? Reverend Bender was one among several who would turn their attention to that challenge.

40 | Upstanding work

The most immediate challenge was one of upliftment: to ensure that the most vulnerable of the new arrivals did not descend further into outright destitution. It was a nobly charitable commitment but also driven by an urgent wish to erase the spectacle of Jewish poverty, and the embarrassment it caused.

Various charities set to work, both galvanised and unsettled by a sense of polite repugnance. The Jewish Ladies Association, for example, sent their social workers to 'the dismal slums and congested areas where, amid unhealthy and uncomfortable surroundings, a poor Jew or Jewess needed succour, help, advice or encouragement. Social and philanthropic workers coming into actual contact with this phase of life often found it difficult to carry on their labours, but the workers of the Philanthropic Society and the Ladies Association carried on courageously to assist those who had fallen by the way. They laboured in common to maintain our poor.'[166]

Reverend Bender – champion of such philanthropic initiatives – also offered his services at the vanguard of a strategy of anglicisation, intended to bring the Easterners into the Western colonial fold. Bender, wrote Louis Mirvish, 'despised "foreigners" – which included Russian Jews – and considered the old forms of religion to be outmoded. Yet his kindness overcame his prejudice and he was ever ready to help a needy individual or a deserving cause.'[167] Louis Mirvish was a son of Rabbi Moses Mirvish, who arrived in Cape Town from Lithuania in 1908 and ministered to the *Beth Hamedrash Hachodosh* congregation, favoured by the beleaguered Russians. Louis would become a colleague of Bender's at the University of Cape Town, where he lectured in physiology until 1929, and was also actively involved in Jewish public life. His reading of the illustrious Bender, then, is likely well informed: as one who was convinced of the superiority of his version of Jewish life and was both compassionate and determined in his efforts to spread it around. The kind paternalistic version of Western Jewish contempt for their oriental cousins.

Much of Bender's energies were directed towards the children of the immigrants, encouraged as far as possible into English-medium schools with appropriately colonial curricula. Bender saw to the creation of various clubs and associations that would familiarise children with colonial ways and interests.

His purview included adults too, especially in helping them to learn English. Bender had already organised the first English night school in District Six, opening in 1897. He understood perfectly well the imperative of learning the language as a first and crucial step in lessening the cultural distance the newcomers would have to manage. The then Jewish establishment was entirely of like mind: as far as possible, Yiddish was to be replaced by English, the language of the colonisers. In 1903, an editorial in the *South African Jewish Chronicle* – vigilant in its mission to rehabilitate the Jews from the East – insisted that 'anything which cultivates the art or practice of Yiddish speaking in a European colony is actually detrimental to the Jewish people and their cause'.[168]

Morris Alexander also played a critical role in smoothing the integration of the new arrivals into the life of the colony – in his case, as a lawyer willing to engage the colonial courts on the Easterners' behalf. By the early 1900s, Alexander already had a reputation as an eminent professional. After his first legal degree at the University of the Cape of Good Hope in 1896, which earned him a gold medal, he secured his second degree from the University of Cambridge. Returning to Cape Town in 1900, he turned his attention to the plight of the immigrants from the Pale. At his instigation, the Roeland Street synagogue was set up for new arrivals, with Alexander (although not a rabbi) leading the congregation.

The Immigration Act of 1902 – which prohibited any further entry to the colony of those who were not recognised as 'European' – galvanised him further. After Jews in Johannesburg had established their Transvaal Board of Deputies to represent their interests, Alexander moved to do likewise in Cape Town and became its first president. Wearing this hat, in 1903, he seized an important victory, prevailing upon the Cape legislature to accept Yiddish as a European language.

Here was a rather breathtaking irony. At the same time as the settled Jewish establishment embarked on a mission to banish the 'jargon' of Yiddish as a backward tongue, Alexander heralded Yiddish as boasting the badge of the civilised West. Confronting the Cape legislature, he argued that Yiddish was an offshoot of German – which he demonstrated by asking a non-Jewish German speaker to read and translate some Yiddish. His case was incontrovertible, and succeeded in keeping the gateway into the Cape colony open to the Yiddish-speaking Easterners.

Alexander had effectively situated the Eastern Jews within the 'European' camp, as required by the Immigration Act. In the emerging racial parlance of the day, 'European' would be tantamount to 'White'. Alexander's intervention was decisive in enabling Yiddish speakers to claim legally protected citizenship and the opportunities and privileges of Whiteness that went with it.

As historian Riva Krut points out, this was not Alexander's doing alone. Usefully, his goal aligned closely with the interests of the politically more muscular Donald Currie. Panicking at the prospect of more holes in the holds of his steamships and the loss of income this would cause, Currie used his connections to keep the Cape open to his Jews from the East.[169]

Alexander was a liberal and professed his support for a non-racial franchise in the Cape. During his legal career, he would take on anti-racist causes, and stood with Mahatma Gandhi, his friend, in Gandhi's fight for non-racial recognition.[170] But in tackling the Immigration Act on technical grounds – to find a place for the Jews under the mantle of 'Europe'– rather than opposing it as a matter of non-racial principle, Alexander's focus was on the Jews alone. The gates would close on the Asians and Africans.

Others on the two boards of deputies had no liberal qualms at all, their views amplified by the *South African Jewish Chronicle*, set up to be the main mouthpiece of Jews in the country. An article in this increasingly authoritative publication asserted one fundamental principle that should bind all Jews, irrespective of their political party allegiances and their countries of origin. 'The Jews ... if they wish to act up to their name, are pledged to maintain the superiority of the White man in this country. As Jews, they object to being put on the same level as the Coloured races.'[171]

A declaration of colonial loyalty, this was also a call to Jews from the East to see where the light came from, and to align with it, even if 'the White man' still judged them dark, dirty and distasteful.

41 | 28 Longmarket Street

Another consequence of the mass immigration from the East troubled the respectable Jewish establishment, pulling its reputation down into the gutter.

There were brothels aplenty in Cape Town at the turn of the century. Sex work criss-crossed racial and ethnic lines, bringing in Jews too. Some walked the streets and slunk into alleyways when the opportunity arose; others operated from a variety of brothels dotted around in the architectural mix. Some operations were low-key and home-spun. Others were writ large on global maps of the international sex market: locations for 'consignments of women-mongers and girls'[172] involved in the White slave trade, many of whom were Eastern European Jews. Even more compromising, some of the leading pimps were too.[173]

Charles van Onselen has drawn some of these maps in vivid detail in *The Fox and the Flies*, an account of the life of Joe Silver, a notorious Polish Jew who made South Africa the capital of his sprawling prostitution racket. Van Onselen surmises that while living in London prior to this, Silver may have been the monstrous Jack the Ripper.

Silver owned several brothels in Cape Town, including a house at 28 Longmarket Street – the very house to which Bere likely had brought his family in June 1902. In Silver's hands, it would become one of his smartest brothels, a 'French-styled *maison*', designed to keep out the sex-seeking dregs. 'A peephole at the front door enabled the *madame* to cast an eye over the would-be clients before admitting them …. Reception rooms had printed cards bearing the names of the ladies of the house, a move away from the low-price, high-turnover strategy.'[174]

Silver had taken possession of 28 Longmarket Street on 31 December 1903 – one and a half years after Beila and family had moved in. It had cost Silver in the region of £800.[175] He bought it from Harris Plein, who then moved three doors down, to number 34.

Although I can't be sure, I assume that the Posel family accompanied Harris to his new house at number 34, since the move was so soon after they arrived, and Harris would still have wanted paying tenants. If so, the convergence of their lives, however fleetingly, with the heinous Joe Silver makes me gasp. Did Bere and Beila make his acquaintance as he visited to survey the property, just an ordinary visit from one Yiddish-speaking resident of District Six to others? Could the Posels have made friendly small talk with the ignominious Silver? I have no way of knowing, but the historian in me marvels at this unexpected discovery of the moment at which a crumbling, neglected house of the past is reinvented as a structure of globally notorious substance.

Organised Jewry, however – in both Cape Town and Johannesburg – were on a different sort of mission. The White slave trade was a global issue, drawing mounting condemnation. It was well known that South Africa was a lucrative node in the operation, and that Jews were centrally implicated. The local Jewish establishment felt the urgency of shutting it down – in line with their counterparts in other parts of the world blighted by the same problem – and threw in their lot with local authorities of like mind on the matter.

It wasn't an easy operation. Many in the police were complicit with criminals such as Silver, not least for the kickbacks they enjoyed. But in 1904, the authorities did ultimately prevail, using the services of a Jewish detective to trap Silver.[176] Under threat in other parts of the country too, Silver – sensing his moment in South Africa had passed – left the country in 1905.[177] At least one part of the Jewish prostitution blight was erased, even if not all of it.

42 | Choices

As the first decade of the new century was ending, a landscape of opportunity for newly arrived Jews in Cape Town had taken shape. Accepted legally as White, they could naturalise as British subjects, own property and enjoy legally unfettered access to financial credit. They would encounter no barriers to education (including access to university) or health care – in fact, no formal official disadvantages at all. Economically, the colony now saw a period of expansion after the depression of the war years and their immediate aftermath, offering the Jewish immigrants many openings – some small, others more sizeable – into burgeoning consumer markets.

And yet the terrain was also jagged and hostile. Antisemitic prejudice would persist – in the hostile judgements, the contemptuous rhetoric, and sometimes worse. Socially and culturally, it was clear: the Jews from the East were 'dark' White; second-class Whites, inferior to the colony's White-Whites, the Western Christian mainstay of 'civilisation'. It wasn't surprising, then, that Beila's permit of entry to the colony had recorded her complexion as 'dark'.

Whiteness was a hierarchy, after all; social class and culture would define the rungs of its ladder and the actions required to ascend it, one step at a time. Progress was not guaranteed, however; it was not impossible that the dark Whites would stay low, if they did not do what was required to lighten their way.

Bere would have faced a range of options on how to proceed. There he was, in District Six, able to converse in Yiddish, comfortable enough with fellow Jews from the Pale, as well as some from his home town of Pumpian. I've been able to track at least four other families from there who settled in District Six, including those of Messrs Sandler and Furman, who ran one of the local kosher butcheries. Having initially done a roaring trade, their prospects plummeted, and they went insolvent in 1910. Bere was one of their customers, who owed eight shillings one pence on the eve of the insolvency, and paid up[178] – the one and only act that inserted Bere into the colonial archive, apart from his death.

Getting ahead was far more likely had Bere been willing and able to breach the informal walls of District Six's Yiddish comfort zone. Naturalising as British would have been a big step ahead, opening the door to formal advantages enjoyed by White colonial subjects. Learning to speak and write in English – normally a prerequisite for naturalisation – would have made an enormous difference. A document for prospective Russian immigrants, published by the Jewish Colonisation Association based in St Petersburg, had underlined the point. 'The whole country is opened up to a person who can speak English; he may look for a job everywhere he is able to.'[179]

No doubt all of this would have been easier for younger people, who had more energy and determination to succeed than the older arrivals like Bere – already beyond middle age. But making the most of the colony's opportunities was also a matter of character: what we would recognise today as emotional intelligence. A willingness to take risks, an ability to engage with strangers, an affable demeanour, savvy insights into the ways and character of others, a confidence to endure the slights of prejudice. These traits would be necessary to enable the foreigners to link up with helpful cultural and linguistic interlocutors, build business partnerships and establish networks, including reaching beyond their own people. Today's public sphere is replete with phrases that describe these prerequisites effectively: a matter of 'good people skills' and the ability to build 'social capital'.

During the nineteenth century, back in the Pale, this discourse was unknown, of course, but the imperatives and preconditions were very familiar. Life for the Jews there had made similar demands and created opportunities along similar sorts of lines. For anyone entering the marketplace, mixing with cultural strangers was *de rigueur*. Transacting across cultural boundaries had been good for the stability and dignity of Jewish communities amid the habits of hostility and suspicion that prevailed in the Pale. And before the harsh strictures of the late nineteenth century, porous economic boundaries had rewarded those with an entrepeneurial bent who ventured out into faraway places.

Back in the shtetl, Bere had displayed little of this kind of skill or inclination. Even his enterprising, socially adept father had seemingly failed to motivate or educate his eldest son to reach out and up. The odds of Bere leaping into action in a strange and demeaning setting were surely low from the start.

Perhaps his old wounds were reopened too, as the shtetl hierarchies that had pushed him down made their presence felt in District Six. Louis Mirvish wrote that the Russian immigrants 'brought with them the caste system that used to exist in the shtetl'.[180] In religious gatherings, for example, or the discussion groups arranged by the new arrivals, people were assigned seats according to their perceived status. Yet again.

Bere did not naturalise as a British subject. Letters of reference vouching for the 'good character' of the applicant were required. Perhaps Bere was an abidingly unlikeable man for whom such letters were not forthcoming; I don't know. I suspect that a key reason for his having remained a Russian subject was that he could not sign his name in English. He might have accomplished a smattering of spoken English, or Afrikaans (easier to learn for a Yiddish speaker than English), enough to exchange a greeting or two with others beyond his own tribe. My suspicion is that Yiddish remained his lingua franca and that his working life was largely confined to the inhibiting familiarity of Jewish life in District Six.

43 | Carrier

Early on in my research into Maurice's family, I headed off to the Western Cape government archive in Roeland Street, Cape Town, in search of one of the few official documents that bore his father's name: Bere's death certificate.[181] I knew it would provide some basic information about my great-grandfather's life, including his line of work while alive.

There it was. A line in the document noted: 'Occupation in the life of the deceased: carrier'.

I confess that taking in that line in the busy silence of the archival reading room evoked many emotions. Bewilderment – what on earth was a carrier? Bemusement, even some incredulity – a carrier? Really? Disappointment – was that all he could manage? I could see my own snobbery unwittingly on show.

Back home, I googled 'carrier'. Most of the search results referred me to carriers in Victorian Britain. A list of Victorian occupations in London in 1891, for example, includes this: 'Carrier: a person who drove a vehicle used to transport goods'. Did colonial carriers go on foot, or were wagons also in regular use? Did Bere have a wagon? Not when he died, according to his estate papers. But by then he was likely long retired and would have disposed of any such thing.

I scanned the *Early Cape Town Jewish list*, compiled in the first decade of the twentieth century. It's not comprehensive, but contains several hundred named immigrants and their occupations. I see no one is listed as a carrier. In other historical material I read, I see references to 'Natives' as 'carters': people who carted things around from place to place, usually with wagons. Carters and carriers must have been one and the same; also in some contexts, a 'cartage contractor'.

In 2012, Cape Town's Jewish Museum held a special exhibition on the Jews of District Six. It recorded the presence of at least one other Jewish carrier/carter who lived there. One early resident, a child at the time, recalled him as a figure of fear. 'There was a cartage contractor – a huge coarse man with an extensive vocabulary of Yiddish swear words. He used to refer to his wife and his horse as "*klatche*" (mare) and as he approached his house after a day's work he would shout out "*klatche!*" and we children never knew if he was referring to his wife or his horse.'[182] Thankfully, I am sure that this could not have been Bere; there are no genes for huge people in the Posel family. If and how he swore at his wife is another matter.

I gleaned nothing more about Bere's working life. It is most likely that he acquired a wagon and a horse or two, and transported a variety of goods. The harbour was close by. Perhaps he became one of those people who transported the new Jewish arrivals with their meagre baggage into the rough and tumble of District Six. Perhaps he hired labourers and assisted the Jews who moved out and up from there, into more salubrious parts of town. There were many possible permutations, all compatible with him being limited to the confines of his colonial illiteracy.

I am certain about one thing though. His was a menial occupation, which must have paid relatively little, offering nothing by way of a step-up on any ladder of social reputation or prominence. As a man of work, he would remain entirely insignificant and invisible in any greater scheme of things. Ne'er one of the *balebatim*, not even close.

On my reading, Itsyk's and Chaia-Sora's oldest son had headed out of Pumpian with a load of failed expectations. Already a carrier, so to speak. He had surely hoped to make something more of his life. But the load was too heavy.

44 | Smous

A range of economic opportunities presented themselves to immigrant Jews willing and able to move beyond their Yiddish enclaves. The most familiar one – and the iconic figure of the start-small version of Jewish success – was becoming a travelling salesman of some kind. As historian Hasia Diner writes, this was the course followed by millions of immigrant Jews from the East in other parts of the world too: 'literally, the most pedestrian segment of world Jewry, the peddler, making his way on the new world's many roads'.[183] In South Africa, he – I have not encountered any female peddlers – was commonly known as a smous.

Unlike in the USA, relatively few Jews who arrived from the Pale entered the proletariat by taking a job in a factory or sweatshop of some kind. Many more went into one or other form of trade. For those who arrived 'with nothing' (as is commonly told), or thereabouts, becoming a smous was a predictable place to start.

Likely having to borrow a small amount of money to get started, a smous sold his wares in towns or beyond, trudging the dusty streets or rural pathways with his merchandise bundled on his back, or – as his fortunes improved – riding a wagon with bigger bundles than his back could have borne. If his wagon trade had gone well, he might have set up a shop, and in rare cases, moved on to what would become a gigantic commercial enterprise.

The Jewish Museum in Cape Town offers a tribute to this figure. 'The footsore smous, the itinerant trader who trudged and trundled between farmsteads selling all manner of articles to farmers and their families, has become a figure of legend within South African Jewish memory.'

Traders had been criss-crossing the vast South African hinterland for over a century, supplying the basics to outlying farmers and their families, but also bringing some of the extras that fired the consumerist desires of people longing for more: soft, shiny, shimmering things like lace, ribbons, buttons and mirrors. When the Jews arrived, their ranks were full of men who were willing – whether they liked it or not – to head for the hills and try their luck selling all manner of things in unknown parts.

It took courage and emotional stamina. Many a smous travelled long gruelling distances through remote and uninhabited parts of the countryside. These journeys were dangerous: laden with goods, smouses could be robbed or, worse, violently attacked or killed. Activist and writer Lorna Levy discovered that her grandfather, a smous who lived in Kimberley, was murdered by his two hired assistants as they headed out of town.[184] His progeny – including Lorna – had been entirely ignorant of this family tragedy. As she realised while she was researching the incident, her family was likely not the only one to have silenced and suppressed the occurrence of a murder: 'bad news was not something to communicate.'[185] So strong was the drive to do well, and to be seen to do well.

We do not know how many others smouses had faced a similar fate, or a violent attack that led to serious injuries. There must have been others and there may well have been many, erased from memory.

The experience of a largely solitary life on the open road could also take its toll psychologically; some were undone by the anxiety and stress. In her history of Valkenberg asylum in Cape

Town, Sally Swartz notes several admissions of single men who had been trying to make a living as smouses. 'Business worries' were typically listed as the main cause of their psychological distress, exacerbated by their having been alone and intensely lonely, with no family or friends offering financial support or emotional succour.[186]

Thousands of new capillaries of rural trade grew off the main arterial routes. And by then, there was oh so much more stuff to sell: fruits of the Industrial Revolution and its technologies of global circulation. Big and small, expensive and cheap: something for everyone, a salesman would say. From bicycles, cameras, typewriters, telephones and sewing machines, lights and lamps, to small trinkets, beads, mirrors and cheap ornaments; the latest in crockery and cutlery, household furnishings and 'fancy goods', as they were called, through to inexpensive eating utensils, pots and pans; new trends in women's, men's and children's fashions, as well as more humble clothes and shoes; pills and potions, soaps and detergents, cigarettes, chocolate and champagne. A lot of this stuff would be city bound, but the desires of far-flung consumers were changing too. Jews would be the most frequent agents, and beneficiaries, of that change.

For South Africans, all these new things were the fruits of the world of Empire, courtesy of Great Britain. For the smous, they also opened doors to different relationships in its more troubled outposts: in the homes of Afrikaans speakers who despised the British, even if they enjoyed partaking of their stuff. Many stories are told of Afrikaner farmers welcoming a smous into their homes, as fellow 'people of the book'.

Whether this was a shrewd business tactic on the part of the Jews or a ritual of meaningful connection – and perhaps a mix of the two – it has infused the memories of some whose ancestors started out as a smous. Harry Ostroff's father, for example, was a religious man who travelled with his prayer book. 'When they arrived at an Afrikaans farmer,' he recounts, presumably as his father had recounted to him, 'for the first two days they were entertained and in the evening there was a Bible session, with my father bringing out his *Tnach* [Hebrew version of the Old Testament] and the farmer bringing out the Bible. Through the bush telegraph the other farmers were told, "come, the smous has arrived", and then the surrounding farmers could come along, and they would do business.'[187]

As the conflict between the British and Boers gathered momentum, through and beyond the South African War, most Jews aligned with the British, but there would be Jews on the side of the Boers, partly as a result of these kinds of encounters. And some Jews would settle in Afrikaans-speaking communities, the first of those who became known as the *Boere Joode*.

Proud recollections of the resourceful smous have their limits, however. Historians Richard Mendelsohn and Milton Shain sound an appropriately cautionary note: 'the smous has been romanticised in South African Jewish memory', ignoring the extent to which the smous became 'a figure of derision'.[188] Articles in the press and reports from state officials portrayed the smous as 'dishonest, cunning and exploitative';[189] the 'bloodsucking' smous also made his way into some novels of the day.[190]

Sometimes – perhaps often – he was simultaneously welcomed and derided, by people liking what he brought but not he who brought it. Novelist Francis Brett Young writes about 'the little Jewish smous' who was 'welcomed by every farmer and farmer's wife ... as the sole purveyor of imported luxuries and cheap European merchandise, which he brought to their doors in his donkey-wagon'.[191] But Brett Young goes on to describe the smous as less than human – 'an insect', small, wiry, cunning, repulsive. An ugly bearer of beautiful things.

The fact that Jews worked hard to make their goods available everywhere, to satisfy everywhere the longings to consume them, meant that they too were everywhere. Sometimes too much so for the locals to stomach. The smouses' commercial wins created other kinds of losses. They had to live with both.

45 | Good eggs and bad eggs

For Jews with grit and savvy, some useful transnational connections, and a big chunk of luck, there were many opportunities to earn a living – and sometimes achieve the status of success – beyond the well-trodden pathways of the smous. Most of these have remained unknown, falling outside the remit of established economic histories. I have crossed paths with a few, adding to the surprises of ordinary life among the first generation who came from the Pale.

The egg market in Cape Town at the turn of the century was a case in point. Here's the first surprise: most of the eggs consumed at Capetonian breakfast tables at this time were imported. Hundreds of thousands of eggs arrived at the docks every month, packed in cases of around three hundred eggs each. They had been ordered by wholesalers, who sold them to retailers, who sold them over the counter, or to peddlers who trudged door to door, a few eggs in hand. The second surprise is that this market – from the wholesalers through to the peddlers – was dominated by Russian Jews.

Three wholesale companies met much of the town's demand for eggs. Two were wholly owned by Russian Jews. The third was co-owned by a Jew and a Portuguese man from Madeira. A court case in July 1903, duly recorded and meticulously filed in the colonial archive, opened an unexpected window for me on how this market worked.

In January 1903, the Table Bay Harbour Board made a mistake, delivering twenty-nine cases of eggs, worth around £64 and consigned to Berman, Grolman and Co., to one of their competitor companies instead.[192] Sacks, Chiat and Cumes took possession of the eggs, without paying for them. Berman,

Grolman and Co. claimed against the Harbour Board for the value of the missing eggs and were duly compensated. The Harbour Board then tried to extract the money from Sacks, Chiat and Cumes, who offered them a payment of £43. It was £21 short, so the Harbour Board took the matter to court.

The trial begins. Several participants in the egg trade are called to testify. Samuel Berman (of Berman, Grolman and Co.) is first and explains how their business works. 'We do a large business in imported eggs. We dispose of about 100 000 weekly. Our firm, the defendants, and another, are the largest importers in Cape Town. In February the SS Kanzler brought 190 cases of eggs from Lisbon for us. There were 297 eggs in each case. Of these, it was found that 31 cases were short, and it was found that 29 had gone to the defendants.'

Berman is cross-examined by Morris Alexander, acting for the Table Bay Harbour Board – the same Alexander who would soon make his most significant legal intervention, persuading the colonial government that, like all these eggs, Yiddish was 'European'.

In response to questions from Alexander, Berman continues. 'Madeira, Lisbon and English eggs come into this country. Lisbon eggs are always the cheapest. The Kanzler eggs were very, very good. They cost roughly 7/ per hundred. I sold these eggs at different prices. I sold the Kanzler eggs at 18/ per hundred.'

Clearly a substantial profit is possible. A mark-up of eleven shillings per hundred eggs offers a whopping return of around 157%.

Retailers who bought the eggs from these wholesalers are also called to testify. All are Jewish. One of them, Lewis Levin, mentions inter alia that he recently bought eggs from a different wholesaler, Klein Brothers and Plein; also Jewish.

The court rules in favour of the Table Bay Harbour Board. Sacks, Chiat and Cumes are ordered to pay £60 plus costs.

As it turns out, Harris was the Plein in Klein Brothers and Plein. It must have been he who supplied Bere and his family with their breakfast eggs, hopefully at a wholesale price, in their home in Longmarket Street.

In 1903, Chatzkel – Bere's brother – would set up home in Marshall Street, in the heart of Johannesburg's heaving inner city. His house would be part of the slum yard – Posel's Yard – that I had brought to Gertrude Posel's attention in 1994. Barnett Cumes – of the wholesalers Sacks, Chiat and Cumes – would live opposite him on that same street. One of Cumes' nieces would marry Aaron, Harris Plein's oldest son. Benjamin Grolman – of Berman, Grolman and Co. – would later move to Johannesburg and, after several years, would marry my mother's grandmother Chaia – his second marriage, her third. A familiar Jewish social geography, with all its serendipity.

46 | Nothing ventured, nothing gained

For those immigrant Jews with the appropriate character – risk-takers at heart – earning a living could be a matter of improvisation: chancing their luck and living with the odds, pushing through some of the small gaps that opened, falling through others, on the edges of the law, sometimes falling outside, clawing up the first few rungs on a precarious social ladder, even if only to fall again. Theirs was a life of boom and bust; surprising successes could fizzle out and die just as quickly and unexpectedly as they came to be. Many went bankrupt and liquidations were frequent; some achieved satisfactory returns, a few became rich.

Residents of the Cape in the late nineteenth/early twentieth century had surprisingly abundant access to financial credit – a significant economic opportunity. Mortgage bonds were readily available across the board, with no restrictions of race or gender. These were monies loaned by individuals as well as banks or other financial institutions, instituted and overseen by a formal contract. Occasionally a Black woman took out a bond; more frequently it was men, and more often than not, White men. Many Jews were among them.

The opportunity was fulsome, but also very risky. Partial repayments were expected half yearly, including interest – the rate often as high as ten per cent. After three years, the lender could demand repayment of the loan in full, at three months' notice. Often, the only way to manage that was by raising another bond – or two – for a comparable value. Many insolvencies arose from debtors being unable to meet the terms of their bonds.

I went through many archival records of such transactions and was struck by the apparent ease and frequency with which Russian Jews took possession of mortgage bonds, and sometimes surprisingly soon after arriving in the Cape. Some did so cautiously and judiciously; others more blithely, even recklessly. From what I saw, non-Jewish applicants typically took a bond in the tens or hundreds of pounds. Jews tended to be a lot bolder, some raising upwards of one or two thousand pounds at a time – husbands and wives both.[193] They then usually used this money to buy residential properties and rent out the rooms to paying tenants. This was one of the most common paths of upward Jewish mobility in the early years of colonial life.

It was not a straight road onwards and upwards, however: more like snakes and ladders. Up, up, down, sometimes up again, as business cycles produced property declines, and sometimes collapse, as in the case of the economic depression that set in right after the South African War. For the more inexperienced, taking their chances in a world of colonial business they ill understood, their fate would lie with the luck of the market's dice.

The working life of one Jacob Cosay tells of the turbulence of confident – and naïve – daring. A Russian Jew, he came to the Cape in 1896 at the age of nineteen from Mogilev in Belarus, a flourishing city, rather than a beleaguered shtetl. Maybe that provided some of his brash bravado. When he applied for naturalisation as a British citizen in 1899, he described himself as 'an importer'.[194] To some extent, he was. A minor importer of small things. Fancy goods, so-called, which were much in demand among consumers in the countryside.

Jacob Cosay became a smous. He gathered his imported fancy goods, along with other wares he bought on credit from local wholesalers, and off he went, in search of sales. But he rapidly became more besides. He began taking out mortgage bonds, which he used to buy properties that he then rented out. Some of the rent paid for his wares; the rest he reinvested in more properties, some residential, some shops, along with more bonds to up his investment game with each step he took.

Cosay started his loan-taking with a bang: his first bond, which he secured just one year after he had arrived in town, was for £1 300. Two years later, he had mustered five bonds, all in the thousands of pounds. But then he came unstuck. He owed the venerable Cape Town wholesaler J.W. Jagger and Co. the sum of £121, which he could not repay. The case came to court, and Jacob's assets and liabilities were publicly probed. During just three years in the colony, he had accumulated all of this: 'some fancy goods and shop fixtures valued at £200, and six houses and shops in Caledon Street and a piece of Land in Mill Street at £4 050. He also had debts to the value of £297.'[195]

The court sequestrated his estate. Jacob had to start again. This he did in 1900, with vigour and aplomb. By 1904, Cosay had taken out a staggering seventy-seven bonds! Most were in his own name; some were in the name of his wife.

Imagine the vertigo. The Cosays were now so flush with cash that they both became money lenders themselves, giving mortgage bonds to others.

Then, in October 1904, as the post-war economic depression was taking hold, Jacob died – 'somewhat suddenly'. It may be that he took his own life, overwhelmed with shock and shame; that same fate befell others in those difficult times. His wife had to face the demands of their debtors. She owed £400 on one of the mortgage bonds, a payment that she could not afford. Once again, the matter was heard in court, which is where I find the trace. By then – a mere eight years after he had arrived in the Cape – Jacob Cosay's assets had ratcheted up to £36 150. Most were land and property, a little in money lent out. Sadly, his liabilities had soared even higher, to £47 169 – mostly bonds on properties that had not yet been paid off.[196] Mrs Cosay's estate was sequestrated. She lost everything.[197]

47 | Business in the mix

Most Jews imagine that Jews went into business with other Jews: an ethnic thing, and the source of many a *farribel* too. But that wasn't necessarily the case. Many commercial partnerships crossed over into non-Jewish territory; and sometimes they would reach beyond the familiar trade routes of South African colonial commerce too, breaking the predictable mould.

The immediate attraction of these sorts of business partnerships could have been the solution they offered to the immigrant Jews' language problem. Those recently arrived from the Pale spoke Yiddish and would usually take some time to master English. Many of the non-Jews they encountered likely spoke much better English and could write the language effortlessly. In a colony that had introduced a legal requirement for businesses to keep their books in English, as another way of keeping the aliens out, finding an English-speaking partner could be a smart move.

For example: Harris Chiat – of the egg merchants, Sacks, Chiat and Cumes – also went into business with one Joseph Debs, far more worldly and well travelled than he. Debs, a 'wholesale merchant and importer' born in Lebanon, was fluent in English. He had spent five years living in Trinidad before journeying for another five years in parts of Europe and America before arriving in the Cape.[198] Here was one invisibly ordinary biography of remarkably far-flung mobility and improvisation on a global stage. Jewish partners could jump into the slipstream of people like this, people with links in distant places outside the South African colonial mainstream.

Jose Taxeira, another global itinerant, was born in Madeira and spent six years on the Mercury Islands (off the coast of New

Zealand) before migrating to Cape Town. Arriving in District Six, he was on the lookout for a business partner and found an eager Jew. He and Shalowsky set themselves up in the egg trade, but they ranged more widely too, importing fresh fruit and other produce from Madeira. Taxeira's brother, based in Madeira, arranged financial support on his end.[199]

I could tell you about many other partnerships – but with one glaring absence. In all the business ventures in these early years of the twentieth century that I have tracked, I haven't yet discovered a case of a Jewish person going into business with someone the colonial authorities deemed 'Non-European': a Coloured, Asian or Native partner, as they were then known.

District Six was nothing if not mixed. People – at least some of them – transacted, socialised, loved and married across racial lines. The place was also a hive of trade, and many new business associations were made there, in that motley cosmopolitan hub. The 'Non-Europeans' living there were eligible for credit in the form of mortgage bonds, as were the Jews. Abdullah Abdurahman – eminent doctor and elected the first so-called Coloured city councillor in the Cape in 1904 – was just one among the Coloureds of District Six who availed themselves of that opportunity.

Setting up a business required applying and paying for a trading licence. Colonial authorities were more inclined to grant trading licences to White traders than others; Asian traders had to walk a particularly rocky road. But to my knowledge, in those early years of the twentieth century, there was no law that prohibited an inter-racial business.

If so, then in that first phase of Jewish working life in the mix, no law was necessary. The barriers were self-imposed – obstacles of mistrust and distaste. The manual on colonial status-making was making its presence felt. And maybe not always from one side only. Would an aspirantly respectable Coloured man seeking to advance his business prospects have looked askance at a 'dirty Jew' too?

48 | Ways for women

It was an irony of patriarchy in the Pale that Jewish girls typically enjoyed a far more worldly education than the boys. That was thanks to the closeted world of the *kheyder* being largely off limits to them: girls were neither required nor expected to study the Torah. This difference equipped some of those girls to challenge and question the world of their childhoods, in quests for wider horizons.

Some of the women who left the Pale for far-off destinations – particularly women of the *maskilim* – were literate and assertive, with an eye to new futures. Other women emigrants were of more traditional bent, shaped in the mould of the *kleyn-shtetl-vayber*: experienced dealers in the daily produce markets, accustomed to interactions with cultural strangers, speaking their language. Few of the women of the Pale who took to the seas were of the stay-at-home type – even if some aspired to do more of that.

The British colonies offered a softer landing to women who were longing for more bourgeois ways of family life: men at work as the main breadwinners, women preferably at home to take care of children, taking a job to supplement the family income if necessary. This was the preferred White colonial way, after all. It reflected the preferences of the Anglo-German Jews of the Cape too. Part of the anglicisation strategy favoured by the Benders of the town was to put the Russian women in their place (in both senses of the term) – in their homes and with their children as far as possible, their husbands as head of the household.

For the women who had grown accustomed to the cut and thrust of the marketplace, with their young sons out of reach in the *kheyders*, colonial life could be either a rude shock or a welcome reprieve. For better or worse, their role as mothers was substantially redefined. Most Jewish children in Cape Town – boys and girls – attended secular schools; religious education was an after-school extra, usually at private Talmud Torah schools created for that purpose. The all-day *kheyder* had given way, and as a result, a *melamed* was no longer a dominant presence in the boys' lives. Mothers would move into some of that space, spending much more time with their sons than had been the shtetl norm. The caricature of the overprotective Jewish mother smothering her sons is a product of the modern diaspora, not of the shtetl.

Of course, this had a class component to it. This way for women depended on the sufficiency of their husbands' income. For many immigrant families, that was not the case. Some women would work from home, often as seamstresses. Others would help out in their husband's store. A few were more enterprising and started businesses of their own – a boarding house, for example.[200] The most successful among them would have transferred their shtetl skills to the new colonial milieu.

Alongside the resourceful women who adapted with flair, however, were many others who floundered, unable to find their feet on the new colonial ground. Beila was one of those.

Her surname, Rabinovich, was common, and without knowing where she was born, it has been impossible to trace any of her lineage. Her marriage to Bere was probably arranged, either with the services of a matchmaker or directly between her parents and his. He had been married once before, and already had four children, so perhaps some compromise on Itsyk's and Chaia-Sora's parts was necessary. Still, I imagine there was some similarity, status-wise, between Beila's parents and Bere's. Middling, at the very least, if second best was required; 'well-to-do', if the better outcome. In either scenario, the young Beila would have learned to read and write Yiddish – either with the help of a personal tutor, or at a school for Jewish girls, private or state-run. She probably also learned to read and write in Russian and maybe studied the basics of history and chemistry. Not an illiterate or entirely uneducated woman, then.

Some of this is borne out by the fact that Beila signed the permit for entry to the Cape, issued in Libau, with an assured hand, clearly the mark of a woman who had had a basic education at the very least, sufficient to enable her to master the Yiddish script.

In Pumpian, she could well have been one of the outgoing *kleyn-shtetl-vayber*, particularly since her husband seems to have been an unreliable breadwinner.

In Cape Town, I find no sign of the *kleyn-shtetl-vayb* in Beila. When she joined her husband in District Six, she might have considered finding ways to supplement the family income – particularly since Bere's job surely generated little. But helping her husband out was likely not an option: his was not a line of

Beila Posel's signature. Permit for entry to the Cape Colony, 1902.
Author's photograph of original document in author's possession.

work to which his wife could contribute. Doing anything else would have required some initiative and stamina on her part, and courage to take on an unfamiliar setting.

Beila's death certificate records her occupation while alive as 'housewife'.[201] There is no indication there of a time frame, but I am inclined to think that she was a housewife throughout her Cape Town life, remaining meek and retiring in a colonial setting that churned her stomach. The colonial archive led me to discover that, like Bere, Beila's limitation would have been her failure to move beyond the confines of Yiddish.

In 1928, after Bere had died, Beila had to sign a particular form in the process of settling his estate. I found that yellowed paper in the Roeland Street archives. Reading through it produced a dramatic revelation: the ageing Beila could not sign her name in English. The place on the form reserved for her signature was marked with a cross (noted as 'her mark'). Above it, an official had written out her name on her behalf. After no less than twenty-six years in the colony, Beila had still not learned to read or write in English.

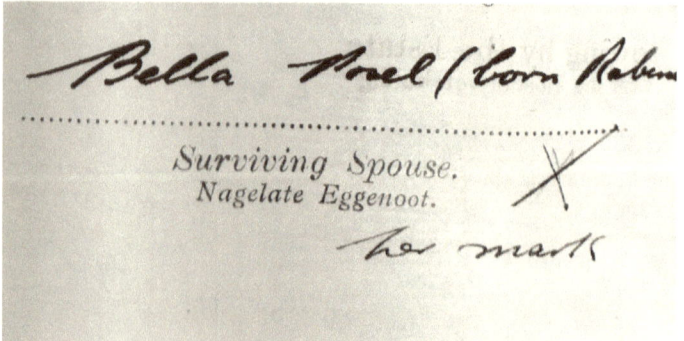

Official form for settling Bere Posel's estate with Beila's X. Western Cape Archives and Records Service. Author's photograph.

An exceedingly short woman of alien tongue. Alas, I can't see her striding out, making her way in that new world with any confidence or conviction. After a life of hustle and bustle in a small crumbling shtetl, I suspect she made a quiet retreat into the recesses of an ever-foreign, affronting town.

49 | Love and marriage

Already wobbly in the Pale, the old traditions of love and marriage took a harder knock in the move to the West.

Colonial life in the Cape delivered a blow to the Jewish case for arranged marriage; here, arranged marriages were associated with darker peoples, lower down the supposed scale of civilisation. Many young Jews took heart and insisted on choosing their own spouses.

Some of the more stubborn and tenacious Jewish parents were undeterred and married their daughters off in the old way, with or without the services of a paid matchmaker. One resident of District Six recalled matchmaking discussions around the fish carts on the street.[202] Some of these marriages took root and grew, but many withered. Local Yiddish writers told stories of arranged marriages going awry.[203] Still, a few dwindling die-hards stood their ground. In researching the lives of Jewish immigrant women, Veronica Belling discovered cases of arranged marriages persisting until a few decades later, as women sought help finding husbands who came with money and status, even if they were older and their shoulders sagged.

The biggest challenge for the faithful was Jews 'marrying out'. Amidst the human variety and dense proximity of District Six, love could subvert the discipline of the faith; and then what? Novelist Patricia Schonstein Pinnock tells a lyrical story of a Coloured woman who spent her early adulthood in District Six of old in the arms of a Jewish man from the East. A man needing love and a warm embrace, which he was lucky enough to find outside his tribe.

'Ouma met Mr Bauman when she was a young girl in District Six. He had just arrived from Russia. Stepping from a tossing ship onto the still earth at the foot of Table Mountain. He was running from sorrows and from things my Ouma never spoke about. All she said was that he was poor and alone and that he owned a coat and the clothes on his back. When she met him, his eyes were already deep and stained by the sad things of life. My Ouma held him and let the sun warm his back. She rocked him and put away his pain and helped him make his life again.'[204]

The story is fictional, but entirely plausible. As Mandy Sanger, of the District Six Museum in Cape Town, commented, District Six was 'one of the few places in the world where you'd find Muslims with Jewish surnames such as Benjamin or Levy'.[205] Some of these were originally slave names;[206] but not all. Noor Ebrahim, who worked at the District Six Museum, grew up in the area before District Six was razed to the ground from the 1960s by apartheid's bulldozers. His neighbours, he told me, were Levys, the offspring of a Jewish father and a Moslem mother.[207] And in earlier times, Betha Padovich, who grew up in District Six after her family arrived from the Pale in 1910, recalled having a 'Non-White friend in the early days; she lived near me, a beautiful little Coloured girl ... she was from a Jewish father and a Non-White mother.'[208]

Betha remembered 'a great many Jews ... marrying out of the faith'. For her parents and their adult acquaintances, it was 'painful', and difficult to speak about.[209] Another one of those erasures: the uncomfortable realities of immigration that were best forgotten.

The challenge extended well beyond District Six. Jewish men in far-flung places, lonely and isolated, made their lives among non-Jewish others; many fell in love there and married, including across the colour-line. Some of these husbands approached the nearest synagogue hoping to convert their wives to Judaism, but seldom with any luck: 'the policy of the congregation usually was to refuse such requests for fear of encouraging intermarriage or for other reasons, and only to permit those sanctioned by the Chief Rabbi.'[210] For the local Jewish community, intermarriage was tantamount to social death; the rabbi and the family sat *shiva* (went into mourning).

A Jew who married a Coloured person was lost to 'the White race' as much as to 'the Jewish faith'. Typically, in those early years, the Western Jews were more preoccupied with the former, while the Easterners were more focused on the latter. Conveniently for all concerned, much of the time these imperatives would align, even if their priorities would differ and the distaste across the line from East to West and back again was palpable. It's likely that the majority of Jews remained in the fold.

For the Posel family, rooted in the mix of District Six, the score card on marriage went up and down. Sarah, Bere's oldest daughter from his first marriage, took the hand of one Solomon Ginsburg, a fellow Jew from the Pale. They married in 1911; she was nineteen and he was thirty-one, already a merchant living in Rustenburg, in the Transvaal. Perhaps someone arranged an introduction; Solomon was getting on, after all, and would likely not have crossed Sarah's path socially in District Six. The outward signs point to a stable marriage. They stayed together; he did reasonably well, owning a shop and investing in a few properties that he rented out. When he died in 1951, he left Sarah and their two sons comfortably provided for. So far so good.

Bere's younger daughter Leah, on the other hand, was far more troublesome. Her chosen match – which I'm sure was not arranged in any way – was a man called Maurice Livingstone. They married in Cape Town in 1916; she was twenty-one, he was twenty-three. He had been the manager of a tobacco company in Swakopmund, in German South-West Africa.[211] By then, she had renamed herself Lydia. One – or both – feet out of the shtetl-that-wasn't.

Not only was this husband not Jewish; he was also a convicted criminal – twice. In 1920, Maurice Livingstone was sentenced to eighteen months' hard labour, having been found guilty on eighty-four counts of fraud and forgery. Livingstone had been practising as an accountant. Boris Kaplan, 'dealer in bones' and an Eastern Jew, was one of his clients. For almost a year, Livingstone had written out and cashed a series of cheques, totalling many hundreds of pounds, in Kaplan's name, forging his signature. The bone business was busy; perhaps that's why it took a while for Boris to see the scam. The court record showed too that Maurice had come to the Cape Town court with a previous conviction in Johannesburg in 1917 already in hand: also on charges of forgery and fraud, with a sentence of two terms of three months' hard labour, served concurrently.[212] The newly-wed Livingstones must have headed north to Johannesburg to start their married lives, but then fled back to Cape Town to escape the shadow of Maurice's conviction, only for him to darken their lives once more. A son-in-law jailed twice: not what Jewish in-laws would see as a *chap* (a good catch) for their daughter.

I'm not surprised that this snippet of family history was entirely hidden. Grandfather Maurice never made any reference to a sibling in Cape Town; it was as if she had never existed. Perhaps Bere and Beila heaved a sigh of relief that Livingstone was White; things could have been worse.

50 | One of those who froze

The fact that twenty-six years in Cape Town could not turn Beila's hand to writing English has weighed on my mind. It must have been abundantly clear to her that to unlock the colonial door, some mastery of English was essential: the key, in fact. Why did she choose not to do it?

It was not for lack of opportunities; there was more than one avenue to a colonial signature. If Bender's school for adults did not appeal, there were others. The Jewish Culture Club and the Dorshal Zion Association – organisations run by Russian Jews in District Six[213] – both offered English lessons.

Informally, too, there were fellow immigrants who had arrived earlier, knew something of the lie of the land and were willing to show the newcomers the ropes, linguistically and culturally. One of those ministering that sort of help recalled it in touching detail. 'It was people like us that helped the Greeners [new arrivals] that came from Russia to speak English, to understand the life, how it had to be in a strange land, because we knew what it was like to live in a strange land …. We taught them a little bit of English, we taught them that they have to send their children to a Christian school. We taught them that they've got to mix with people, they mustn't take notice because we are anglicized instead of being *Eastern Europekeit*. And they began to learn from us. They began to understand that you took a person in and how you give them a cup of tea, how to give them a piece of cake, you know, all of this.'[214]

Beila was not one of their takers.

Amidst the success stories of the immigrants who made good, often extraordinarily so, it's easy to forget the degree of dislocation and social alienation suffered by others: those who did a far less impressive job of putting down roots and ascending the social ladder into positions of prosperity and respectability. 'Acute homesickness' was common, writes psychologist Hannah Hahn, in her book *They Left It All Behind*, on the experiences of Eastern European immigrants to the USA.[215] Veronica Belling translated many Yiddish poems and stories written in South Africa that wail with longing for home – the real one. Intense loneliness was a prominent theme.[216]

Some were completely undone by it, finding refuge in a mental institution removed from the demands of daily life. Psychologist Sally Swartz has written about the Jewish patients admitted to Valkenberg in Cape Town from the late nineteenth and into the early twentieth century, among whom were several struggling with the 'melancholia' of their displacement.[217]

For those who managed to keep going from one day to the next, there were two ways of dealing with the emotional pain. One was to disavow and repress it, retreating into a silence born of denial, in a dogged attempt to 'move on'. Many generations later, families still comment on how little their ancestors spoke of their experience of immigration, of what they left behind and what they came to.

Another was an emotional freeze, stuck in the thick of that loss, unable to process the pain and refusing to engage with the new realities of living home-less. Beila must have been one of those who froze, her colonial illiteracy a marker of a traumatised failure to adapt and accept where she was and what was required of her. A woman who had lost her way and did not have the emotional wherewithal to find a new one.

Trauma has become a much-overused word, but it's appropriate, I think, in making sense of Beila's Cape Town life. Hannah Hahn makes a useful distinction between 'big T' trauma and 'small t' trauma. ' "Large T" trauma refers to events such as war, predatory violence, sexual abuse, which cause such horror and threat that they permanently alter an individual's coping ability; "small t" trauma, while not threatening to life or physical safety, are instead "ego-threatening"; they can cause helplessness and may have a cumulative effect. "Small t" trauma can include ongoing poverty, daily discrimination or abrupt relocation.'[218] Beila's refusal to leave the cultural and emotional space of the Yiddish world of District Six was surely a case of 'small t' trauma, which she was unable or unwilling to deal with.

Beila's dedication to the preservation of her ticket to sail and her permit to arrive now starts to make sense. For a woman so invisible, and so marginalised, these documents may have provided a kind of testimony she felt she needed, for herself and for her progeny: official evidence of her colonial existence, which was otherwise an unconvincing ghostly approximation thereof. Or the documents may have become more like totems, with the power to light up the past, rekindling memories of what she had given up back home in undertaking the journey that the ticket required of her. Here was proof in writing of the cause and trajectory of her loss; an ironic reminder of the woman she had abandoned, lost somewhere along the way.

51 | What's left behind

Bere died on 23 April 1928, without a will. This meant that his estate had to be managed by the Supreme Court. I presume it was because Beila could not communicate effectively in English that the master of this court appointed her step-daughter Leah, the only one of Bere's children resident in Cape Town, as the executrix.

Bere left a meagre contribution to his family's financial well-being; but it was not nothing. After deductions for various expenses, a little over one hundred pounds remained. The master of the Supreme Court decided that it should be distributed equally between his widow and four children.

This simple matter would take an inordinately long time to see through to its conclusion, however, producing a flurry of letters between Beila's Maurice and a remarkably responsive master of the Supreme Court, all neatly slotted into Bere's estate file. I marvel at the punctiliousness of the official archive, and the ordinariness of the record;[219] there was no necessary relationship between the copiousness of the correspondence and the magnitude of the issue.

The dry back and forth in the paperwork so carefully filed also opens an unexpected window on the texture of relationships in this family. When Bere died, only Leah was living in Cape Town; his other children in the country – Sarah, Gershon and Maurice – had all relocated to Johannesburg. This left Beila largely at the mercy of Leah and her husband Maurice Livingstone. Things would soon turn nasty.

The root of the delay in settling Bere's estate was a conflict in the family, with Beila, Maurice, and his half-siblings Sarah and Gershon, ranged against Leah and her man. Given Livingstone's record of fraud, it's unsurprising that the family took fright on discovering that the amount remaining in Bere's estate (modest as it was) was paid into Leah's post office savings account on 14 July 1928, on the understanding that she would distribute it within the family – and nothing happened.

Beila's Maurice wrote repeatedly to the master of the Supreme Court urging respectfully that he prod Leah into fulfilling her duty. Maurice feared 'that the small amount would be squandered'. The master obliged, sending a letter to Leah.

By early October, no payments had materialised, and Maurice's brother-in-law, Sarah's husband Solomon Ginsburg, sent his own letter to the master. 'Mrs Posel is now here under our care. She complains that Leah Livingstone with her unsavoury husband, sold up her home [I assume this means the contents of her home, since she did not own any property] while she was in hospital and that they have converted the money to their own use. They used violent threats towards her if she interfered with their plans, which they told her was to obtain the estate money for their own children.'

The master replied, dutifully promising another letter to Leah. But again to no avail. At the end of October, Maurice wrote again: 'I have written on three different occasions to the Executrix, Mrs Livingstone, yet all my letters are ignored.' The master wrote to Leah yet again.

Still nothing. Maurice prevailed on the master at the end of December to take the matter in hand, once and for all.

The meagre monies were finally paid out, twenty-six pounds and three pence each, in March 1929.

The matter ultimately reached a satisfactory conclusion; no money went missing. Perhaps that was why it never became a full-blown *farribel* added to the family canon and duly passed down to the next generation. But it explains to me why I had

had no idea of Leah's existence; she was entirely excised from the family memory, as if she had never been.

Beila died a year and a half after her husband, on 19 October 1929. Her health had declined precipitously during the period of conflict with her step-daughter, and the upset of being removed from her home, reassigned by Leah and Maurice Livingstone to the Jewish Old Aged Home in Cape Town.

Bere and Beila were buried in the old Jewish cemetery in Maitland, Cape Town. I have visited their graves, which are not far apart and have identical-looking gravestones. Unlike the nearby gravestones, which stand tall, with texts memorialising the dead person's links with apparently loving kin (or at least those intent on being remembered as such), Bere's and Beila's gravestones are conspicuously small, lying flat, with minimal text. They were likely the cheapest stones available at that time.

Bere's gravestone, Jewish Cemetery, Maitland, Cape Town. Beila's looks exactly the same. Author's photograph.

There were some resources among the siblings at that point: at the very least, Sarah's husband was a reasonably prosperous businessman. That no one seemed willing to fork out for the cost of a more elaborate memorial is telling. As is the text of the message carved into the stone, a précis – surely – of strained relationships and attenuated feelings. Recorded for posterity with their colonial masks on, 'Barnard' and 'Betsy' Posel are declared 'deeply mourned'. Nothing more. There is no mention of any children or other relatives desiring to be named and wishing their grief to be noted.

Inscription on Beila's gravestone, Jewish Cemetery, Maitland, Cape Town. Author's photograph.

52 | Mothers of loss

Solomon Ginsburg provides the last trace of Beila in this story. In his letter to the master of the Supreme Court, Solomon described his mother-in-law as 'decrepit, toothless, of swollen limb'[220] – a woman floundering, in the throes of giving up on the world.

Would Beila's life, so distant from home, have taken its meaning – such as it was – from the lives of her child and stepchildren, and their prospects? Was it her lot, as much as her purpose, in the lonely confines of a place she could not fathom, simply to mother? To be a Jewish mother? That concentration and compression of purpose and identity might have been enough, under the circumstances – or not. After all, it was a role much valourised in Jewish history, all the way back to biblical times, and even more so amidst the disruptive migrations of more recent times. In 'collective memories of prejudice and persecution, of wandering and exile,' writes Adrienne Baker, 'the woman's place as wife and mother has been central in maintaining the continuity of the Jewish people.'[221] Particularly if fathers devoted themselves to a life of religious learning, it was mothers who glued households together. And if fathers took to the road or the seas, absent for long periods, it was mothers who had to plug the gaps.

But how much did this motif of the Jewish mother – as strong, resilient, resourceful and ever caring – conceal or overlook the pain and damage sometimes unwittingly transmitted to children in the drive to survive, with gritted teeth and dissociated determination, or in that frozen state of emotional paralysis and despair? I have no wish to detract from the strength and triumphs of many of the women who shouldered onerous burdens, but is there a mythology that erases more complex personal consequences of women's lives under pressure?

Beila's only biological child Maurice did not grow into a man at peace with himself or feeling safe in the world. No doubt there are many different reasons for this. As Bere's son, Maurice was likely fathered by doubt and insecurity. Beila must have played her part in it too. And, surely, she was not the only mother with children who took to their new world feeling inadequate and vulnerable, with an emptiness within. As a mother myself, I am struck by the daunting difficulties of mothering for a woman like Beila, who had lost herself, somewhere at sea or in the crevices of the strange colony. How could she prepare her children for their lives ahead in a world she failed to comprehend, a world in which she didn't speak the language, couldn't read the codes, and didn't have a presence? As her children learned English and began to understand the social texts of colonial life a bit more each year, did they become the interlocutors and gatekeepers to the outside on her behalf? Was she ever more the child in the colony, dependent on her and Bere's offspring for succour and protection?

There is nothing inevitable or given about the emotional capacity to mother. Immigrant women's journeying into strangeness and insecurity made sure of that.

53 | Longing to be let in

Despite the limits of what his parents could offer and the scars of his childhood, the young Maurice was not without opportunities. First and foremost, he had access to a far more worldly education than would have been possible in Pumpian. Maybe that included a more humane classroom than the *kheyder* of his earlier years – or maybe not; corporal punishment in schools was the way of the world at that time.

Maurice told my father and us grandchildren repeatedly – and proudly – that he had attended the South African College School (SACS), which was then the most prestigious school for Jewish boys in Cape Town. In fact, according to my father, this was the only piece of information about Maurice's childhood that he had shared with his son over the years. As if the young Maurice growing up in Cape Town had been nothing if not a pupil at SACS.

The school's website celebrates its Jewish enrolments going way back, with 'Justice Albie Sachs, Lord Solly Zuckerman and Lord Leonard Hoffmann ... [as] a few of those who, in the words of the School Song, have "swelled the fame" '.[222] This was a public school, but it was relatively costly, more so than the more modest schools for the Jewish children of District Six. SACS offered some bursaries and scholarships for the most talented applicants.

I called SACS to find out about Maurice's schooling there. The school, I was told, has kept comprehensive records of its pupils from the first decades of the century, except for one year's worth which were destroyed by a fire. Maurice's name does not appear anywhere in these records.

It took a while to take this in. That Maurice had been a SACS boy had been a family 'fact', giving at least some definition to an otherwise empty version of who he had been and how he had grown up. It had never occurred to me that he would have made it up.

After the call to the school, I realised that the only scenario that could have accounted for Maurice matriculating at SACS was that he had joined the school during that final year alone – and that that was the year for which school records had been lost. An unlikely case. It also became clear that he could not have been a pupil there for a protracted period; he would then have shown up somewhere in the school archives. Perhaps he did attend the school for all or part of the one missing year and nothing more – just a brief taste, but sufficient for him to have felt entitled to claim the school as his own.

Historian Howard Phillips, with whom I discussed Maurice's schooling, thinks that he may well have been a SACS boy for at least a short period because he liked to play cricket as a child (I knew this from my father, who had to endure Maurice's dogged and at times punitive insistence that his only son should master the sport too). Cricket, Howard stresses, was the quintessential boys' sport in the Cape, a marker of young colonial belonging. SACS made sure to bring all its boys on board.

Or maybe Maurice never attended SACS at all. If he was not a sufficiently able or promising pupil to have secured a bursary – which I think was probable – his father's earnings likely could not have encompassed the regular school fees. Maurice was one of four children in the Cape Town family; school fees would have been paid for all of them. Perhaps Maurice just kept dreaming, his longing intense and desperate enough to have produced a myth, as much for himself as for his progeny. A version of himself that warmed up some of the chill of his childhood.

54 | A colonial education

If not at SACS, Maurice would have been educated at one of the other schools that the Jewish children of District Six attended. The most likely was the Hope Mill Hebrew Public School, which had a good reputation as a well-run school providing a worthy education, much less prestigious but also far less costly than the SACS equivalent.

Although not himself a teacher, Reverend Bender kept a watchful eye there. 'There was hardly a boy of that generation who did not benefit by his advice and very often by concrete assistance,' wrote Louis Mirvish. 'He was the embodiment of the perfect English gentleman of his generation and his greatest ambition was to make the younger members of his community fit into the same patterns of manhood.'[223]

Young Maurice would have been clay in the venerable Bender's hands. For boys whose parents couldn't see through the colonial fog, Bender created a clearing: a way to see into the future, what lay ahead if the rules of advancement – all clearly laid out – were followed. *In loco parentis.*

I imagine Bender might also have offered Maurice a source of emotional attachment, even if sparse and at a distance: someone to look to – and to look up to. Some solace for his young soul in the strangeness. Bender never married and had no children of his own. Willing and available to engage with the pupils of District Six, maybe he too found some satisfaction – even the occasional ripple of joy – in being a proxy-father to many youngsters who needed a colonial role model. I have looked in vain for a biography of Bender; I would have liked to have known more about his own emotional interior.

Hope Mill School must have also provided Maurice with at least one ardently British teacher dedicated to the cause of the English language. Maurice's adult pride in his command of spoken English entirely devoid of any Yiddish accent, and in his conscientiously grammatical written English, was surely seeded at school. As was his unmistakable handwriting, another facet of his youthful homage to a grandiose British canon.

His flourish was out of kilter with the early twentieth century trend, which had moved away from the elaborate swirl of the Victorian era to the Edwardian script that was more streamlined and efficient: the italic script, as it became known. At least one of Maurice's teachers must have indulged a nostalgia for the older mode. As in the past, it would have required a dedicated curriculum to instruct the pupils in the various stages of this craft of handwriting. And this pedagogy typically came with another adage of the Victorian age, for good measure. 'In the nineteenth century,' writes Tamara Thornton, 'writing masters regarded penmanship training as a way to form legions of that Victorian favourite, the man of character.'[224]

A man of character. According to historian Dan Gorman, this was 'something of a national preoccupation in the late Victorian era ... If late-Victorian Britons agreed upon anything, it may have been in their valuation of "character" as the basis of British success ... particularly so in the case of Empire.'[225] The meaning of the term was usefully loose and flexible, but those who used it were thinking across a spectrum of ideas like being disciplined, courageous, loyal and dutiful, and being of strong moral fibre.

I don't recall Maurice using that phrase himself, but it captured some of his aspiration to colonial belonging. A 'man of character' was the man he wanted to become; a colonial grafting onto the stem that had rooted in the shtetl.

This was Maurice's signature. How far it was – and how much of an emotional wrench – from Beila's diminished cross on the page.

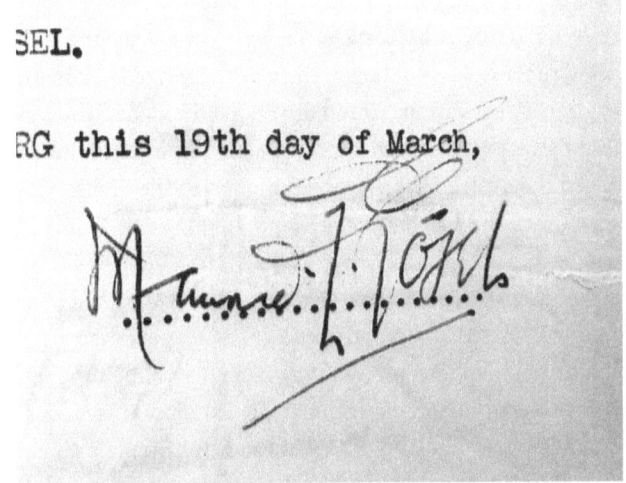

Maurice Posel's signature, taken from a letter in the author's possession. Author's photograph.

55 | Carruthers Beattie

For all the Jews from the East, learning to speak and read the King's English was a big step into a different cultural space, with its own literary exemplars, standards and benchmarks. Crucially, it would open the way to a prized – sometimes prestigious – education. Colonial schools in Cape Town, with some famously skilled teachers from the imperial motherland, nurtured the aspiration to proceed higher, to the South African College (later the University of Cape Town) or to a university abroad.

Jews' access to a university education in Russia had become severely restricted. After an initially more permissive policy during the mid-nineteenth century, which saw the numbers of Jewish university students shoot up, legislation passed in 1887 changed course, imposing drastic quotas limiting Jewish enrolment in Russian universities. This led many young Jews seeking to study to leave for universities abroad.[226] In the Cape, a respectable university college opened its doors, with no such restrictions; not even for the beginnings of a medical education – the highest prize of all. Several children of the Russian immigrants would proceed to study medicine in Cape Town and then specialise in well-known English or Scottish hospitals – an opportunity few would have had in the Pale. Their parents would have worked hard to make this happen and would feel intensely proud and grateful; it was a cherished opportunity. Among the best of what 'Britishness' had to offer.

Bender would have emphasised the prize of the university to all his flock. The institution, and the doors it opened, were close to his heart. His father Philipp, a Hebrew teacher and religious minister in Dublin, had taken the unusual step of reading for a doctorate. It inspired him to apply for a professorship in Hebrew at a university there, with his candidature widely supported among influential figures in Dublin. He was not already a member of academic staff, however, which invalidated his application. His son Alfred would make up for it, becoming the first professor of Hebrew at the University of Cape Town.

At the heart of Maurice's searing *farribel* with his first cousin Max was the promise of the university. Max had gone to university. Maurice had not. And he never recovered from the shame of it. This was not – as I see it – because he longed to learn. Somewhere, somehow, during his childhood, Maurice had realised that a university education was the key to the kind of recognition and status he longed for. Perhaps some of this message came from his parents, although there is no trace of any yen for study on their parts. I suspect a more powerful and well-informed prompting came from Bender. This was part of the message that Bender imparted to all his youthful progeny: to embrace a colonial education and make the most of its opportunities, with the university at its pinnacle. Maurice surely heard it loud and clear.

I can't know exactly how Sir Carruthers Beattie came into Maurice's life, but here is a possible – even likely – entry point. Bender and Beattie were both professors at the South African College; they must have known each other and associated as colleagues. Given Beattie's standing, Bender may well have invited Beattie to visit one of his favoured Jewish schools, to give a speech at a prize-giving or make an appearance at another such ceremonial occasion. Bender might have referred to Beattie in his own chats to the children, as he attempted to fire up their aspirations and imaginations. Beattie's glowing name and status may well have floated into the consciousness of Bender's young Russian flock.

With Beattie's name already illuminated, teenage Maurice might have read about a speech given by the vice-chancellor in the *Cape Times* – I suspect Maurice was an ardent reader of that colonial mainstay by that time – or heard him on a public platform. As a member of various scientific boards and civic organisations, as well as the esteemed vice-chancellor, Beattie was an eminent public figure in Cape Town, photographed and quoted in the newspapers.

One or other way, Maurice must have heard some inspirational words from the man at the pinnacle of his city's university, a man who embodied the link between social standing and education as much as he proselytised about it. Here was a promise of joining the colonial *balebatim*.

56 | What a shame

The anglicisation process often came at a heart-searing cost. Not just for Maurice, but within the Russian diaspora at large.

The writer Alfred Kazin produced a poignant memoir of growing up as the child of an immigrant Jewish family from the Pale in the neighbourhood of Brooklyn, New York – 'a place that measured all success by our skill in getting out of it'.[227] It was drummed into Alfred's young head that doing well at the public school he attended was the key to that. 'I was awed by the system, I believed in it, I respected its force ... I realized ... that it was not for myself alone that I was expected to shine, but for my parents – to redeem the constant anxiety of their existence. I was the first American child, their offering to the strange new God; I was supposed to be the monument of their liberation from the shame of being what they were. And that there was shame in this was a fact that everyone seemed to believe as a matter of course.'[228]

Mastering the English language was upfront – but in a very particular way. 'A "refined" "correct" English ... was peculiarly the ladder of advancement. It was bright, clean and polished. We were expected to show it off like a new pair of shoes.'[229]

In Cape Town Bender worked hard to ensure that his young charges too were neatly shod in English – and then all spruced up in British manners, learning to doff their new hats to British colonial norms. No doubt some emerged better dressed than others; not all their shoes were as shiny as Maurice's.

Psychologist Hannah Hahn has written up her research among other Jewish immigrants from the Pale to the USA who were also 'weaned away from the culture of their parents'. 'The pain this caused parents and children,' she writes, 'was immense. The children were ashamed of their parents' foreign accents, of their mothers dressed in old-fashioned clothes, of their fathers who shuffled around the house.'[230]

The distance between generations could grow wide and deep – like 'a chasm of silence, which neither affection nor goodwill could bridge', as Irving Howe put it. 'Inner shame, outer irritation, a rare coming together in grief – life ripped people apart.'[231] Within families, immigration could be a wrenching emotional dislocation, not merely a geographical dispersion, elasticating the connection between generations to breaking point.

Well aware of how indebted they were to their parents, immigrant children also understood that 'they were expected to shine. In high school, we used to think that if you got less than ninety on a maths test, you had disgraced God, Country and Home,'[232] said one of Hahn's informants. The symbolic load of success could be heavy – the weight of familial and communal redemption, no less.

It was a script for immigrant honour written for all the destinations to which the Pale Jews travelled where the marks of the alien East offended the sensibilities of the British West: Canada, Australia, Britain, Rhodesia, South Africa.

Some children emerged less wounded than others. Alfred Kazin was one who found some softness between the jagged edges. He retained a strong, warm bond with his mother, and developed a love of reading and music that nurtured his imagination and creativity. Maurice was one among the many others who were less lucky, suffering what Hahn sees as the intergenerational transmission of trauma. 'Because the traumatized parent cannot provide a containing, empathic, holding environment, the child's developing psyche is damaged.'[233]

Think of the enormous scale of Jewish migration from Russia – almost all of it Westwards – and an unfamiliar picture emerges: a diaspora of damage, the hidden accompaniment to the stories of triumphant assimilation.

Bere's and Beila's gravestones shout out in their silence that there was no deep attachment between Maurice and his parents. He made his way without them, turning his back on them and what they stood for. That's why he never spoke about them to his wife or his son; why he had no memorabilia, no family photographs or letters that perpetuated the memory of his parents and where they came from (with two exceptions). His would be a traumatic erasure, a repression of his early past. It left a big black hole; all the dark we grandchildren saw.

There were two exceptions, then: the first being Maurice's hanging onto his mother's ticket, bound to her permit to enter the Cape. It's unclear how and when he would have taken possession of it. Did she want him to have it, as a residue of her life that her son would value: certification of her rightful place in the venerable colony after all? Maurice left Cape Town before his mother died; perhaps she handed it to him as a parting gift, as a reminder of her contribution to the direction his life was taking. It was something that he clearly wanted to keep all along the way; a small, jagged shard of who he was could not leave his mother behind entirely. Keeping the ticket became its symptom.

The second exception was the two written prayers. Maurice would never lose his faith, one enduring legacy of his early shtetl life, but it would be transformed in ways of which Bender would have approved. Maurice's most intimate, personal prayers that he recited every day throughout his adult life were always in English.

Part Five

57 | Brothers

Sir Carruthers Beattie gave oxygen to Maurice's aspirations for success; his *farribel* composed a lament for how they were snuffed out.

Maurice's story of the *farribel* begins by presenting the relationship between Bere and his brother Chatzkel with striking symmetry, as if each was an equal half of a nice round whole. Each had a son who wished to study at university, and each brother lacked the means to fund this on his own. Each was fully supportive of his son's ambitions, so they turned to each other, to put each son to work in service of the other. It's a parable of sturdy brotherly love: as if they could count naturally, and exclusively, on each other. And it resonates with the triumphalist tales told among Jews about their immigrant successes: families held together and offered sustenance; Jews worked first and foremost with others in the family; brothers helped each other out.

But then came the unthinkable, unbearable betrayal that broke it apart. Bere and his son Maurice honoured their commitment, but Chatzkel and his son Max cheated on it. The family failed to support its own.

The story has all the hallmarks of a mythic invention, a story created for the purpose of a moral message rather than empirical truth. It's stylised and simple, no ifs and buts, no circumstantial complexities, no emotional nuances. Just a pared-down tale of unmitigated wrong-doing on one side, and wholesale victimisation on the other.

It's already clear that Bere and Chatzkel had grown up in Pumpian to inhabit different sorts of lives. The adult Bere was diminished and undistinguished compared to his younger brother, who was more of a man on the move. The brothers planted their respective feet on South African soil as dissimilar sorts of people, of disparate means and talents. There was no reason to assume that they would naturally turn to each other rather than go their separate ways, simply because they were brothers. And surely they were not alone in this breach of familial loyalty. The romance of resilient family ties was often more resilient than the family ties themselves; these were not ethnically inevitable.

It turns out that as the brothers' South African lives took root and grew, the contrasts between them were confirmed and magnified, in ways that Maurice must have found unbearable.

58 | Modern Jews

Around the turn of the twentieth century, Cape Town, as we have seen, showed Eastern Jews how to find a place in a foreign British colony, on the lower rungs of its hierarchy of Whiteness. There were lessons to be learned on the streets and in the house, on the body and in the mind.

Cape Town's school of White life, however, would be a more complacent, slower-paced affair than its counterpart in Johannesburg. The city of gold was brash and bold from the start: a minefield of the new, in which the tempo was faster and more aggressive than anywhere else in the country. The majority of the Jews from the Pale would settle in this burgeoning city, with its own manual of modernity.

Yuri Slezkine, historian of Russia, has penned a bold book about Jews and modernity. Others before him had presented Jews as archetypically 'modern', personifying the qualities that many historians see as key in transforming pre-modern lives into modern ones. Slezkine starts off similarly – albeit with his own, sometimes maverick, spin. 'Modernisation,' he writes, 'is about everyone becoming urban, mobile, literate, articulate, intellectually intricate, physically fastidious, and occupationally flexible. It is about learning how to cultivate people and symbols, not fields and herds .... It is about transforming peasants and princes into merchants and priests, replacing inherited privilege with acquired prestige.'[234]

Jews, he claims, were 'model moderns'[235] and ahead of the curve of history. By the start of the twentieth century, generations of Jews had long been 'service nomads', as he puts it: people who were modern in their mobility and adaptability, in the industrious pursuit of trade, crossing borders, sometimes ranging globally, well networked beyond their immediate confines, effective interlocutors across cultural and geographical boundaries. Even in 'ghetto times,' says Slezkine, Jews 'travelled far and wide, well beyond the edges of peasant imagination.'[236]

Cape Town's egg importers, as well as the other Jewish merchants who forged unfamiliar and innovative routes of sale, along with the ubiquitous smouses who redrew the maps of rural trade, often while based in a city or town, would modestly make Slezkine's point.

Over time, Slezkine writes, Jews had put all these qualities to singularly good use, not merely in the spheres of commerce but in the professions too. 'Some of the oldest Jewish specialties – commerce, law, medicine, textual interpretation, and cultural mediation – have become the most fundamental (and the most Jewish) of all modern pursuits.'[237]

But then, Slezkine makes an unfamiliar move, taking a familiar line of argument to a new extreme. 'The Modern Age is the Jewish Age,' he posits, 'and the twentieth century in particular is the Jewish century.' Put even more starkly: 'modernisation is about everyone becoming Jewish.'[238]

His claim is metaphorical rather than literal, of course – as in, modernity makes everyone Jew-*like*. If Jews were quintessentially modern, then all modern subjects resembled – or aspired to resemble – Jews (even if they had no desire whatsoever to be Jews). For Slezkine, it is Jewishness that became ubiquitous in modern times – what the Jew represents – rather than Jews themselves, who were always a small minority in the modern world.

Still, it's a wild overstatement, as Slezkine's critics have said. There are many ways of being modern, just as there are many ways of being Jewish; the fabric of history is densely woven. But it's a fascinating provocation nevertheless: changing the familiar optic on Jewish history, moving 'Jewishness' from the margins of the early twentieth century to its epicentre: in the vanguard of change, setting the tone, not merely a languishing adjunct battling the odds. And that is a suggestive place from which to think for a while.

Johannesburg would become South Africa's archetypically modern city and beacon of the country's future. 'The general impression given by Johannesburg,' wrote one of the many visitors at the turn of the century, 'is that it is the pivot upon which all South Africa turns.'[239] He was not wrong. Johannesburg was a little over a decade old when it surpassed Cape Town as the fastest growing, richest place in the country, centre of its innovation, heart of its entrepreneurship. And in the early decades of the life of this city, Jews would find themselves at its forefront, with some far-reaching opportunities to shape what it became. In popular parlance, Johannesburg became 'Jewburg'. In Slezkine's terms, the making of Johannesburg was about Jews taking a lead in its people becoming Jew-ish.

59 | Money

Modern or not, there was a big difference, of course, between being Jewish and being Jew-ish. It was the Jews who had to bear the burden of bigotry – a burden imposed by those, amongst others, who would become Jew-ish. That burden was heaviest in relation to the quest for riches – the very essence of Johannesburg in the making.

In the litany of antisemitic prejudice, surely the most deep-seated and inflammatory was also the oldest, long pre-dating the modern catalogue of antisemitism produced by the supposed science of race. This was the accusation of the intimate and contaminating relationship that Jews had to money – as if Jews and their Jewishness could be reduced to clamorous and powerful greed.

Jewish prominence in finance and trade has been an artefact of history. In medieval times, Jews dominated the money-lending business at the behest of Christian kings, since the New Testament prohibited money lending by Christians. Jews took on the job, which enabled Christian notables to take loans, at the same time as taxing the usurers on the interest they charged. As anthropologist Claudio Lomnitz puts it, Jews became the Christian version of a *shabbas goy*: enabling Christians to keep a religious prohibition intact while enjoying the benefits of its breach by religious outsiders. 'The supposed fiscal immorality of the Jews was in fact indispensable for the proper functioning of the Christian economy.'[240]

Powerful Christians – kings, noblemen – also sought connections to Jewish bankers and merchants, operating on a global canvas. The wealthiest Jews famously bankrolled voyages of discovery and major wars; many kings were dependent on their Jewish benefactors.

The occupational niche was, in some ways, a gift: conferring some prestige and prominence; power, too, in becoming economically indispensable.[241] But this was also a curse. When things turned sour – an economic downturn, a calamitous defeat, a loan called in at a bad time – Jews were easy scapegoats. As if, when Jews were in control of the purse, it must have been their doing when its contents dried up.

Modernity recast both the gift and the curse.[242] As capitalism flourished in the nineteenth century, Jews looked well placed for success: economically fleet-footed, with historically well-developed skills in the marketplace. Yet, for exactly that reason, it was easy to blame Jews for rapacious extract of profit and rampant exploitation. Karl Marx made the point that capitalism presented itself to those who lived within it as a somewhat mysterious, abstract system, driven by impersonal, inscrutable forces that were difficult to predict and control. It became more scrutable, more intelligible, when imagining a cohort of maliciously powerful Jews manipulating the system in line with their own selfish schemes. 'The abstract domination of capitalism,' writes anthropologist Moishe Postone, 'is personified as the Jews.'[243]

Johannesburg would give life to this antisemitic caricature too. Jews would be gifted with unusually open opportunities to shape the place and cursed with the conspiratorial prejudice that went with it.

60 | 'Like insects to the light'

The first flurry of excitement at the prospect of fortunes to be made from South Africa's gold did not amount to much. In 1884, some alluvial gold was found in Barberton, in the eastern Transvaal. Thousands of prospectors arrived but did not find the treasure troves they were looking for. Then, two years later, an unremarkable prospector from Australia made a remarkable discovery that made all the difference, when he discovered gold on the farm Langlaagte on the Witwatersrand.[244]

The gold deposits along the Witwatersrand were large – even more so than the diggers grasped at the time. Excited news of the discovery spread fast. According to historian Eric Rosenthal, 'no gold rush in history attracted such numbers'.[245] 'Like insects attracted to the light,' wrote Leibl Feldman, who was one of the Lithuanian arrivals,[246] and for no greater cause than the lure of Mammon. 'We are none of us here for the benefit of our health,' declared one of the (non-Jewish) diggers; 'money-making and money-grabbing is the alpha and omega of those resident on these fields.'[247] That's what gave the place its burning energy, its hot haste.

Like boom towns birthed by gold rushes elsewhere, Johannesburg arose from the dust, *de novo*. Founded officially in 1887, it had no prior history, no layers of different pasts, no social hierarchies already in place, no traditions to protect or give away, no sentimental attachments. It was a place shining, and dirtied, with gold; nothing more nor less.

Its growth was extraordinary, mutating at speed from the ramshackle camps of motley diggers, labourers and traders, to a modernising town unlike any other in the country. This was partly a consequence of the rocketing pace at which the gold-mining industry expanded. In 1886, the Witwatersrand contributed less than one per cent of the world's gold. Three years later, that figure had soared to twenty-seven per cent[248] – producing explosive expansions all round.

In 1887, one year after gold was discovered, around three thousand hopeful prospectors had gathered on the Witwatersrand goldfields, with Ferreira's camp as its heart. A mere nine years later, that number had ballooned to over one hundred thousand.[249] In the township of Johannesburg itself, the number shot up from around eight thousand to forty-two thousand in the space of the six years from 1890 to 1896.

The same sense of breathless acceleration drove a building boom. Amid a frenzy of investment and speculation in the fledgling mining industry (after recovering from a temporary setback), the first substantial structure to grace the grubby town centre was the Stock Exchange. In place by 1888, it was bold and bombastic from the start, 'with its Corinthian pilasters, attic pediments and palatial pretensions'.[250] One year later, Johannesburg boasted three hundred and twelve hotels and bars, four theatres, a host of sports clubs and three social clubs – including, pre-eminently, the Rand Club, an establishment that anyone of substance wanted to join.[251]

By 1893, the quaintly named *Guide to South Africa for the Use of Tourists, Sportsmen, Invalids and Settlers* had no hesitation in recommending Johannesburg to visitors as a place with precociously grand ambitions. 'Enormous sums of money have been expended on buildings and the many stately piles of offices and stores which adorn the town ... The beauty of some of the shops and the size of the plate glass in some of the windows are most remarkable.'[252]

In the next four years, an impressive array of three-, four- and even five-storey buildings would go up in the town's main streets: headquarters of its burgeoning banking, mining and finance companies. One of the new arrivals at the time declared his 'astonishment' at the 'almost lightning speed' of this accomplishment.[253]

Johannesburg's consumerist pulse was also already racing, as varieties of shops came to life. This included the largest department store, Stuttafords, replete with elaborate ironwork – very fashionable in the British empire at the time – all along its street frontage, on the corner of Rissik and Pritchard streets. 'The Arcade', also in Pritchard Street, the town's main shopping street, boasted 'a long tunnel with glass panes' built from cast iron and steel, with a central decorative dome, to house a series of smart shops. 'Inside there were galleries on either side and the richly ornamented cast iron construction was extended into the frontage of many of the little shops.'[254] It was absolutely in line with the architectural and shopping fashion in the stylish capitals of Europe, even if it arose in the dirt and dust.

'The mushroom growth of Johannesburg has astonished the world,'[255] proclaimed the venerable *Guide*, which was another way of saying that the world was taking note. Johannesburg came to life under an international spotlight: a global modernising city in the making from the outset.

61 | Jews in front

By the late nineteenth century, South Africa's development was being heated up by two cauldrons of change. The first is commonly called the country's mineral revolution, which followed the discovery of gold and diamonds. It set the forces of industrialisation in motion, spewing out new opportunities for work, income and economic growth, transforming South Africa from a colonial backwater into a jewel in the British imperial crown. Accompanying the mineral revolution – and thoroughly intertwined with it – was what I like to call a consumer revolution, which dramatically transformed the pace and scale of trade in consumer goods. Steamships and railways ferried many thousands of new consumers into and across the country. Legions of traders emerged from the ranks of the immigrants, who created new spaces and networks of trade that criss-crossed the country. And they offered consumers a then astonishing variety of things that recent techniques of mass production had made possible.

These fires of change would be hottest in Johannesburg, the city of gold. And Jews would be close to the heat, stoking the flames of both.

In his book *The Jews of Johannesburg*, Leibl Feldman wrote the story of Johannesburg from the perspective of its Jews. He went looking for them and found them all over. They had been in the area even before 1886, he claims, which partly explains why Jews were among the first prospectors to secure prospecting licences – including, remarkably, one Fanny Rosenstein, 'a Jewish businesswomen and pioneer of Pretoria'.[256] (I can't find anything more about her, unfortunately, but the mere reference to a Jewish woman prospector jolts my thinking; the conventional historical accounts tell only of men. Tenacious researchers have revealed feisty women prospectors at work during the gold rushes in New Zealand, Australia, Canada and the USA at this time; South Africa might be another case awaiting that kind of digging.)

A Jew could also be in the right place but at the wrong time. Sammy Marks – who would become one of the headline entrepreneurs enriched by gold – started out as a Lithuanian immigrant, arriving in the Cape in 1868, a year after the discovery of diamonds. Sammy and his cousin Isaac Lewis made good money on the diamond fields, but didn't realise how close they were to a far bigger win, a lot earlier than they could have imagined. In 1881, when Sammy ventured to the Witwatersrand for the first time, he turned down an early opportunity to buy the farm Driefontein for a mere eight hundred pounds. It turned out to contain a large chunk of the Witwatersrand's main gold reef.[257]

From the start of the gold rush, writes Feldman, Jews made their presence felt at the heart of the emerging town. 'There were Jews trading with the farmers in Turffontein, Doornfontein and Braamfontein and Jews owned bars and hotels in and around Ferreira's camp, on the Turffontein farm.'[258] Joffe Marks – who would go on to establish the Premier Milling Company, one of the largest milling companies in southern Africa – was one of the earliest Jewish traders in Johannesburg, arriving in 1887. 'We got hold of a few sheets of corrugated iron and built ourselves a store in Ferreira's camp. It was very small, but big enough to trade in. We slept on bags and on part of the stock, and after we heard about the many robberies, we saw to it that we had a revolver or a gun lying nearby.'[259] Jews were among the first to set up hotels, bars, pharmacies, butcheries and bakeries, as well as general trading stores. And they were among the first to secure lucrative licences to sell alcohol.[260]

The mining and the commerce went hand in hand. As the pace and scale of gold-mining soared, trade boomed, not least in meeting the needs and wants of the burgeoning workforce. Jewish traders were among the first to spot the opportunities to set up shop, especially among the lowliest consumers, who had to feed and clothe themselves with whatever bits of cash they could muster. Trade with the working poor sustained the pulse of the place; the large proletarian rump of the city's wealth would grow with it.

Jews were among the earliest prospectors for gold and discovered various parts of the reef. Isaac Sonnenberg, for example, hit lucky on the farm Kromdraai. According to Feldman, this became 'the first gold field proclaimed by the government in the district of the Witwatersrand'.[261] And Jews were among the first financiers to fund the gold prospectors. Alfred Goldberg was one of the first to form a company to sink deep shafts to attempt to reach the gold. When the first building stands were offered for sale in 1886, Jews were among the first buyers. Feldman thought it propitious too that the first passenger to step off the first train that arrived in Johannesburg from Cape Town in 1892 was a Jew named Leopold Lowenthal – apocryphal perhaps, but for Feldman, a sign of a canny timeliness.

As it became clear that extracting the gold was too big and expensive a job for individual prospectors and large mining companies formed to take on the task (and each other), Jews were once again in the vanguard of these changes. Lionel Phillips and Otto Beit – partners in Hermann Eckstein's mining company – as well as Sammy Marks and Isaac Lewis were among the so-called Randlords who made fortunes on the gold mines. Hermann Eckstein and Company (then a private firm, not a public company) raked in a profit of four million pounds in 1895 alone.[262]

The prize for the most dramatic Jewish entrepreneurial success in those early years would have gone to Barney Barnato. His was the archetypal Jewish rags-to-riches story: from a life of poverty in London's East End to becoming one of the world's richest industrialists by the age of thirty-seven. Having made a fortune on the diamond fields of Kimberley, Barnato moved to Johannesburg in 1888. He rapidly became a public figure, well known for his ebullient confidence in the future of gold-mining and the growth of Johannesburg as a major colonial city. When others worried that the promise of the goldfields might fizzle out and Johannesburg would wither, Barnato pronounced otherwise and invested very substantially and very quickly, igniting global interest in the future of Johannesburg's gold. Barnato's enthusiastic example helped to steer the course of investment in that gold, and with that, the tempo of the city's expansion.

Just as formative was Barnato's own investment in Johannesburg's development – a spectacle that hit the headlines in Johannesburg and abroad. 'Barnato purchased ground in every direction … He floated the Johannesburg Estate Company, the Consolidated Investment Company, the Barnato Buildings Company, and the Waterworks Company, besides floating and reconstructing some of the leading gold-mining companies on the fields. It is said that in two months he put over £2 000 000 into lands and gold properties. His interests in the Transvaal are now gigantic; and his profits, realized and prospective, may be described in the same terms.'[263] 'In barely three months,' wrote Richard Lewinsohn, one of Barnato's biographers, 'he had made himself the greatest landowner and industrialist on the Rand.'[264] His imprint on the burgeoning city would undoubtedly have been even greater but for his premature death in 1897 at the age of forty-five.

In most parts of the world, as the prominent entrepreneur Mendel Kaplan pointed out, when the Jews came to a city, 'it was a place that had been established by others',[265] with ground rules and boundaries already in place. In the late nineteenth century, Johannesburg was different: unbounded and unruly, an unusually open and fluid scenario for the Jews who gathered there. There were no restrictions on Jews taking a lead; they could make their mark unapologetically.

Exactly that would maximise the cost. For their detractors, Johannesburg's Jewish pioneers simply confirmed the toxic stereotype of Jewish money lust. As if no others in this place were similarly inclined. Many of the mining magnates were not Jewish; many of the wealthiest commercial beneficiaries of the gold rush were not Jewish; leading bankers and financiers were not Jewish; the poorest peddlers and storekeepers were not exclusively Jewish either. Jews were doing what many others were doing in this dusty mecca: trying to get ahead. Even the lowly diggers acknowledged that theirs was a dogged pursuit of money, shorn of any other more elevated purpose, in a city coming into being without one.

62 | Chatzkel's luck

Chatzkel landed in Cape Town in 1895 and headed straight for the Witwatersrand. He was following in the footsteps of his brother-in-law Harris Plein who had made the journey five years before, in 1890. Harris had followed his older brother Solomon, who must have been among the earliest of the Russian Jews to have reached these goldfields.

Harris's and Solomon's long treks northwards to the Witwatersrand goldfields would have been far more gruelling than Chatzkel's. The railway from Cape Town to Johannesburg had been completed in 1892. Chatzkel had the good fortune of arriving three years later, which spared him the slow and arduous trek by ox wagon that travellers in years past had to take, spending several weeks to months on the move, depending on the surprises sprung on the way. The train journey, on the other hand, was likely a three-day, two-night affair, suggests Gordon Pirie, historian of the early railways, although unscheduled stops and interruptions could have made it a lot longer.[266] For the rapidly expanding mining industry – and the country at large – this innovation would revolutionise the importing and exporting of people and things, a key ingredient in the recipe for Johannesburg's dramatic rise.

There's no knowing whether Chatzkel's train arrived in Johannesburg at night or during the day. Had he arrived after dark, he would have been stunned by the electric lights that dazzled in the town centre. Remarkably, the first central power station had been established by 1890 – only four years after the discovery of gold. Streetlights were duly installed, including in Pritchard Street, the already fashionable shopping street, with its cutting-edge glass and steel arcade.

It must have been a magical sight – not least because it was entirely unexpected. Approaching Johannesburg by train at night, one P.E. Bodington found it alluring: 'one is weirdly impressed by the blaze of electric light which bursts from the otherwise opaque blackness of the lonely African night.'[267]

Bodington was visiting from Britain; he would have seen electric lighting before. Not so for Chatzkel. Electrification in the Russian Empire had been slow; by the end of the century, only Moscow and St Petersburg had made any progress.[268] Reb Yehuda Schrire, a fellow immigrant from the Pale, was captivated by encountering electricity for the first time in Johannesburg; 'electric fire',[269] he called it. There's something obviously metaphorical about seeing a scintillating sparkle in the pitch dark for the first time – if Chatzkel was inclined to see the light in this way.

Had he arrived during the day, Johannesburg would have shown itself more honestly: more brash and brutal than magical. The air was dirty. Every traveller complained of the ubiquitous dust, a mix of sand blown in from the mine dumps and the sand churned up by the horse-drawn carts on the unpaved streets. According to the well-heeled Florence Phillips (wife of mining magnate Lionel Phillips), 'the place was very dirty and fearful odours abounded'.[270] Undeterred, the pace in town was brisk and busy; even in its early years, 'the bustling crowd was quite different from anything else in South Africa'.[271] It was a burgeoning city in a hurry; its tempo of impetuous speed was palpable.

Johannesburg was edgy too, a sense of menace circulating with the dust. Florence Phillips commented that firearms were commonplace, carried openly. Some of the ladies of the town also resorted to guns to protect themselves. Florence was a member of the Ladies Revolver Club and owned her own gun, which she insisted her (White) domestic servants carry as they went about their errands in the town.[272] Maurice Harbord, who took up a commission with the Transvaal Police in the late 1890s, was convinced that the town had a 'larger criminal population for its size than any other town in the world'.[273]

Crime spanned the spectrum, from the work of well-organised criminal syndicates and gangs to more opportunistic cases of property theft, gruesome assault and murder. All were at risk. Wealthy home owners and prosperous shopkeepers could be robbed, often violently. Lowly mine workers could be assaulted and robbed of their meagre wages.[274] Dishevelled proprietors of modest stores on the edge of the town could be 'disemboweled and decapitated'.[275]

Sjamboks and whips were common sights, typically in the hands of the self-appointed guardians of the emerging racial order. In 1894, the Sanitary Board (the municipal authority that had formed to govern the place) made it an offence for 'Natives' to walk on the town's pavements. The penalty for breaking the rule was two pounds or ten lashes. 'As most of the Natives could not pay the fine, lashes were freely inflicted.'[276]

Violence would be part of Johannesburg's lingua franca from the outset.

As Chatzkel stepped away from the railway station and began exploring, his gaze would have taken in a landscape of blistering inequality already taking shape. Walking to the east and north of the railway line, he would have glimpsed the distant outlines of the ample houses and their spacious gardens belonging to the town's elite, set in the neat suburbs of Parktown and Doornfontein. Had Chatzkel headed off to the south and west, beyond the central business district, his visitor's eye would have alighted upon the ramshackle dwellings of the poorer classes, already congested and overcrowded. Charmless corrugated iron structures they were, many of them simple one-room shacks; home to most of the hapless arrivals struggling to get their bearings.

The cost of living in Johannesburg was notoriously high and many lived with the risk of destitution. Most of those crammed into these desperate parts were single men, who spent their spare time 'drinking, whoring and gambling'.[277] Olive Schreiner, then a resident of Johannesburg, was one among many appalled by this vortex of vice. 'I have lived on various places on earth, Monte Carlo, London, Paris; I have worked among the outcast women and drunken sailors in the East End; but anything so appalling, so decayed I have never seen. One realized in Johannesburg what the tone of society must have been in the reign of Charles I. The whole moral fibre relaxed.'[278]

Chatzkel would have noticed and understood from the start that this was a place for hustlers and adventurers. The going would be tougher than in Cape Town, but the promise of reward that much greater. It seems to me entirely appropriate that of the two Posel brothers, it would be Chatzkel who settled in Johannesburg, while Bere remained in Cape Town. I can't help thinking that early Johannesburg would have eaten Bere and Beila alive.

63 | Whose gold

The immigrants who headed to the gold reefs of the Transvaal in droves in the late nineteenth century imagined that they would be southern Africa's gold pioneers. They were wrong.

Nine years before the discovery of gold on the Witwatersrand, Cape Town convened its first International Exhibition. It was the town's inaugural effort to participate in what had become an international trend, following the Great Exhibition at Crystal Palace in London in 1851. These exhibitions became occasions to display local craft skills and industrial prowess, typically as monuments to the technical and aesthetic greatness of the British Empire. Cape Town's first effort was a rather half-hearted affair, with very few local exhibits. Amidst the dullness of the display, an unexpected glint of gold caught the eye of a journalist who was covering the exhibition for the *Cape Times*. Looking more closely, he was stunned to see a 'very pretty chain worked out of virgin gold with very rough tools by the uncivilized Natives of the Zambezi'.[279] It was an instance, said the venerable newspaper, of 'superb workmanship' on the part of these 'Natives'.

The history of gold in southern Africa went way back to the kingdom of Great Zimbabwe, where an abundance of alluvial gold had sponsored a prosperous trade in gold artefacts along the East African coast for several centuries. But this was entirely unknown to White Capetonians visiting the exhibition in 1877. Surprised, even shocked, by what they had seen, they had to ponder the question: how could 'uncivilized' people produce such beautiful 'civilized' things, without any assistance from those more 'civilised' than they were? Did this presage the possibility that all 'Natives' could be uplifted to 'civilisation' and was this what the Cape's colonial project should undertake?[280]

While the issue resonated with the Cape's long-standing liberal tradition of thought, it did not gather sufficient momentum to unsettle the colony's strengthening racial hierarchy. Its underlying assumption of immutable 'Native' inferiority would remain intact. But the presence of the question in respectable public circles signalled a striking difference between the Cape and the Witwatersrand. Such questions would have no traction whatsoever among those who steered the future of Johannesburg. The presence of gold here – reportedly plentiful but vexingly difficult and expensive to extract from the rocky underground – made the racial issue a lot starker, with no room for any ambiguities or doubts. 'Civilisation' here would be for Whites only – unequivocally. Black workers, payable at a far lesser rate than any White counterparts, were essential to the viability of the mining project. They would be sent underground to extract the gold, to which only Whites could lay claim. No Black people would be given permits to prospect for gold. And in line with that same racial logic, no Whites would be permitted to undertake the menial manual work of mining underground; their role would be elevated to that of supervisors and overseers.

The discovery of gold inaugurated a racial order in Johannesburg premised from the beginning on uncompromising White supremacy, built on the back of cheap Black labour. It would be an integral part of the aggressive harshness of the place.

64 | Jews and 'the Blacks'

For many of Johannesburg's Jews – and especially those from the Pale – relationships with 'the Blacks' had a particular trajectory, not quite the mainstream.

Had there been no Black people in Johannesburg, Jewish prospects there would have been pale and wan – as the Russian Jews understood especially well. Many of these Jews were traders and many more Black people were their customers. Their interactions across the racial divide were shaped by the terms of this commerce.

On a mine, Black mine workers would be subject to brute force, and the unmodulated power of White managers and their overlords. Pursuing a sale with these mine workers – or any other Black people for that matter – was best served by a different kind of interaction. Doing business involved a transaction, not an instruction. Whiteness had the upper hand; some deference was expected. Still, a would-be customer could refuse to engage or choose not to buy; no one could be forced to part with hard-earned wages. Treating Black people with even the tiniest modicum of kindness or decency was good for business, if nothing else.

Luckily for the Jews, all that gold locked in the rocks lured Black people to the Witwatersrand in droves. Almost all the new arrivals were men, coming from near and far in southern Africa. Most came to work on the mines, compelled by recently imposed poll taxes – payable in cash – to pursue a wage. Their numbers ratcheted up dramatically, from fourteen thousand in 1890 to ninety-seven thousand in 1899.[281] By 1904, Black Africans constituted the majority of those on the Rand, at nearly sixty-eight per cent.[282]

Explosive growth in the size of the population triggered a comparably explosive growth in trade. The commercial landscape of the Witwatersrand – once sparse and dry – now flourished. The place of gold was also a place of cash – as much at the lower end of the economic spectrum as at the top. However meagre his wages, every Black mine worker was also a consumer. He needed food, drink, clothing and shoes; but he also wanted to buy a lot more, making his paltry wage stretch as far as possible, to include things such as cutlery, bedlinen, tablecloths and blankets, brushes and combs, candles, beads and tobacco.[283]

That little cornucopia, modest as it was, was a godsend for the Jews, who would make sure to keep it filled and available wherever it was wanted. And that made the Jewish traders a godsend for the Black consumers too, who were never short of an opportunity to buy.

Even in this sparsest of Jewish pursuits, however, there was a hierarchy. The most precarious of the Jewish immigrants had to begin on the lowest rung of what became a commercial ladder. So low, in fact, that almost all other White traders were not willing to stoop so far.

At the bottom of the immigrant heap were the poorest of the Russians who really did arrive 'with nothing' and who lacked the leg-up of supportive kin already in town. Their survival often depended on their willingness to serve the poorest of Black people under the worst of conditions – an inversion of the accepted racial order of things that was considered utterly contemptible by the White mainstream. 'White South African racist attitudes held in contempt any occupation that provided basic services for Blacks but prevented the opening of such trade to black entrepreneurs,' writes Joseph Sherman.[284] Desperate Jews could eke out a living in the space that this anomaly opened.

White people working in so-called *kafireaters* – sordid canteens selling the cheapest offal to hungry Black mine workers – were considered the lowest of the low. Almost all the *kafireatniks*, as they became known, were Russian Jews: people who needed a place to start, and who didn't yet carry the racial baggage that would have ruled it out. In later years, however, the shame of the occupation typically snuffed out its memory: few of these men chose to reveal it to future generations.

A step up, bedraggled Jewish peddlers plied their trade in old clothes and shoes on the dusty streets, pitching to the poor. Some customers were other lowly immigrants at the end of their luck. Many, if not most, were Black people.

Jews who could afford a trading licence to set up some sort of shop were better off, and especially if in the vicinity of a mine. Meyer Dovid Hersch, another Jewish inhabitant of early Johannesburg, made the point in 1896, writing about the fledgling city. 'As soon as the Natives commence earning money at their work on the mines, the gold pounds begin to fly into the pockets of the shopkeepers or the liquor shops or both ... These Blacks are the pivot of the trade in Johannesburg and its surroundings.'[285]

Everyday commercial transactions between Jews and Black people became *de rigueur*, with small insertions of a mutual humanity inserted into some, maybe many, of them. And perhaps not all of this followed a transactional logic; perhaps elements of friendship, a sense of shared beleaguerment, developed too. But the wider politics of race would make itself felt. It would discount this on-the-ground reality and largely delete its memory among future generations.

Yiddish newspapers had been flourishing in Johannesburg from 1890 – the main source of news and commentary for the Russian immigrants. This included observations and debates on the racial order taking shape in South Africa. Some disapproved strongly.

Historian William Pimlott gives the example of Benzion Hersch, a frequent contributor, who wrote critically about Harry Solomon, a 'prominent Jewish politician and member of parliament, who proposed that "coloured" people should not be allowed to travel in the same wagon as White people'.[286] Other readers saw their future with the likes of Solomon, recognising that the way ahead for them looked brighter with an uncompromising Whiteness.

I referred earlier to the *South African Jewish Chronicle* – leading publication of the emerging Jewish establishment – seeking to dispel any doubts or ambiguities on the matter, aligning Jews with 'the superiority of the White man in this country' and 'objecting to being put on the same level as the Coloured races'. This intervention was particularly apropos the Jews in Johannesburg: 'it may seem strange that this comment should appear in a Jewish paper of all places, but in reality it is quite fitting. It is the Jews of the Rand who are primarily concerned in [sic] this question and will be among the first to be affected by the levelling process going on between White and Coloured.'[287]

It had become clear to the Jewish establishment intent on promoting the respectability and legitimacy of Johannesburg's Jewish peoples that an unambiguous embrace of the ways of colonial Whiteness was required to dispel any doubts about the Jews' political loyalties.

65 | Chatzkel on the move

Back home in Pumpian, Chatzkel had been a flax trader who had done reasonably well: 'well-to-do' by shtetl standards. In Johannesburg, as a foreigner arriving with no English, whatever money he came with could talk, but not in full sentences. He too would have to start relatively low.

He headed first to Fordsburg – an area to the west of the town centre, home to a miscellany of Johannesburg's poor hopefuls. Alice Rallis spent her early childhood years there, and in her memoir *Daughter of Yesterday* remembered 'the Chinese vegetable vendors ... the Armenian women who carried exciting trays of bright trinkets, brooches, cottons, tapes and beads ... the old Jews plying their humble trade of buying old clothing, bottles, sacks and newspapers on the streets'.[288] Fordsburg was also notorious for its criminal gangs, bars and brothels – one of the nodes of Johannesburg's thriving, not-so-hidden underworld.

Harris Plein was on the Rand too; I don't know exactly where. He and Chatzkel did not go into business together – not yet anyway; they would buy property together in later years, after the South African War. Instead, Chatzkel met up with one W. Gordon (not a name I encountered again in this story) and together, feeling the pull of the Black mine trade, they headed east to the Driefontein farm, near the Driefontein mine. There they bought a small stand, acquired a trading licence, and set up shop.

The stand was fifty feet by fifty feet. The shop, which they set up on the stand, would have been built from iron and wood: a very basic structure, with no insulation and no running water. Chatzkel lived there; perhaps Gordon did too. It would have been intensely hot in summer – especially for a recently arrived immigrant from Russia. Perhaps he found the freezing winters easier to deal with. But the summer months offered the biggest prize, as Christmas approached and the mine workers stocked up on the things they would have been longing to take home for the celebration.

There Chatzkel lived, inside his shop, for nearly three years, until after the outbreak of the South African War in 1899. Then things changed. Britain and the South African Republic, led by Paul Kruger, went to war largely for control over the lucrative goldfields. The British expected a rapid victory, but they were wrong: the war would last for nearly three years, as the Boer guerrillas put up an unexpectedly fierce fight against His Majesty's army. As mentioned, it was only after Kitchener arrived, with his bounty of troop reinforcements, that victory was finally assured in May 1902.

At the outset of the war, most of the Transvaal's Jews fled, seeking safety elsewhere. Those who owned properties or shops abandoned them fearfully; many would be looted by soldiers on both sides. Most of those in flight headed for the Cape colony. Chatzkel did too. He left the Transvaal in October 1899 and spent the next year or so in Cape Town, before returning to Pumpian. He had come to South Africa in 1895, without his wife and three daughters. The war must have been a prompt to return home and reconnect.

It was a fruitful visit; his only son Max was conceived, and born on Christmas day, 1901. Chatzkel would spend almost all of 1902 watching his only son's early milestones, but by November he was off again, back to Driefontein. Perhaps he was under financial pressure, perhaps less inclined to spend his time doing little or nothing in the shtetl while his shop languished and his customers spent their meagre wages elsewhere, perhaps determined not to miss the Christmas rush.

In July 1906, his wife Chane, three daughters and son joined him in the Transvaal. I can't be sure what their living arrangements were once the family arrived. Much like Bere's immigrant family, Chatzkel's would leave no trace of their lives for future generations: no photographs, letters, no memorabilia that I know of. I've had to rely on archival documents I have traced by other means, but this makes for a partial picture with several gaps.

Chatzkel naturalised as a British subject in 1907. His papers show that in that year, he had two residential addresses: plot 215 in Driefontein, and 27 Marshall Street in Ferreirastown, central Johannesburg. After returning from Pumpian, he must have bought the stand in Marshall Street. At some point, he divided it up into dismal shacks and rented them out – creating the Posel's Yard I had stumbled on in the archives all those years ago and exhibited in the Gertrude Posel Gallery. Before that – or maybe at the same time – he likely installed his family there while he went back and forth to Driefontein to run the shop.

In 1909, Chatzkel and his co-owner applied for permission to enlarge their Driefontein stand on the grounds that '50 x 50 is too small for a house with a married man with children, and also for a store'.[289] A more substantial extension was granted, of up to six hundred and twenty-five square feet. Perhaps by then, Chane and her girls had had enough of the conditions in Marshall Street; or Chatzkel had decided that their services were required in running the shop, and he built them an appropriately sized home.

Chatzkel's son Max, however, stayed with his father in Ferreirastown. In 1909, he was eight years old, already at school and set to continue. He would start high school at Jeppe Boys – close to Ferreirastown – in 1914. The school register of new pupils recorded his home address as 27 Marshall Street.[290] It was an address that would come to haunt him.

66 | Obscene extremes

After the war ended, Johannesburg – now part of a colony under British rule – flaunted its extremes even more obscenely than before.

An economic depression set in, sending food prices and rents skyrocketing. Earnings fell and many jobs were lost, but immigrants continued to arrive, making the competition for work and accommodation even more intense. Among the poor, the 'limitless, confused mass of slums and shacks' – as visiting magistrate and well-known writer W.C. Scully put it – sprawled even more.[291] These were home to grim and desperate lives. A spate of hastily convened private charities attempted the emergency work of containing the destitution.

At the other end of the spectrum, Johannesburg was experiencing its own Gilded Age. It was in the USA, in the late nineteenth century, that the spectacle of gargantuan fortunes and extravagant consumption had been at its most garish. 'There is no doubt,' wrote one American commentator of the day, 'that money ... is the romance, the poetry of our age.'[292] He was referring primarily to the country's burgeoning *nouveau riche*: property barons, trade and finance tycoons, captains of industry and others who had achieved stratospheric success as the USA industrialised during the nineteenth century and made sure everyone knew about it. By 1880, the USA had around two thousand millionaires who had made their fortunes at inordinate speed and chose to flaunt their success as conspicuously as possible. Many had started out with little; theirs was 'the ostentation of upstarts',[293] rather than the decadence of old money passed down from one generation to the next.

In Johannesburg, the excesses of the *nouveau riche* were more muted – but loud nevertheless, particularly given that this was still a startlingly new place. Here, too, money bulged in the pockets of 'upstarts' who were living in 'houses of banknotes'[294] (as Yehuda Schrire, newly arrived from the Pale, put it) and flashed their newfound wealth without restraint. When Baron Ferdinand de Rothschild visited in 1895, he noted in his diary that 'great fortunes have just been made, and the Johannesburgers are in a high state of exultation'.[295] If initially dulled by the effects of the war, their jubilant spending frenzies resumed once it ended.

This explains why some visitors described post-war Johannesburg as 'an extravagant pleasure city';[296] 'there is everywhere a novel appearance of luxury and wealth'.[297] In these circles, ostentatious parties and balls, with 'epicurean' wining and dining, were *de rigueur*,[298] as was the sight of 'many women dressed to the top-notch in the latest fashions' at all hours of the day and night.[299] One of the mining magnates was said to have worn a new pair of trousers every day of the year.[300]

Once completed, the Carlton Hotel would sit at the acme of this excess. 'We like to talk in superlatives, and everyone has been talking very largely about the Carlton,'[301] wrote an enraptured journalist on the eve of the hotel's much-anticipated launch. The project had been initiated by Barney Barnato's nephew Solly Joel in the 1890s but was delayed by the onset of the war. It finally opened its doors in 1906. Commentary in the first edition of the *Sunday Times* covering the moment was hyperbolic. 'It isn't merely a hotel; it's a miniature city insofar as it contains the whole of those comforts to which the luxury-loving modern aspires.' The London edition of *The Star* newspaper also waxed lyrical. 'The building itself is magnificent. All the glories of the place cannot be described ... in this Palace of Luxury.'[302]

Many newspapers in South Africa reported on the hotel's impact on the social lives of Johannesburg's elite. Reporters' responses ranged from captivated to aghast, as they foraged for ongoing stories of outrageous extravagances at this place of plenty. The hotel manager was known to oblige. 'Lord Rocksavage, a fashionable young officer of the 9th Lancers, would spend an average of £1000 to £1500 per week. His parties were unbelievable, with expensive liquors flowing like fountains. Every three months, we needed four hundred new cases of champagne.'[303]

As the inequality festered, so too did the antisemitism.

Russian Jews found themselves the target of a public horror at the rot that pervaded the lower reaches of the town. These unfortunates became known as 'Peruvians' – a term of contempt already in circulation before the war, wielded by more respectable types, Jews and non-Jews alike.[304] Much like elsewhere in the country too, poverty-stricken and unsightly Eastern Jewish strangeness was judged to be a moral blight, but nowhere as aggressively as in Johannesburg. Meyer Dovid Hersch, writing in 1896 to discourage would-be Jewish immigrants from heading to Johannesburg, made the point bluntly: 'our people are detested by the local inhabitants. The malignant plague of antisemitism has spread to ... all the spheres of everyday life and the struggle for survival. Even the courts are infected by this pestilential evil.'[305] By the late 1890s, writes historian Charles van Onselen, the 'Peruvians' were 'the unhappy recipients of the most vicious class and race prejudice that society could muster'.[306] The worsening economic situation after the war did nothing to improve matters.

A rampant illicit alcohol trade, along with a brothel boom, added a particular sting. The sale of alcohol had been an economic niche for Jews in the shtetls, as we've seen, so it's not surprising that the trade attracted many Jewish hopefuls in Johannesburg. Initially, trading licences were issued freely by the Transvaal authorities, but in 1896, after the mines complained about excessive drinking among mine workers, the trade was prohibited. It persisted illegally nevertheless – an open secret – and was denounced as the source of untold vice, blamed on the Jewish traders who kept it going. The flourishing sex trade hit the headlines too, amid anxieties about the White slave trade. In the public mind it, too, was an Eastern European Jewish scourge; many of the sex workers, as well as the pimps who dominated the business, were known to have made their way to the Rand from those parts.

After the war, as the economic malaise deepened, so did the distaste. It was well known and noted in the Yiddish press. If the Jews in town had not already experienced it first-hand, they would have read that 'the English officials look upon Russian subjects with disgust'.[307]

The figure of the Jew offered a précis of what Johannesburg's rapacious growth was doing to its vulnerable humanity at the bottom of the heap – in a way that offloaded the problem as an ethnic affront.

A similar kind of appalled displacement occurred at the top end of the social spectrum. Olive Schreiner spoke for those who shared her vehement contempt for Johannesburg's *nouveau riche*. 'The mass of ill-gotten wealth obtained without labour and squandered with recklessness [is] the true source of evil,' she declaimed.[308] She was echoing the sorts of distaste provoked by the flamboyant rich in other parts of the world too, where the spectacles of the *nouveau riche* became hallmarks of poor taste and cultural vulgarity. Jews were an easy and obvious target of such disgust: the crass, supposedly semitic, love of all things monetary offered a ready-made explanation for the offence of such excess.

In late nineteenth century France, for example, one of the many expressions of rising antisemitic sentiment was in the novels of the day. Many included one or other version of a rich Jew, 'depicted as a foreigner emerging from poverty and squalor to insinuate himself into the highest circles of power and prestige'.[309] The spectacle of the *nouveau riche* – of people who had risen dramatically from shabby insignificance to flashy social prominence – prompted suspicion of ill-gotten gains and crude fakery. The iconography of Jewishness contained a ready explanation: masqueraders at heart, Jews' newfound wealth could not disguise the derelict and dishonest schemers that they really were. In Great Britain, the Jewish Randlords were regarded as suspect for the same sorts of reasons.[310] Being *nouveau riche* was an instance, apparently, of the most vulgar version of Jewish fakery.

In Johannesburg, the first such murmurings were triggered by Barney Barnato – a Jew who had started out poor in London's East End and enjoyed flaunting his newfound wealth. Barnato Park – the house he commissioned in the suburb of Berea, and unfinished at the time of his death – was purportedly built at an exorbitant cost, excessively decorated with 'marble columns, mosaics, plate-glass windows, alabaster mantelpieces, painted ceilings and other extravagances'.[311]

Barnato made no bones about his lack of what the British called 'culture', making no apology for his low-class origins and his often-uncouth mannerisms. Other Jewish Randlords were at pains to acquire the cultural capital of the British aristocracy, investing in substantial art collections, along with aristocratic titles where the opportunities to purchase arose.[312] Barnato had no such pretensions; his was money entirely without style or sophistication. Notoriously, he was blissfully ignorant about the world of Art. As told by Louis Cohen (one of Barnato's contemporaries on the diamond fields) and repeated many times at Barnato's expense, he was once with Barnato 'in an art dealer's "sanctum". An assistant entered and whispered audibly to his employer that "the Constable" had come. As the picture seller hurriedly left the room, Barney inquisitively said to me, compressing his lips, "What's the copper here for, I wonder?"'[313]

Another mark of Barnato's refusal to kowtow to dominant cultural conventions was his marriage to a Coloured woman – referred to in lofty social circles, where a euphemism was necessary, as a woman of 'dusky' complexion. He and Fanny Bees had met in Kimberley, when Barnato was making a name for himself trading diamonds, beginning to get rich. She was a barmaid; he was an enthusiastic customer. By all accounts, their relationship was strong and supportive; she remained at his side as he grew ever richer and more famous. In the eyes of the establishment, this was another sign of Barnato's *nouveau riche* vulgarity: the mark of an ignorant upstart, his failure to appreciate the cultural texts of colonial privilege.

Conflating the *nouveau riche* with crass Jewish excess grew even more bitter after the end of the South African War. It was widely dubbed a 'Jews' war'. Many among the war's opponents in Britain regarded the war as irresponsible plunder on the part of powerful British Jews driven by capitalist greed. The sentiment was shared within some of the officer corps of the British army, who blamed the war on 'rich self-made men', *nouveau riche* Jews who had bought their way into British high society.[314] When General Sir William Butler, of the Welsh Regiment, referred to Johannesburg as 'Jewburg', he had in mind 'the most corrupt, immoral and untruthful assemblage of beings at present in the world'.[315]

After the war, 'Hoggenheimer' arrived on the scene, to prejudicial acclaim. The cartoonist D.C. Boonzaier borrowed the character from a musical depicting a *nouveau riche* Jewish financier living in London's opulent Park Lane. The musical opened in London in 1902 and then travelled to South Africa. In Boonzaier's cartoons, Hoggenheimer became the archetypal Jewish parvenu – flashy, loud-mouthed and uncouth.[316]

Brazenly antisemitic, W.C. Scully described Johannesburg after the war with this character at the heart of the place. 'Vapour-driven cars and coughing motorcycles speed up and down. A huge automobile glides, hooting furiously, down the street and halts close to where I stand. In it sits a portly man wearing a fur-rimmed overcoat and smoking a big cigar. Arrogance seems to exude from him, to be as evident as the petrol fumes his monstrous car gives off. Surely this must be the much-caricatured Hoggenheimer with which Mr Boonzaier has made us all familiar.'[317]

Boonzaier's Hoggenheimer cartoons appeared in a raft of South African newspapers for nearly forty years.

67 | A deferent retort

Trying to assuage all this hostility would prove far more difficult in Johannesburg than had been the case in Cape Town. In Cape Town, British and German Jews had had forty or so years to set themselves up, with relatively stable institutions and an established communal infrastructure, before the Easterners arrived. These Westerners had achieved some public respectability, having proven their colonial loyalty, with rituals of deference to the British crown to prove it. The situation in Johannesburg was very different, with no pre-existing apparatuses of respectable community to work with.

At the turn of the century, Johannesburg's Jews were anything but a cohesive community. Eastern Jews arrived at more or less the same time as their Western counterparts. Most of the Westerners were more affluent, better educated and more secular than their oriental cousins, with whom they had little, if anything, in common. Scorn and mockery were lavishly traded, in both directions. As was the case in Cape Town, the Eastern Jews turned their noses up at the 'ignorant English types' who observed 'corrupt ways and customs', as Russian immigrant Yehuda Leib Schrire put it,[318] at the same time as the anglicised Jews showed their disdain for the unsophisticated, slovenly habits and religious anachronisms of the Yiddish speakers.

Class schisms between the flashily rich and the doggedly poor were more pronounced in Johannesburg than in Cape Town, and initially the more affluent were disinclined to direct their monies in any easterly direction to help out.[319] Religious conflicts erupted often too. Groups of the discontented broke away from one synagogue to set up another; accusations and counter-accusations about delinquent interpretations of the faith abounded.

Neither the Easterners nor the Westerners formed a united, cohesive group among themselves. They had different loyalties and allegiances in the local politics of the place: during the South African War, some had remained determinedly neutral, some had supported the Boers, others were more inclined to go with the British. Many among the most recent arrivals from the Pale came with experiences of political activism in pre-revolutionary Russia, and would gather and organise in Johannesburg too, taking secular stands against the religious orthodoxies of their anachronistic brethren.[320] Nor were these secular Jews on the same ideological page. While some were ardent Zionists, a Yiddish-speaking branch of the International Socialist League in downtown Johannesburg took a strongly anti-Zionist stance. *Landsmanschaftens* – clubs for immigrants from the same shtetls or towns in the Pale – drew emotional maps of the borders that pulled some Jews together and left others out.

Each group wanted as little as possible to do with the others. By 1904, the *South African Jewish Chronicle* could not contain its frustration. 'A demon of discord has lodged itself with exceptional tenacity in Johannesburg's Jewish population.'[321] A shared sense of Jewishness was a remote, even preposterous, idea.

Disparate and fractious the town's Jews may have been, but in the eyes of the more mainstream, affluent and well connected among them, it would serve all the Jews' interests (and especially their own) to have an organised faction (at that stage, it could not have been more than that) to articulate and defend (what they saw as) Jewish interests in the hostile prejudicial milieu of the times. It would be a strategic initiative, speaking back to the local non-Jewish public and colonial authorities in a social and political language they would understand: their own, the language of imperial Great Britain.

Think of it, then, as a tactically deferent retort to the colonials – with the added advantage of seizing the initiative, with its attendant powers, from the embarrassing Easterners. Max Langerman, one of the German Jewish Randlords with strong affections for the British Empire, proposed activating his contacts with the Anglo-Jewish Association in London to set up something comparable, and connected, in Johannesburg. A meeting of interested locals ultimately came up with a different proposal, not out of kilter with the first: to set up a local Board of Deputies instead, with a mandate to bat for Jews in the colonial game, across their many divisions and whenever threats from the outside arose.

Predictably, the move was soon contested. Langerman and his friends then brought in Rabbi Hertz – who ministered to the Anglo-German Jews in Johannesburg but hailed from Eastern Europe and therefore straddled some of the divides. Could he mediate and soothe the argument?[322] Yes, he could. The proposal would prevail, if precariously.

The board took shape as a social and political device, more than a cultural one: making moves to rehabilitate Jewish respectability in the eyes of the Johannesburg public by undertaking something of a moral clean-up, tackling issues of illicit alcohol and sex work, encouraging Jewish philanthropy to deal with poverty, and promoting the education of Jewish children. The cultural diversity among Johannesburg's Jews would be less of an issue in the first instance. But over time, as the board grew in confidence and muscle, it would play its cultural hand too, calling on Jews to look to Britain as their protector, and to take out British citizenship as a demonstration of colonial loyalty – much the same line as had been taken in the Cape.

In the interim, however, Johannesburg's Jews would remain a culturally disparate lot. Many of the Russian Jews would continue looking inward and homewards, to try to ward off the stinging rebuffs of their obvious difference.

68 | Ferreirastown

Ferreirastown was where Johannesburg began, in a multitude of tents for myriad prospectors. It didn't take long for the tents to give way to a mix of iron and wood structures, some brick homes, bars and hotels. Johannesburg's first hotel, bar, brothel and barber shop opened in Ferreirastown, as did the first circus, school and bank. Despite harsh official pronouncements about the need to keep different races resolutely apart, the place was mixed and cosmopolitan, with people converging there from various parts of Europe, Great Britain, Asia and southern Africa. Location, location, location: the place was close to the mines and the central market square, convenient for prospectors and mine workers, as well as the traders who set up shop to cater for all those locals. By 1904, the population density in Ferreirastown was comparable to the most congested areas of inner London.[323]

All the accounts of Ferreirastown that I have read depict it as a thoroughly degraded space: dirty, destitute, a criminal stronghold and den of vice. 'The name of the place became synonymous with everything that is vile and violent about Johannesburg.'[324] It didn't help that Jews recently arrived from the East had congregated there: seen from the outside, the place was a lair of repugnant 'Peruvians'.

For most of its inhabitants, Ferreirastown was tough and the resources it afforded were sparse. Leibl Feldman gives a glimpse of the harshness in the so-called Yards, in which a mixed population rented spaces of minimal comfort. 'The Yards,' he wrote, 'were large courtyards that were empty in the middle. On the periphery small metal shacks were erected close together. Inside the shacks it was very hot in summer and very cold at night, especially in winter. The furniture in the rooms consisted of old broken beds, a big crate for a table and a small one for a chair. On the "table" stood a primus, a few cooking pots, and a tallow coated candlestick. Every Friday they would put seven newspapers on the "table" and tie them together with a piece of string, so as to be sure of having a "clean tablecloth" for every day of the week. There was no running water or electricity.'[325]

Bernard Sachs and his family, in flight from the Lithuanian shtetl of Kamaai, settled in Ferreirastown in 1914. In his memoir, Bernard – younger brother of the more famous Solly, communist activist and trade union organiser – recalled the rigours of daily life in that 'weary and drab' place, worn down by the perpetual noise of the nearby mines. 'Cage after cage screeched along the cables from the shafts bringing dusty loads which were emptied onto the heap [of the mine dumps]. The din of the stamp-batteries crushing the gold ore persisted through the night.'[326]

But there was more to life in Ferreirastown than its grinding austerity. Bars and brothels there were, in abundance, but also butchers, bakers and food stalls; booksellers and theatres; and churches and synagogues too. Political associations and social clubs formed. Many of the inhabitants were single men, but there were families as well. The first school opened in 1896 with twenty-one pupils.

The Jewish presence was especially conspicuous. According to Leibl Feldman, 'from Ferreiras to Fordsburg, one saw Russian Jews everywhere'. Typically, their lives were arduous, sometimes dark, but lit in unexpected ways: theatre and music added sparkle. Bernard Sachs explains, with witty irony: 'those were the days of the *chevraleit* (the gentility), a euphemism for the White slavers.[327] Sauer Street was lined with their emporiums, where all manner of amenities were made available.' Clearly, the Board of Deputies still had their work cut out for them. 'Strangely enough, the *chevraleit* did not allow the squalor of their pursuits to rob them of their aesthetic sensibilities. Sarah Sylvia [internationally famous Yiddish singer and actress] told me that without the munificent subsidies of these *chevraleit*, there would not have been any Yiddish theatre – here were the real patrons of the Arts.'[328]

The Jews of Ferreirastown were not of like mind, not religiously nor politically. The strongest node of Jewish life there was orthodox, the traditional religious identities and rituals resolutely in place. Another node was secular and socialist, with outspoken Jewish activists at odds with their orthodox neighbours, not least the rack-renting landlords of the Yards. The Yiddish-speaking branch of the International Socialist League set up in Ferreirastown. Solly Sachs recounted how 'a little Communist Jew of about five feet in height … assuming a Napeolonic stance would declaim in ringing tones that echoed down the labyrinthine backyards. "Sklaffen (slaves) why don't you fight for your freedom?"' [329]

Some Jews had strong networks and connections with their kinsmen; others were more solitary. Feldman tells of 'friendly relationships' that developed between 'the lonely Jews and the lonely Blacks'[330] – all newcomers and strangers, whose paths crossed regularly in the forlorn eateries or in the busy trade of humble things. Bernard Sachs's family was 'friendly with the Coloured family living two rooms next door to us – the camaraderie of the rootless'.[331]

For many of the Russian Jews, Ferreirastown was an enclave of home, and a refuge amid all the alien hostility. There they lived with 'their friends and fellow countrymen close to the Jewish bookseller and the Orthodox *mesmedresh* [place of worship]. The special Jewish dishes, kosher meat, fish, pickled herring, kitke, beigel etc were available there. There they could live out their lives in their mother tongue – Yiddish. There they felt more at home than anywhere else.'[332]

Chatzkel and Bere both chose to live in areas where their connections to a sense of home would remain strong. But they did so in very different ways. Bere's horizons remained limited, as if the Britishness of his new colonial world had to be held entirely at bay. Chatzkel, on the other hand, brought lessons for prosperity learned in the shtetl – to engage beyond one's own – to his life in the colony. He applied for, and received, naturalisation as a British citizen. He learned to speak, read and write English. His commercial life took him into daily contact with the non-Jews who bought his goods and rented space in his yards. He understood what the colonial bureaucracies required of him – and complied. The Blacks in his yards had the requisite permits. He kept a detailed list of his tenants and their rentals which he could present to the authorities if and when they came to visit. Indeed, his records were impeccable, even if on disreputable-looking scraps of paper – as I had discovered in 1994 when working on the exhibition in his disapproving daughter-in-law's gallery. The authorities issued no complaint. Culturally, however, Chatzkel could be as Russian as he pleased; mixing with Russian friends and neighbours; eating shtetl food and chewing the fat in Yiddish.

69 | Prospering in Ferreirastown

None of the accounts I have read imagine that the people of Ferreirastown, including the Jews, were anything but pitifully poor, or deviant thugs. Undoubtedly, poverty and vice marked the space – poverty in particular. Many, probably most, of Ferreirastown's people eked out an existence, ever precariously. Jews too. Some clawed their way up a little from the dusty ground onto a more secure ledge; a few others hauled themselves all the way up and out. The surprise for me was to discover some who started out there and stayed, despite having had more than enough to enable them to leave.

Here are profiles of three Jewish men who prospered in Ferreirastown without resorting to crime, accumulating enough money to buy a home in a prestigious part of the town, and who chose not to. There's no reason to assume that they were the only ones.

Chatzkel is the first of the three. He made his money through a combination of the sales in his Driefontein shop, and by buying property, on which he set up scant structures that he rented out – both in the Driefontein area and in Ferreirastown. By the time he bought his first stand in Ferreirastown, he already co-owned a stand and a shop in Driefontein. He then bought another two stands in Driefontein (one with his brother-in-law Harris Plein), extended the first one and built a house on it. And in addition to the yard that he set up at 27 Marshall Street, he bought another four stands in Ferreirastown that also became yards. 'The letting of rooms in the yard,' writes historical geographer Susan Parnell, 'was allegedly the most lucrative form of property dealing in Johannesburg.'[333]

Chatzkel's yard on 27 Marshall Street was cramped, but not as badly as some of the others. The Johannesburg municipal authorities, beginning a process of surveillance in Ferreirastown, offered an unusually detailed description. 'In Posel's Yard, a White family occupied the cottage fronting onto the street. A kitchen and room behind the cottage were let to a White man and similar facilities to the rear were rented to a family of six "Syrians". To the west of these buildings were individual structures that housed four Coloured, two Indian men, five French-speaking "Native Madagascans", a Coloured woman, four Africans with permits, and the owner's domestic servant. There were also two unoccupied rooms.'[334]

That makes a total of twelve rooms, in addition to Chatzkel's home. Ridgeways Yard, elsewhere in Ferreirastown, on the same size stand of fifty by fifty feet, had twenty-five structures on it; Chatzkel's was on the low end of the average of ten to twelve per yard.[335]

Conditions in the yards were challenging: freezing in winter, intensely hot in summer.

Ventilation was poor, drainage was bad. Sanitation arrangements must have been rudimentary. The relentless dust of early Johannesburg settled everywhere, and when it rained, the yards turned to mud.

I have wondered how a 'well-to-do' Jew from a status-conscious shtetl adapted to life under these conditions, living so intimately with others who were teetering on the edge. Did he need rituals of one-upmanship? Did he wield a metaphorical whip against any tenants struggling to pay what they owed him, or did the harshness of the place elicit some compassion?

There were a few signs of slum snobbery. The survey of Posel's Yard reveals an unexpected detail: Chatzkel's family had a domestic servant. His 'cottage' stayed clean; his family's clothes were washed and ironed. I suspect this helper was not paid to extend his or her services to the others living in the yard.

Max, Chatzkel's only son, attended Jeppe Boys High School – one of Johannesburg's most prestigious boys' schools of the day. Each day he would have stepped out of the family home in his neat school uniform, a reminder of what was possible for him and likely unthinkable for most of the other children in the yards.

Chatzkel's death certificate records his occupation at the end of his life as a 'retired gentleman'. Was this what he felt himself to be, the sense of self that paraded in his head as he surveyed his dilapidated yard with its tatty tenants?

Were details such as these daily reminders of a miniature class hierarchy, even in the dirt: a drama of minor differences, played out intensely because it was so precarious? They were all living in a slum, after all.

By the time Chatzkel died, he had accumulated a respectable stash to pass on to his children. His assets – a combination of the land he owned and the rentals he took in – were just short of five thousand pounds. He had achieved what all new immigrants aspired to do: to ensure that his children would have substantially better opportunities in the country than he had had. And in Jewish eyes, his son would bag the highest accolade, studying to become a medical doctor. At a top university, in the heart of the British capital. What more could an immigrant father have asked for?

The second man who flouts the typical picture of Ferreirastown's down-and-outers was Chatzkel's neighbour living across the street at 28 Marshall Street. This was Barnett Cumes – of the Cape Town egg trade, one of the three who 'mistakenly' took delivery of an egg consignment bought by others. Arriving in South Africa as a child in 1884, Barnett had spent his early adult years in Randfontein (near one of the mines) as the co-owner of two properties. On one of those, he had set up house and ran a shop. At the outbreak of the war, he fled to Cape Town, leaving his stock and property behind, and entered the egg trade with Chiat and Sacks.

Like many other Jews who returned after the war to find that their belongings had been looted, Barnett claimed for compensation against the new colonial government, to the tune of nearly nine hundred pounds. The claim was refused, on the grounds that he and his business partners had left their goods for safekeeping with other traders who had subsequently sold them off.[336] His profits from the lucrative egg trade would come in handy as he repositioned himself back in Johannesburg.

A younger man than Chatzkel, Barnett was twenty-three when he bought his stand in Marshall Street in 1902, as a newly married man. He arrived there just a month or two before Chatzkel. It's not impossible that they had already met in Cape Town after 1899 and made a joint decision to buy property in Ferreirastown on returning to Johannesburg and live as neighbours. On his return, Barnett also retrieved his properties in Randfontein, jointly valued at five hundred and fifty pounds, and rented them out. And the partnership with Chiat and Sacks continued, adding the importation of seed potatoes from the Canary Islands to their repertoire.[337]

I don't know exactly when Cumes left Ferreirastown. By the 1930s – when the area was cleared and resettled for 'orderly' White occupation – he was still living in Johannesburg, continuing to invest in property on the goldfields and loaning money to Black people to buy homes in Sophiatown,[338] extracting interest on the loans. By 1943 he had moved to Cape Town, and he died there in 1948 an avowedly rich man, with an estate of nearly one hundred and fifty thousand pounds.[339]

The third man who did well for himself living in Ferreirastown was Wulf Cohen, a compatriot of Chatzkel's from Pumpian. Wulf first made a name for himself as a shrewd salesman after a catastrophic dynamite explosion in Johannesburg in 1896. Glass windows were shattered all over, and Wulf – advised by 'a fellow countryman' – gathered glass panes and went house to house offering to repair windows. 'On the very first day, he earned five pounds,' writes Leibl Feldman. 'He immediately sent this money to his impoverished family. When the money arrived in Pumpian, it caused a sensation' – proving that if Johannesburg could yield five pounds in a single day, it truly was a ' "golden land" '.[340] Wulf then turned his attention to baking *matzah,* offering an affordable alternative to the *matzah* that was imported into Johannesburg at a hefty cost. His business flourished, enabling him to set up the Rand Steam Matzo Factory Ltd, producing enough *matzah* 'for the needs of the whole of Transvaal Jewry'.[341]

It turns out he had some friends in high places too. 'During the Boer War, when the British were advancing in the Free State, Mr. Cohen was granted a special permit by the Boer Government which enabled him to travel to Bloemfontein for the purpose of obtaining supplies of Kosher flour.' And in Johannesburg, 'Boer troops attempted to commandeer Mr. Cohen's supply of flour, but the plan was frustrated by Dr. (now Mr. Justice) F.E.T. Krause, who at that time was commandant of the town.'[342]

None of these three men needed to live in Ferreirastown to keep their business dealings alive. It was surely the sociality of the place that kept them there: a sense of solidarity and even some feeling of domestic mastery, keeping at least some of the colonial demons at bay, despite the degraded infrastructure of daily life. I imagine the camaraderie amongst these three and their other brethren in the yards was strong. In addition to his large *matzah* factory, Wulf Cohen set up a bakery in his yard on Marshall Street, known as 'Cohen the baker's yard'. 'On Friday night,' wrote Feldman, 'the Jews from [the] Yards would come to put their pots of *cholent*[343] in Cohen the Baker's oven, to cook overnight. Every *shabbas* when they had finished praying, they would come to fetch their pots. This scene was reminiscent of the small religious villages in the old country.'[344]

There were social and familial connections between Chatzkel and Barnett too. Barnett's niece would marry Chatzkel's nephew, Aaron Plein – son of Chatzkel's brother-in-law Harris Plein. Aaron, with whom Chatzkel had regular contact, was an ambitious entrepreneurial type from his teenage years onwards and would go on to become the most successful of all of them, setting up a lucrative international shipping company.

Under these conditions, the colonial cultural codes of upward social mobility mattered little to these men. Yet I suspect none of them was inclined to pass any of this on to their offspring, for whom the idea of slum origins would have had a very different, more conventionally colonial, meaning. Better to keep *shtum* [silent].

70 | The *farribel* undone

Many of the fiercest *farribels*, locked in the tightest of secrets, have to do with inheritances and wills. Yet individual wills and deceased estates are public documents, freely accessible to anyone who chooses to consult them in the national archives. At least some of those secrets can be prised open.

Reading Chatzkel's will was a revelation to me, exploding the family narrative about how Max's university education was funded.

Chatzkel died on 21 March 1916, aged fifty-two; his wife Chane had died four years previously. His immediate family at the time of his death comprised his three daughters and one son. His oldest daughter, Jane, was married to Morris Elliot and lived in Germiston; his second daughter, Gertie, was married to Philip Owitz and they lived in Piet Retief. Sarah, his youngest daughter, was unmarried; I'm not sure of her home address. Max had been living with his father in his yard.

Chatzkel's will provided for all his children, but he took especially good care of his son, who was allocated one third of his father's estate. Max would continue at Jeppe Boys High School until he matriculated in 1918. After his father died, he likely became a boarder at the school, since both of his married sisters and brothers-in-law lived outside of Johannesburg. Chatzkel left him a monthly allowance to cover these and other expenses, under the guardianship of his brother-in-law Morris Elliot, until Max turned twenty-one.

The school record shows that Max was not a top, prize-winning pupil, but he was good enough to matriculate and to proceed to study medicine at St Bartholomew's Hospital in

London. Perhaps he already knew he wanted to become a doctor while his father was alive and they had discussed how to make this happen; perhaps not. Either way, it's clear from Chatzkel's will that there was ample provision made to fund Max's university education abroad.

All in all, after all the necessary deductions and settling of debts, Chatzkel bequeathed a sum of five thousand three hundred pounds. Of this, a little over one thousand seven hundred pounds would go to Max, with most of it assigned for when he turned twenty-one. It makes sense, then, that Max left Johannesburg for London in 1921, initially drawing his monthly sums from his father's will but on the cusp of the full bequest set to come his way.

Here is the fiction in Maurice's story of the *farribel*. It is patently clear that Max's opportunity to study medicine did not depend in any way on contributions from his cousin Maurice. There had been no obligation of sacrifice imposed on Maurice; Max hadn't needed him at all.

What, then, of the family story? Was it simply a brazen and outright lie, a malicious deception, or are there shards of truth that jut out, to be extracted and interpreted anew?

I find myself returning to the story of the blood libel in Pumpian: factually, also a falsehood, but moored in a bed of uncomfortable truth and an occurrence of trauma. Surely Maurice's *farribel* followed a similar logic. The factual details were invented, but with some plausibility in the narrative arc of the story, and an emotional injury at its heart that was powerfully real.

The way Maurice told the story implied that Bere and his brother were not estranged; there must have been some sort of brotherly relationship between them for anything like a mutual arrangement to have been thinkable. Bere would have known that Chatzkel's financial position was vastly different from his own. Perhaps there was some expectation on Bere's part that Chatzkel would have contributed to his nephew's education – a good brotherly thing to do, in such an unequal situation. A good Jewish thing to do too, showing familial compassion and care, for which Jews want to be known. Perhaps there was also an understanding between Bere and his son that without any such largesse on Chatzkel's part, going to university would remain a pipe dream for Maurice – unless he could conjure up ways and means of his own.

Chatzkel died before his brother, who would soon have been confronted with the contents of the will. Perhaps the first iteration of the *farribel* was Bere's creation: a parable of his injury at the hands of a miserly brother. Then Maurice made it his own and cast it in stone.

In 1916, Maurice would have been nineteen years old. He had likely recently finished his last year of high school: a momentous point in his life to have received the news that nothing from his deceased uncle would be coming his way. Maurice was not scholarship material. He might have been eligible for bursaries on the grounds of his financial need but no doubt the competition for such resources was strong and his academic abilities likely did not position him at the forefront. Did Maurice then give up on his plans for university in a fit of pique and frustrated entitlement, and choose to shift the blame for this decision to his uncle and first cousin?

Maurice was not a man of grit and determination. If something got in the way of a plan he had hatched, he was far more likely to have marinated in a sense of grievance and injury than picked himself up and come up with another plan. If he felt his path to a university education had been thwarted by his uncle and cousin, then so be it: it would have been their fault, and the plan would have died entirely, suffocated by Maurice's seething fury. His sense of injury, however, would flare and flame. All the ingredients of a *farribel* for life.

71 | Max

I didn't meet Max, of course, and know little about him. Before starting on this book, all I saw of him was refracted through the prism of the *farribel*: Max as Maurice's nemesis. Max had everything that Maurice wanted: he was schooled at a top school; secured a prestigious education at a top university, reaching the pinnacle of professional distinction as a medical specialist; he enjoyed social standing and professional recognition, and married into a family of substance in the Jewish community. And Max bought himself a seat in the Wolmarans Synagogue, the grandest of Johannesburg's shuls.

I can add a bit more now to what I had already known. His daughter and niece confirmed to me that the practice of medicine had been at the centre of his world and his daily life. He took great pride in his profession and chose to spend his time with his medical peers, or others whom he regarded as comparably accomplished. It gave him great pleasure that Carol, the elder of his two daughters, studied medicine. All of this must have been salt to Maurice's wounds.

But there is another side to the Max story that had previously been hidden. Having spoken to Max's daughters in the course of researching this book, I am struck now by the similarities between the two M's. Both were rather taciturn and antisocial; both were men who spoke little and did not take up much social space. Both were British loyalists: sentiments likely anchored in their schooling. The one aspect of Max's childhood that his children had been told was that he had gone to the then prestigious Jeppe High School for Boys. Given Maurice's deceitfulness about his schooling, I felt the need to check the facts in Max's case too.

As it turns out, there was no lie: he started there in 1914 and stayed until he matriculated in 1918.

Jeppe Boys School was one of the so-called Milner schools: beneficiaries of the decision by Lord Milner – then governor of the Transvaal – to provide free schooling for White English-speaking children – or children who desired to become English speaking. It was part of his anglicisation strategy, linked to the nurturing of colonial loyalty and British manners among the youngsters of the town. In Max's case, these early leanings strengthened after his stint in London as a medical student. I'm told that on his return, he revealed his penchant for pin-striped suits and hats; they matched his upper-class British accent.

Both Max and Maurice, I now know, had banished their younger selves to dark inner closets, firmly locked away – as if their childhoods had never been. None of their respective children knew anything about where and how they had grown up. If any of them had asked, I have no doubt they would not have been told.

Max had been one among the children of a slum, a place perceived from the outside as a den of undesirables, 'Peruvians' prominent among them. Viewed from the outside, his father would likely have been seen as one such delinquent. I suspect that even as a young boy, this was not a detail about his life that Max was happy to publicise in his activities beyond Ferreirastown; at his well-mannered school, for example. Even more so as he grew older and ascended the social ladder. For a man of his station, acutely conscious of the stature he had achieved, admitting to a contaminated childhood must have been a social and psychological risk he was not strong enough to have taken.

I'm not at all surprised, then, that one of his daughters described her father to me as man of secrets. 'He kept it all inside,' she said and put it down to his 'Eastern European roots': 'They had a complex about their history. They found it shameful.' But she had no idea that he had grown up in a colonial slum – an aspect of his early life as shameful as his 'dirty' Eastern origins. Another among his many secrets.

The most revealing trace – or symptom – of Max's repressed inner life must surely be one of the lines in his entry in the Jewish *Who's Who* – a register of the South African *balebatim*. Max's father is described as a 'Rand Pioneer', a version of the man that his secretive son would have supplied – to assuage his shame.

# Part Six

72 | A Johannesburg man

Maurice left Cape Town after finishing high school and headed for Johannesburg. Once he reckoned that the doors to the University of Cape Town had closed to him, I imagine he decided to leave home in indignant haste and try to make something of himself in a different setting, far from his parents and their Russian blemishes.

He moved in – at least for a while – with one of his own. Chave – Bere's and Chatzkel's sister – had emigrated to South Africa in 1909, already married to her husband Max Farfel. They settled in Potchefstroom in the Transvaal, where Max ran a store. Their son Sam studied medicine at the University of the Witwatersrand, before heading to London to specialise. Maurice got on reasonably well with his first cousin Sam, so much so that he lodged with Sam in his house at 42 Regent Street in Yeoville until Sam's departure for London in 1923.

Little about Maurice's life during those early years in Johannesburg comes into focus, other than the fact that by 1930 – the year of his marriage – he had succeeded in purchasing a house in the suburb of Bez Valley, had cash savings of one thousand pounds, and furniture and household effects to the value of five hundred pounds. These are items specified in his and Erna's antenuptial contract, as 'gifts' that he agreed to hand over to his wife on the occasion of their wedding. He must have had a reasonably well-paying job, collected rent from tenants in the house he owned, and saved furiously.

Maurice's story is drenched in longing. Longing for the respect and status he did not have; longing to be someone other than who he was. Perhaps for a short time, in Johannesburg, he arrived where he enjoyed being and felt whole; maybe he was beginning to feel he belonged. The only photograph I have of him prior to his marriage tentatively suggests so.

The image offers a fleeting, perhaps ephemeral, glimpse into his Johannesburg bachelorhood. He's looking confidently into the camera, and has struck an assertive, even cocky, pose, his right arm crooked and his mouth suavely set. He seems to be holding a cigarette in his left hand – a flash of worldliness that was nowhere in evidence in his later adulthood. Here, momentarily, I see a young man of the world, even a tad dandyish. With an air of defiance, maybe some defensiveness with it, claiming his space.

Maurice Posel as a bachelor in Johannesburg. Author's collection.

I'm keenly aware of how unexpected and unusual this image is in the small visual archive of the Posel family. The photograph was preserved and passed down, rather than discarded or destroyed. There's something in it that Maurice wanted to hold onto and transmit – a brief message, if inchoate and ill-formed – for generations that would not otherwise have known.

The injury of his *farribel* would have flared most painfully when Maurice felt judged: seen through the eyes of others who made him feel that he did not measure up. I sense that this image captures a version of Maurice when he felt free of that feeling of surveillance, standing tall. Maybe he was having a good time; and maybe that could have continued. Maybe the wound of the *farribel* could have healed, and Sir Carruthers Beattie would have receded into the distance.

It was not to be. The first knife to Maurice's wound must have been meeting the family of the woman he chose to marry.

To trace the trajectory of his pain, we must switch tack, to the border between the Transvaal and Portuguese East Africa in the first decade of the twentieth century.

73 | 'One man with four girls'

On 5 November 1909, a short spurt of energy unsettled the usually more lethargic police station at the Komatipoort border with Portuguese East Africa (renamed Mozambique in 1976). Smelling a rat, the police sergeant on duty that morning fired off an 'urgent' missive to the chief immigration officer in Pretoria. The night before, five Austrian persons – 'one man with four girls' – had crossed into the Transvaal. Their train had stopped at the border, where the man – seemingly travelling without a passport – presented a merely 'informal pass'. It had been issued the previous day by the Transvaal Immigration Office in Lourenço Marques, the capital, supposedly at the request of the Austrian consul there.

Sergeant Gerome was worried about several things. Why was a foreign man crossing the Komatipoort border in the company of four young women? The White slave trade was much on the official mind, and Lourenço Marques was notorious for its many 'ladies of easy virtue'. Unsurprisingly, then, Gerome suspected the man's motives. But he couldn't be sure. 'I had a slight doubt as to their bona fides,' he wrote. 'It seemed strange to me to see one man travelling with four girls together in a carriage.'[345] Their documentation was suspect too. Informal permits had no photographs or fingerprints attached; there was no way of verifying the identity of those named in them. It was also impossible to prove the authenticity of the permit itself; it could have been forged, as many were. All of which made the business of policing the border notoriously vexing and difficult.

In the previous decade, the borders of the British colonies of the Cape and Natal had been tightening up. Imperfectly, it must be said; but the aspiration was demonstrable in the appointment of new legions of immigration officials, armed with heaps of permits and paperwork, charged with keeping the riffraff out. Efforts to police the north-east border with Portuguese East Africa, however, were altogether more shambolic.[346]

In fact, immigration officials in the Transvaal had been waging an uphill battle at that junction, unable to curb decades-old habits of nonchalant border-crossing. Immigration officials in Lourenço Marques were said to be tardy and unreliable, content to allow travel on the strength of informal permits that had not been officially processed, leaving no proper written trace. Criminal syndicates smuggling would-be immigrants into the Transvaal made effective use of the loophole. Historian Andrew MacDonald has documented the 'traffic in permits', readily forged, sometimes with the collusion of Portuguese officials cashing in on such deals.[347]

The lucrative business of illegal immigration mostly serviced vulnerable Asians, Madeirans and, of late, Greeks and Syrians. Was this Austrian man – accompanying four 'girls' – another face of the same phenomenon? He was travelling supposedly with Austrian consular approval, but who could say for sure?

Six days later (it couldn't have been that urgent after all) Sergeant Gerome received a terse reply from the chief immigration officer expressing his own concern. These informal passes were 'totally irregular', he wrote. 'I shall be glad if you will inform me whether there was anything suspicious in the appearance of these people.'[348]

It took the intervention of one Arthur Long, an agent of the Transvaal's Immigration Department based in Lourenço Marques, to set the record straight, endorsing the Austrian consul's approval wholeheartedly. The Austrian man in question was 'of good reputation and very good character', Long wrote, having served eighteen years in the army of the Austro-Hungarian

Empire. He was travelling, would you believe it, with his daughters. They had spent 'some little months' in Lourenço Marques, where they had set up 'a café'. Now, with savings of two hundred pounds in hand, they were on their way to Johannesburg, where they intended doing the same.[349]

The man in question was Karl Mayer, Erna's father – and therefore my great-grandfather. He was travelling with four of his six daughters, having left the other two, together with his three sons and his wife, in the city of Czernowitz, at the eastern edge of the Austro-Hungarian Empire, near the border with the Russian Empire.

Here was another Jew from Eastern Europe who sought his fortune at the southern tip of Africa at the turn of the twentieth century. But his was a very different journey from that of his Russian brethren, and from a very different version of the East.

74 | 'Little Vienna'

After the Austro-Hungarian Empire collapsed in 1918, the boundaries of its territory were redrawn. Czernowitz – once a city on the inside of Europe, at the eastern edge of the empire – became Cernauti, a city on the other side, in Romania. Then, when the Soviet Union swallowed up Romania after World War II, Cernauti became Chernovsty, behind the Iron Curtain. When the Soviet Union broke up, Chernovtsy became Chernivitsi, part of the Republic of Ukraine. As it is now.

Czernowitz was a city made to die and be reborn several times, perhaps more so than any other city in the world.

It's a city with almost no resonance in my part of the world on the far end of the African continent. Few came here from there. I knew that my grandmother's family had called it home, but little else.

Once I started reading, I ran headlong into the mythical Czernowitz that is now taking shape, the product of yet another memory project, buoyed by what sociologist Karolina Koziura calls 'Hapsburg nostalgia'.[350]

As with many cities in central and eastern Europe that were previously communist, an energetic remaking is taking place. Chernivitsi seeks to reposition itself as a European city looking westwards, shedding its Soviet past.

A narrative is emerging, promoted by city planners, amongst others: a story of a glorious imperial past in which the emperor Franz Josef presided over a vast cosmopolitan land encompassing an impressive diversity of peoples and cultures. Austro-Hungary was modernising, but with an aesthetic flair and amidst a flurry of ideas – encapsulated in the iconic Viennese coffee shops, nurturing deliberation and conversation. Czernowitz was the

Empire's cultural mecca on the eastern border – a 'little Vienna', just as sophisticated as that lustrous capital even if on a smaller scale. And German-speaking Jews were at its forefront, protected by the emperor who had emancipated them and removed the barriers to their progressive advances.

This is a dreamy rewind to the romance of Czernowitz at play during the *fin de siècle,* before the crisis of World War I, when 'the pavements were swept with roses, it was said, and hens scratched poetry out of the sand'.[351] A place 'where people and books lived', wrote the renowned Jewish writer Paul Celan, born in Czernowitz; a place where great ideas came to life in wondrous cafés serving their famed pastries.

The mythical Czernowitz is, and was, the antithesis of the mythical shtetl. The nostalgic shtetl conjures up a comforting world of traditionalist seclusion and argumentatively happy Jewish communalism, pulling inwards against a hostile outside. The glorious Czernowitz was an open place of Jewish assimilation and acceptance, a progressive cosmopolitan hub where Jews could breathe freely, where barriers to the outside had become unnecessary.

This was a story of flourishing absorption, as opposed to the shtetl story of snug detachment – centrifugal versus centripetal versions of Jewish relations with others.

Unsurprisingly, the story of the real Czernowitz – like that of the real shtetl – is a far more nuanced tale.

75 | Jews in the Austro-Hungarian Empire

By the early twentieth century, the Austro-Hungarian Empire was a huge swathe of territory in Europe, second only in size to the Russian Empire. A tenuous assemblage of many different nationalities, ethnicities, languages and cultures – including Austrians, Hungarians, Galicians, Bohemians, Romanians, Croats, Czechs, Poles and Jews – it was overseen by the emperor, Franz Josef II. Taking the reins in 1848 after uprisings against Hapsburg rule in many parts of the empire, Franz Josef set out to bash the unruly provinces into shape, reasserting imperial power, much of it vested in him directly.[352] That was the plan anyway; in practice, rumblings would persist, as nationalist yearnings among the subject peoples grew stronger. Tenacious and dogged, Emperor Franz Josef dug his heels in as the empire teetered, until finally World War I delivered the decisive blow, and the Austro-Hungarian Empire was no more.

After an unpromising start, Franz Josef's accession to power became good news for the Jews. Initially illiberal and conservative, including in respect of the Jews, the emperor conceded the 1867 Edict of Tolerance that paved the way for Jewish emancipation – a process that had begun, albeit falteringly, a century before.[353] Jews could own land, enter the universities, the professions, and the army, unrestricted; all previous barriers on their economic opportunities were lifted. Officially, antisemitic slights and prohibitions were off limits. Particularly in his later years, the emperor made it clear, sometimes explicitly, that he valued the Jews as useful citizens and loyal subjects. Not the usual message.

Unsurprisingly then, many Jews bought in to what historian Daniel Unowsky calls 'the cult of the emperor',[354] assiduously cultivated by the man himself. A theatrical ruler, Emperor Franz Josef staged his authority at every available opportunity. Imperial ceremonies and festivities, performed in spectacular fashion, showcased the man and idealised his empire.[355] Edmund de Waal, writing about this era in *The Hare with Amber Eyes*, quotes Adolf Jellinek, 'the most famous Jewish preacher of the time' in Austro-Hungary, who proclaimed that 'the Jews are thoroughly dynastical, loyalist, Austrian. The double eagle [symbol of the empire] is for them a symbol of redemption and the Austrian colours adorn the banners of their freedom.'[356]

The writer Stefan Zweig – who described himself as 'an Austrian, a Jew, an author, a humanist and a pacifist' – was a case in point. 'When I attempt to find a simple formula for the period in which I grew up, prior to the First World War, I hope that I convey its fullness by calling it the Golden Age of Security. Everything in our almost thousand-year-old Austrian monarchy seemed based on permanency, and the State itself was the chief guarantor of this stability ... Our currency, the Austrian crown, circulated in bright gold pieces, an assurance of its immutability.'[357]

Yet the empire was vast and Jewish life was not cast in a single mould. Most of its Jewish inhabitants lived in Galicia, the poorest part, remote from the pomp and glory of Franz Josef's rule. Pious and observant, these *ostjuden* were allowed the opportunity to work the land, unlike the Jews in the Pale of Settlement. But conditions were harsh, so much so that Galicia was one of the Eastern European capitals of the White slave trade. Throngs of *ostjuden* made their way, if they could, to more promising conditions in other parts of the empire, including Vienna and Czernowitz.

It was the assimilated German-speaking Jews, and particularly those of the Austro-Hungarian bourgeoisie, who benefited most from the imperial order. With all restrictions lifted, these Jews surged ahead economically. Prominent in agriculture, many spheres of industry, commerce and the professions, some also became wealthy landowners. In the dough of Franz Josef's modernising empire, 'the Jews were the yeast that created the ferment',[358] wrote Aharon Appelfeld, born in Czernowitz.

Jews also flourished in the cultural cosmopolitanism of the empire – be they orthodox and religious, free to pursue their faith, or more secular and Germanic in their tastes. But it was the latter – those who were yearning to be 'modern' – who felt especially attuned to the late nineteenth century zeitgeist of the empire. And particularly in Vienna. Enlarged twice before the empire collapsed, with an immigration surge swelling the population, Vienna became one of Europe's largest cities, and a cultural and intellectual lodestar; the city of Gustav Klimt, Gustav Mahler, Egon Schiele and Richard Strauss, Otto Wagner, Sigmund Freud and Carl Jung, Ludwig Wittgenstein, Martin Buber and Edmund Husserl – some of the seminal artists and thinkers of the new century, and several of them Jewish.

Yet there were signs of menace ahead for those who were inclined to look. Even Zweig recognised, in retrospect, that 'the world of security was naught but a castle in the sky'.[359] In the early 1890s, writes historian David Rechter, 'one observer noted that the "antisemitic bacteria" in "beautiful Bukovina" were mostly dormant, but added that one did not need a microscope to detect them.'[360]

The emperor could insist on the empire's inclusiveness all he wanted, but many in his empire regarded Jews as unwelcome outsiders. The racial science of the late nineteenth century added more venom to their bow; poor and rich Jews alike felt its sting. For the down and out *ostjuden*, who poured into the Austrian heartland, it was a matter of being inferior and backward, out of kilter with the progressive dynamism of the times. For the bourgeois Jews, the target of attack was their success. Right-wing nationalist Georg von Schonerer (founder of the pan-German movement in Austria) led the charge against 'the Jew, the sucking vampire'.[361]

Vienna might have been the cultural jewel in the imperial crown, but it was also the first city in the world to have a brazenly antisemitic mayor. Charismatic populist Karl Lueger openly spewed right-wing nationalist bile when talking about Jews. 'Wolves, panthers and tigers are more human compared to these beasts of prey in human form,'[362] he claimed. Nor was it just the politicians. 'Vienna University,' writes De Waal, 'was a particular hotbed of antisemitism', with nationalist student societies taking the lead.[363]

It would get a lot worse, as we know. Until then, many of the loyalist Jews tried to look away, basking in the empire's rapidly fading glow.

76 | Czernowitz and the Jews

Czernowitz, capital city of the province of Bukovina, was Franz Josef's invention. 'Bukovina,' writes historian David Rechter, 'was the eastern border of Austria, abutting Romania and Russia. Geographically, this was eastern Europe. The Austrians, though, were keen to demonstrate that geography was not destiny in this instance, and they set out to establish a beacon of civilization in the wilds of the east.'[364]

Bukovina had been incorporated into the Austro-Hungarian Empire in the late eighteenth century. At that time, it was considered entirely backward, with a meagre population of ill-educated, struggling peasants. Czernowitz was a minor town, with nothing to show for itself. Bukovina began to change from then on, but Franz Josef's plans – implemented from the mid-nineteenth century – were more dramatic and accelerated, and most strikingly in Czernowitz, where he pulled off a wholesale transformation.

Czernowitz shed its old dry skin completely, changing from 'a peripheral, irregular settlement into a city with cobblestone streets, eclectic architecture, and monuments glorifying the Hapsburg emperors'.[365] German became the official language of state; Germanic education was compulsory, much of it in the hands of teachers imported from the west of the empire. An influx of German-speaking professionals and artisans, also from the empire's west to its eastern frontier, strengthened the developing economic muscle.

Jews were among those permitted – and encouraged – to settle there. By 1900, over twenty-one thousand Jews had set up home in Czernowitz – some thirty-two per cent of the city's

Map showing Czernowitz in Bukovina, Austro-Hungarian Empire. Redrawn by Janet Alexander.

population. Jews were more prominent in Czernowitz than in any other city in the Hapsburg empire.[366]

They were not a homogenous lot. The city that the emperor built divided itself between an upper and lower section. Unsurprisingly, the upper section contained the more salubrious parts with the more fashionable, affluent inhabitants. Equally unsurprisingly, the city's *ostjuden* congregated in the lower section. Mostly poor, many of them religious, and almost all Yiddish speaking, these Jews were the city's 'uncivilised' Eastern throwback, an unwelcome reminder of the Eastern foundations upon which the modernising, Westernising Czernowitz had been built.

Jewish wealth lubricated the upper section of the city. Here, Jews were in the economic vanguard: dominant in trade and commerce, prominent in the professions, and among Czernowitz's industrial pioneers too. Their children were disproportionately represented in the state schools, as well as in the elite gymnasiums. Intent on providing elements of a Jewish education for their offspring, some of the city's Jews set up Jewish schools, but with the overriding purpose of guiding the pupils 'closer to civilized Europe'.[367]

At the eastern edge of Austro-Hungary, within spitting distance of the Russian Empire, upper Czernowitz's Jews looked the other way – all the more strenuously and determinedly for being so close to the boundary of 'civilisation'.

Antisemitism in Czernowitz was more muted than elsewhere in the Austro-Hungarian Empire; but by the late nineteenth century, commentators spoke of 'a dark, threatening black cloud gathering on the distant horizon'.[368] On the cusp of the new century, in the late 1890s, that cloud had moved overhead, as an aggressive right-wing nationalism gained momentum across Bukovina. Jews were targeted both for their poverty and their wealth; neither the Eastern nor the Western version of the Czernowitzian Jew would pass muster. Zionism – an expression of Jewish nationalism, a new trend in Austro-Hungarian politics – took root, partly as a counter. Other nationalisms too began to rumble. The uneasy cosmopolitanism of the empire was teetering.

It was World War I that delivered the final blow. Russia invaded Bukovina in September 1914. 'Almost at a stroke, the fabric of Jewish society began to unravel as its leaders were scattered, its institutions ceased to function, and its cities, towns and communities were decimated.'[369]

Karl Mayer and four of his daughters left Czernowitz in 1908 or 1909, well before this collapse. His wife and remaining children, including my grandmother Erna, would stay until 1920, by which time Franz Josef's Czernowitz had all but disappeared.

77 | Bakers for the emperor

Karl and Rosa Mayer had nine children: six daughters and three sons, all with German names. They were an assimilated Germanic family, comfortable rather than affluent, living on Siebenburgerstrasse in upper Czernowitz. This was a relatively smart street, parallel to the glamorous Herrengasse and near the famed Ringplatz; emotionally, if not physically, far away from the poorer Jewish enclaves in the lower part of the town.

The Mayers, it turns out, were a family of bakers. This was a recent discovery for me, despite the signs having been evident long before. Erna and her sisters were all known to be excellent bakers; in the family, their biscuits, tarts and pastries were renowned. As children, we were regularly treated to all this delicious fare. It was clear that this was a family talent – but I hadn't put the pieces together in recognising the occupational niche.

It was one that they shared with many others of their ilk. Austro-Hungarian Jews dominated the café scene and helped to shape the Austro-Hungarian ways of baking. Cafés serving coffee and confectionery were the Austro-Hungarian equivalent of the shtetl taverns: iconic gathering places, of many different shapes and sizes, catering to the mosaic of the empire's peoples. By 1800, cafés had become ubiquitous in their cities. The most celebrated version – the bourgeois café, space of free-flowing debate and probing conversation – was central to the myths of the *fin de siècle* and its romance of 'people and books'.

Not long after her marriage, Erna had told one of Maurice's first cousins that her grandfather – Karl's father – had been a 'baker for the emperor of Austria'.[370] It's unclear exactly what that entailed. Maybe the emperor had had legions of personal bakers, or maybe her grandfather's distinction was more singular. Either way, Erna had made the declaration with an obvious sense of pride, making sure that Maurice's side of the family knew that an honour had been bestowed on her family. I suspect she had told Maurice too, but knowing his gnawing enviousness, I doubt that he would have had any inclination to spread the word.

The Czernowitz street directory for 1898 shows more than one Karl Mayer. My great-grandfather was likely the one listed as a *cantineur* – someone who owned and/or managed a canteen-like café. According to a Romanian friend, the word is commonly associated with an army canteen. Thanks to Transvaal agent Arthur Long, I know that Karl spent eighteen years in the Austro-Hungarian army, and that he had set up a café in Lourenço Marques. These facts, combined with the family's collective skill as bakers, suggest to me that Karl owned and/or managed a café for members of the army, and his wife and daughters likely provided the confectionery that came with the coffee. Karl's journey to Lourenço Marques to set up a café, with his oldest four daughters in tow, then took the coffee and cake a lot further afield.

The prospect of Jewish conscription in the Austro-Hungarian army was initially controversial. As in most other European countries, Jews were at first deemed entirely unsuitable as soldiers: physically weak, unpatriotic and untrustworthy, their unconditional loyalty to a military cause unreliable. From the late eighteenth century, the Austro-Hungarian army was willing to take that chance and began recruiting Jews, following the first steps towards their emancipation. After the edict of 1867, which conferred full emancipation, the numbers of Jews entering the army climbed rapidly.[371]

In 1874, the Russian Empire had introduced a policy of compulsory military conscription – including for Jews. It was one of the factors prompting young Jewish men to emigrate.

The situation in Austro-Hungary was strikingly different. Many Jews – mostly the more secular and assimilated among them – accepted the military opportunity: to demonstrate their worthiness as loyal citizens of the empire, willing to serve. Besides, serving in the military offered the prospect of upward social mobility. Jewish officers could rise in the military ranks, even become generals. This was an unusual opportunity for Jews in Europe. By contrast, 'Germany entered World War 1 without a single Jewish officer'.[372]

By World War I, three hundred thousand Austro-Hungarian Jews were involved in active service. Over five thousand officers among them were killed during the war. 'This made up 67.8% of all officer losses and lay far beyond expectation, given that Jews comprised 4% of the population.'[373]

The commitment to military service extended to Karl's family by marriage. His wife Rosa's father would also serve. Rosa's brother Leon was also a *cantineur*, which makes it likely that he too had a military career. Typically, this involved three years of active duty to start, followed by at least nine years in the reserves. Karl served six years more than the minimum. After the Austro-Prussia War of 1866, the Austro-Hungarian Empire was not involved in major military conflicts until World War I, which meant that a career in the army was 'comparatively comfortable'.[374]

The badge of loyalty to the emperor was worn by the Mayer family at large. Karl made sure that the Austrian consul in Portuguese East Africa was aware of that fact. Before the outbreak of World War I, it would also stand him in good stead as he came under the scrutiny of the colonial British, who were unaccustomed to encountering Jews made in this mould.

78 | Family ties

Unlike the Posel side of the family, the Mayers have bequeathed more than a few photographs. Like many family photographs, each is in some ways an unreliable contrivance: a posed gathering of one moment in a long and dense life together. Even so, the images suggest to me close family ties, of the sort that posing for a photograph could not easily fake.

Here are two images of a family outing – albeit with the adult children only – both taken at the same place on the same day, somewhere in smart Czernowitz.

Mayer family outing in Czernowitz (1). Author's collection.

In the first, Karl stands upright on the right of the photograph, next to his oldest daughter Ischa. His wife Rosa is in the middle at the back, with daughter Lina on the other side of her. Her son Hans is the young man standing with a walking stick on the left of the photo. I'm unsure who the remaining two men are. One might be Ischa's husband Max; they married in 1904.

All seem relaxed and content, at ease in their proximity to each other. Rosa's two daughters stand noticeably close to their mother, their upper arms brushing hers. Hans stands slightly apart but strikes a casual and informal pose. Karl is more upright, but also informal – and benign; there is no assertion of any overbearing paternal authority here, just a family assemblage looking rather pleased with itself.

Their relaxed and comfortable intimacy is even more pronounced in the second photograph. Karl and his wife Rosa lean into each other on the right of the image. Ischa lies close to her mother, as Lina reclines into her sister with her hand on

Mayer family outing in Czernowitz (2). Author's collection.

Ischa's hip. Nor are the men in the picture keeping any physical distance. I'm struck by how much easygoing physical contact there is in the image; not the usual stiffness of the posed photographs of the time. Here are people who seem happily accustomed to lounging around with each other, modern and confident – even avant-garde – in draping themselves so closely together.

I take note too of their modern dress, in the latest Edwardian fashion. Their hats were on trend: 'outing hats' as they were called. Women's wear in those years was more comfortable than the Victorian styles had been, although with some formality persisting. These Mayer women were wearing typically Edwardian 'shirtwaists' (tuck-in blouses), with stiff collars (usually detachable). What look like men's ties and bow ties were also characteristic fashions of the time. Some Edwardian women were still inclined to wear corsets, but the leisurely lounging of these women looks too comfortable and unrestricted for that – another sign of their being confidently abreast of the times.

Lina was born in 1887, Hans in 1888. If the photograph was taken in 1906 or thereabouts, Lina would have been around nineteen years old, and her brother a year younger – which looks about right. Karl (born in 1859) would have been in his late forties, and his wife Rosa (born 1866) on the cusp of forty. This must have been shortly before Karl, Lina and three of his younger daughters left for southern Africa.

79 | Leaving

By the late nineteenth century, the number of Austro-Hungarians leaving home began to accelerate. Most were relocating from one part of the empire to another, typically from rural areas to cities, from less industrialised areas to modernising ones.[375] Others made a bolder move, heading out of the empire altogether. On one count, between 1876 and 1910, around five million people left Austro-Hungary – roughly ten per cent of the population.[376]

The majority left from the poorer provinces of Galicia and Bohemia, and mostly from the areas that imperial projects of progress had bypassed. Many emigrants were single men or women, unable to secure an income at home and venturing afar in pursuit of an elusive job.[377] Most headed to other parts of Europe, or to the USA. Africa was barely on the emigrants' radar, although a few headed to Cairo. One or two of the prominent department stores there were run by Austrians.

A trickle landed up in South Africa. Detailed information about the numbers, and their places of origin in the Austro-Hungarian Empire, is difficult to find. According to Tvrtko Mursalo, 'from the census of 1911, it can be concluded that 1504 people from the Austro-Hungarian Monarchy territories were living in the Union of South Africa.'[378] Of these, an unknown number were Jews.

Karl Mayer's decision to leave Czernowitz for Lourenço Marques does not fit any of these trends, impressionistic though they are. He was a middle-aged family man, ensconced in congenial upper Czernowitz, who made the decision to travel to an entirely uncommon destination with four of his daughters at his side.

Family stories on the Mayer side reveal little about what motivated Karl's decision to up and leave. All that I can glean, via one of his grand-nieces, is that he developed acute financial problems rather suddenly – much like an unexpected illness that required drastic and urgent treatment. Apparently, Karl lost a large chunk of his accumulated savings in a property deal that went horribly wrong. After their emancipation in 1867, the empire's more affluent Jews could invest their capital in property; it became one of their lucrative sources of income. Not for Karl, alas. Perhaps it was a shameful moment too, so much so that a journey far away to redeem his family's standing or honour – I'm speculating – was considered necessary.

He had to leave. But why Lourenço Marques? The choice of destination is so unusual and unexpected that he must have had a very clear idea of where he was going and why. Taking four daughters along with him, the youngest in her teens, adds weight to this supposition: a man going on a more exploratory journey, hoping to stumble on opportunities somewhere along the way, would surely not have proceeded in the way in which Karl did.

There was a small Austro-Hungarian presence in Lourenço Marques, including an Austrian consul. Some Austrian merchants were among those doing business in the city. Karl must have known someone, or known someone who knew someone, with direct links to Lourenço Marques – someone who passed on information that planted the seed of the idea to start a café there.

80 | Lourenço Marques

Lourenço Marques was growing apace when Karl and his daughters arrived there, towards the end of 1908 or early 1909. As historian Andrew MacDonald recounts, 'once a tiny bridgehead to a spasmodic hinterland trade, Lourenco Marques was remaking itself into a self-consciously "modern" colonial city.'[379] A transport and construction boom drove the changes, which produced an architecturally eclectic centre, with little in common with the British-leaning styles of Johannesburg. 'Here is a well-built residence of European architecture, there a mosque with oriental minarets, beyond a gaudy-painted Arab store and next to it an up-to-date café or restaurant.'[380]

Population growth was dramatic: 'the settler population exploded some 5000% between 1885 and 1910.'[381] It was a thoroughly cosmopolitan collection of people. According to an article in a local periodical of 1900, 'members of many nationalities are to be seen there. English, French, German, Portuguese, Arabs, Chinese, Japanese, Indians and Kafirs all jostle each other at every corner.'[382] The large majority were single men, with an enormously skewed ratio of four women to every one hundred men among the Europeans who had settled there.[383] The Mayers added a few more German speakers to the mix, making a minor contribution to easing the gender imbalance.

They also added a modest extension to the city's Jewish presence. A sprinkling of Jews had first settled in Portuguese East Africa during the early years of Portuguese colonisation in the sixteenth century. Most were traders, some had been sailors. A few more trickled in during the nineteenth century, but the biggest single influx of Jews occurred during the South African War, when Kruger's government banished Transvaal Jews who were actively supporting the British war effort. Some headed to Lourenço Marques. One of the first to arrive was Reverend Dr Joseph Hertz who came in 1899, exiled on account of having taken a pro-British stance. He put a positive spin on the situation he encountered: 'here I found Jewish conditions bad enough, but I was not disappointed. As only one or two Jewish people have their families living with them, there is neither *schochet* [ritual slaughterer], congregation nor *Beit Chayim* (cemetery) in Lourenco Marques. My astonishment, on the contrary, was great when I found a prominent businessman a sabbath observer, and another, a subscriber to the Jewish Quarterly Review.'[384]

Hertz left Lourenço Marques after just one week, but during that brief visit, he succeeded in motivating a group of seven men to constitute themselves as an organising committee to establish the first congregation and begin planning for a synagogue and a Jewish cemetery.[385]

By the time the Mayers arrived, the one and only synagogue ever to be built in Lourenço Marques was still a fantasy. It would have to wait until 1926. Until then, a handful of Jews congregated for services in private homes; religious observance was not a mainstay of their lives there. It's more likely that their most convivial gatherings were the times they spent in the city's cafés – 'Levy's kiosque', for one, where Isaac Levy, a member of the organising committee, convened a busy conversational hub for a European clientele.

The Mayers would not have been surprised to find Lourenço Marques divided into an upper and lower section. An informal 'tavern economy' – to use Andrew MacDonald's phrase – dominated daily life in the lower section of this port city, where sailors enjoyed the revelry with other single men and sex-trading women who offered their services in abundance. In the upper section, residents preferred the somewhat more genteel cafés, reminiscent of those in western Europe. As described by Montague Jessett, who visited at the turn of the century, 'as in the tropics, the people mostly lead an outdoor existence, and kiosks and cafes, after the style of the Boulevards in Paris, abound. There, of an evening, Delagoa Bay and his wife turn in to quaff the red wine and eat confectionery.'[386]

Karl Mayer relocated from one café society to another – albeit a pale approximation of what he had been accustomed to. When he chose Lourenço Marques as his destination, he must have known that another café would likely go down well. Maybe he had a hunch that the pastries already on offer were not up to scratch and his daughters could up the standard – and the demand.

It's difficult to say what happened next. According to Arthur Long, their business lasted 'some little months' – so not a long time. They did manage to set two hundred pounds aside; business could not have been that bad. Perhaps they left so soon because Karl decided that the quality of society in the place was not good for his daughters or their virtue. Reverend Hertz found only 'one or two' Jewish families in the place, which was widely known to be heaving with brothels and lecherous men. Karl may well have decided that he had led his daughters down a social cul-de-sac – or worse. Johannesburg would surely offer a range of more respectable options for a family such as his.

81 | Doornfontein

After leaving Lourenço Marques, the Mayer family took up residence in Doornfontein, in Johannesburg. They would have found it far more suitable: an 'enclave' for 'the successful but not yet wealthy Jews',[387] as geographer Margot Rubin puts it – including some who had done well enough to duck out of Ferreirastown and chose never to look back.

A centre of middle-class Jewish life in the city, Doornfontein may have been more religiously oriented than the Mayers required, with a *mikvah* attached to the public swimming pool, many kosher butcheries, and a well-appointed synagogue. The Mayers identified as Jewish, but with relatively little religious observance.

They were lodging with Alfred Elder von Zwiklitz at 36 Upper Page Street. Alfred hailed from Vienna and worked for Orenstein and Koppel Ltd – a large global company based in Germany, with a strong presence in southern Africa, manufacturing railway systems for mines and foundries, as well as steam engines and light railway tracks. It may well have been through Orenstein and Koppel that Karl and Alfred became connected. According to the British consul general in Lourenço Marques, 'Messrs Orenstein and Koppel have, in great measure, controlled the local market in regard to their own special lines.'[388] Representatives of the company likely visited Lourenço Marques often. Given the small number of German speakers in upper Lourenço Marques, Karl likely ran into one or more of their personnel there – perhaps in a café, maybe even his own. One of these contacts might have given Karl an introduction to Alfred as a possible landlord once the Mayers relocated to Johannesburg.

It would be a fateful connection. Karl's eldest daughter Lina and Alfred married in 1911. Their marriage certificate confirmed that they were both living at the same address at the time of their wedding. She was twenty-four; he was thirty-five.

Karl must have been delighted by the romance. Not only did Alfred slot smoothly into the assimilated Germanic culture of the Mayer family; he was a highly desirable match – a Jewish, Austrian blue blood. He inherited his title, 'Elder Von', from his much-decorated father Felix, who had merited the favour of the Austro-Hungarian emperor on several occasions. According to Felix's CV, passed down in the Von Zwiklitz family, 'in 1866 I was working as a legal clerk at the General Directorate of the Austrian State Railway [in Vienna]. In 1870 I became a shareholder in the company Lindheim and Co., Vienna, to which I still belong. In this position, I took a prominent part in Public Works, such as in the construction of the Danube Bridge at Linz and the Crown Prince Rudolf Bridge in Vienna. In 1867, in recognition of my work, I was awarded the Knight's Cross of the Austrian Kaizer Franz Josef Order, outstanding.'

More awards followed: 'the Emperor 1 Russian St, Stanislaus-Order 111 Class, outstanding' for his contribution to public works during the Russo-Turkish war of 1877/1878 and 'the Emperor Russian War medal of 1877/8 for non-combatants'. And then came the culminating decoration: in 1886, he became a Knight of the Order of Franz Josef, with the title Elder Von and his own coat of arms, 'making me a noble'.[389]

Associating closely with Alfred would have drawn the Mayers into the Austrian and German upper crust in Johannesburg. Alfred must have been very well connected even before he came to South Africa. I imagine his father's stature, along with powerful connections in the Austrian railways, had opened doors for him with Orenstein and Koppel at the highest levels. Socialising in Austrian and German consular circles would have been *de rigueur*, mixing with people who celebrated the emperor's birthday and marked the public holidays of their homeland in parties at their embassy; people who spoke German, and enjoyed German and Austrian cuisine, music and culture.

Karl Mayer had successfully moved his four daughters into a far more desirable social circle than Lourenço Marques had offered them: in Johannesburg they would mix with German-speaking men who were typically educated professionals or bureaucrats. These were likely all people who had come to South Africa for economic reasons, but with no affiliation to or interest in the British imperial cause. *God Save the King* was not part of their repertoire.

82 | World War I

For a few years, Johannesburg life for the Mayers must have felt comfortable and congenial – but for the fact that Karl's wife Rosa and the remainder of their brood were still in Czernowitz. The family could not possibly have predicted the calamity that lay ahead, for all of them.

Historian Tilman Dedering points out that the experience of estrangement for German speakers in the British Empire during World War I was not as severe in South Africa as in other parts, given a history of political and social sympathies between Afrikaners and Germans (many of whom had by then intermarried with Afrikaners). In the aftermath of the South African War, the Smuts government was reluctant to enflame British-Afrikaner tensions any further.[390] So, in dealing with the German enemy in South Africa, some restraint was considered politic.

The German speakers on the receiving end of the anti-war measures in South Africa judged their experience bad enough, however, and for many – like the Mayers – it would turn their world upside down.

To start with, German and Austrian men living in the country were interned as prisoners of war – around three thousand in total. Most were sent to Fort Napier in Pietermaritzburg.[391] The regulations specified internment for all enemy men aged up to fifty-six. Karl Mayer narrowly escaped; he turned fifty-six in 1914, before the start of the war. Alfred was interned, along with most in his social circle. This included Emil Einstein, a German friend, who would marry Karl's daughter Anna in 1921.

A few months after he was interned, Alfred began petitioning the authorities for his release, on grounds of ill-health.

He had been hospitalised at the camp hospital in December, he wrote, suffering from chronic rheumatism and with a rapidly deteriorating 'nervous condition'. Repeated letters failed to elicit any change in his situation, until one of the house captains (a German nominated to maintain order in the camps) warned that 'I would not be surprised if he has a complete breakdown.'[392] This secured Alfred's release, and he returned to his home in Johannesburg on 7 May 1915.

Emil Einstein, who was thirty-one at the time of his internment, also petitioned earnestly and repeatedly for his release, but he was a healthy young man and was expected to remain in internment for the full duration of the war. He did that – and more. He was finally set free on 5 July 1919 after undertaking 'on my honour neither directly nor indirectly to take any action in any way prejudicial to the safety of the British Empire'.[393]

Karl Mayer was spared the stress of internment, but he did not come away unscathed by the war. Arthur Long's message indicated that Karl had intended setting up a café after arriving in Johannesburg. Assuming he did, it would have met with a terrible fate in the fierce explosion of anti-German violence that erupted on the streets of central Johannesburg on 11 May 1915.

Tension had been building before the rioting. A few months after war broke out in August 1914, British citizens spoiling for a fight on Johannesburg soil sent petitions to the South African government protesting the allegedly lenient treatment of the enemy, including those interned. The British Patriotic Traders and Consumers Alliance demanded that businesses owned or run by Germans be closed. None of this agitation bore any fruit until a German submarine sank the *Lusitania*, a British passenger ship, on 7 May 1915, killing the nearly one thousand two hundred civilians on board. Angry anti-German riots then broke out in many countries; South Africa would not be an exception.

In Johannesburg, the mayhem began on the afternoon of 11 May, starting with crowds setting fire to German flags outside the Town Hall. The next day, a group of men stormed the well-patronised Anglo-Austrian café in Pritchard Street where 'the crockery and glassware were decorated with the German eagle'.[394] They made sure nothing was left of it, before moving on to continue their trashing spree elsewhere. According to a *Sunday Times* report, 'hotels, beer-halls, bars, private houses, jewellers' shops, bioscopes and the premises of confectioners, butchers and the vendors of all imaginable commodities were torn inside out, with only the bare shells left standing, and a smouldering pile of what were once the contents of the buildings lying in the middle of the street – that is the art of "sacking" as practised by the Johannesburg crowd.'[395] By the end of the day, around one hundred premises had been vandalised and the fire brigade had responded to seventy-two calls.[396]

The police showed themselves to be unable or unwilling to quell the mayhem, which gave further impetus to the angry and boisterous crowds. Their orgy of destruction continued for another two days, the crowds 'numbering several thousand'.[397]

Some of the lawlessness was wrought by a spontaneous mob, but there was a more orchestrated initiative afoot too. Planning for maximum damage, a group within the British Patriotic Traders and Consumers Alliance allegedly produced lists of all the businesses and shops in Johannesburg owned or staffed by German speakers and distributed them amongst the protesters.

The targets of destruction were not restricted to German or Austrian nationals. Anyone vaguely suspected of having pro-German sympathies, or who sold stock from a pro-German country or supplier, was deemed fair game. Many desperate property owners resorted to buying protection from the ring-leaders, who issued notices of indemnity that then seemed to satisfy the otherwise unmollified protesters. It was a lucrative interlude for the Patriotic Traders and Consumers Alliance.

Those on the receiving end of the destruction tried to claim compensation from the South African government. None was given.

Karl, like all the other German speakers who owned commercial premises in downtown Johannesburg, must have lost everything.

In March 1917, Alfred died from heart failure. Before the war started, he had been offering financial support to the Mayers. In addition to the emotional shock – he and Lina had only been married six years – Alfred's death worsened the family's cash troubles too.

Life for the Johannesburg Mayers changed dramatically in the aftermath of the war. They would have realised that their place in their new country had suddenly become more precarious than they might have anticipated – and not because they were Jewish.

83 | A darker world

To her grandchildren, Erna spoke very little about her life in Czernowitz. We didn't show much interest, it is true, but I suspect there were also barriers to fuller disclosures – the sort that derive from the imprint of a horror that would never fade. We had a vague flash of that trauma in a strand of her past that she both shared and withheld. It was the briefest beginning of a story that never progressed beyond an enigmatic fragment.

In Erna's abbreviated telling, she, her mother and younger brother had to escape the Russians, which they did strapped to the underneath of a railway carriage and surviving by eating a 'bread' made of snow and sawdust.

To us children, this was an almost unimaginable episode in our grandmother's life, pushing the limits of our credulity. How do you strap a person (we did not know if she had been a child or a teenager) to the underside of a train? How do you mix snow and sawdust into a concoction remotely edible? At that stage, there was nothing more to say.

For me, now, the story remains fragmented, and its details are still mysterious, but with a plausible context and occasion in the horror that descended on Czernowitz with the onset of World War I.

The start of the war may not have been as dreadful for the Mayers as its middle and end became. They might even have shared the surge of patriotic optimism that buoyed the mood in the empire's bourgeois cafés in August 1914. Stefan Zweig, for example, was initially fired up with excitement on hearing that the war had begun.

'To be perfectly honest, I must confess that there was something fine, inspiring, even seductive in that first mass outburst of feeling. It was difficult to resist it. In spite of all my hatred and aversion for war, I should not like to have missed the memory of those first days. As never before, hundreds of thousands felt what they should have felt in peacetime, that they belonged together... A country of nearly fifty million, in that hour felt that they were participating in world history, in a moment which would never recur, and that each one was called upon to cast his infinitesimal self into the glowing mass, there to be purified of all selfishness. All differences of class, rank, and language were flooded over at that moment by the rushing feeling of fraternity.'[398]

That's often how wars start; the ugly irony of imagined community.

One month later, things changed. Reminding Czernowitz of its repressed eastern edges – now as part of the eastern front of battle – the Russian army invaded Bukovina and its capital city. Even before the troops arrived, rumours of impending disaster sent thousands of Czernowitz's inhabitants into hurried exile. More would follow as the war progressed. 'As the Russian army advanced in the first months of the war, more than half a million Austrians took flight,'[399] writes historian David Rechter. 'The Russian occupation was brutal and venal; upon taking control of the capital, they extorted cash and valuables from the population and swiftly deported much of the local political elite to Siberia ... Between September 1914 and the summer of 1917, half of the city's population either fled or was expelled.' Public buildings and factories were demolished, and transport infrastructure destroyed. The city's food supply dwindled to scraps.

Jews were often singled out, during 'pogroms, executions, expulsions, rape and wanton destruction of property'.[400] According to Rechter, the Russian Jewish writer S. An-ski gave a first-hand account, including stories of 'troops humiliating Jews

A DARKER WORLD

by forcing them to ride naked on pigs [and of] Cossacks manhandling the corpses of Jewish babies'.[401]

Erna's anguished fragment begins to make sense, as a desperate effort on the part of her mother to flee this invasion with her youngest children. Where they went remains a mystery, and the logistics of their escape are still mind-boggling.

The Austro-Hungarians regained control of Czernowitz in the summer of 1917. I assume this is when the Mayers returned. But this would not be a return to normality. After the war ended, the empire disintegrated, and Czernowitz was seized by Romania.

For many of Austro-Hungaria's leading intellectuals, the end of the Empire was horribly momentous – the advent of a darker world order, a mood of uncertainty and insecurity, a sense that the optimism of the past would never return. Freud's lament on Armistice Day was powerful and poignant: 'Austria-Hungary is no more. I do not want to live anywhere else. I shall live on with the torso and imagine that it is the whole.'[402] The horror of the war jolted the philosopher Ludwig Wittgenstein to confront the unsettling indeterminacy of things, the absence of any stable purpose or perspective. "Everything we see could be otherwise. Everything that we can describe at all could also be otherwise. There is no order of things a priori."[403]

Erna was born on 1 January 1900: a child of the new century, opening her eyes in a world brimming with confidence and hope. The accelerated transformations of the nineteenth century had offered the promise of an even more technologically sophisticated, aesthetically elevated and progressive way of life ahead. By the end of the war, Erna was eighteen years old, on the cusp of her adult womanhood. An unimaginably different world confronted her then. What a dreadfully dark looking-glass to peer into, in search of a future.

84 | Cernauti

After the war ended, Rosa and her children suddenly became Romanians; the East had wrested them back. They would stay in Cernauti, as it now was, for two years, until December 1920, living a very different life from their Czernowitz years. For one thing, Romania – along with Tsarist Russia – had been the only European state before World War I to deny Jews their emancipation.[404] This set the tone for the post-war period.

If Erna had had any plans to further her education at a university or technical college, these would have been dashed. As the official language of the city, Romanian was now the language of instruction at all its public institutions, and Romanian nationalists were hell-bent on keeping Jewish students out of their universities.[405]

Unless they could master the Romanian language, many Jews were pushed out of positions they had held in the public service. Anomalously for the Romanians, Jews continued to dominate the Chamber of Industry and Commerce and serve on the municipal council.[406] This would irk the nationalists antagonised by persistent Jewish influence in the city. Antisemitism – already energised in Romania during the late nineteenth century – would gain ground in Cernauti during the 1920s. By 1926, Jewish youth would be the target of overt discrimination in their schools. For example, Jewish pupils could be barred from writing their exams and proceeding to the next year of study. At one such school, a Jewish pupil, David Falik, organised a protest against his exclusion and was murdered by a nationalist student leader for his pains.

Rosa must have read the signs in the early years after the Romanian takeover and decided to leave. But why had it taken her so long? Her husband and older daughters had left at least eleven years before. Perhaps she had not accompanied them then because she had not initially wanted to leave her family in Czernowitz: Ischa, her oldest daughter, then married and a mother of one child; her two sons Hans and Willy; and youngest children – Erna and Herman – still of school-going age; Rosa's parents and her brother. Then came the war, which would have put paid to any travel plans during much of the decade.

Erna's old Austro-Hungarian passport that had emerged from one of my father's chaotic piles of papers was packed full of visas, which reveal the arduousness of the journey that lay ahead for Rosa, Erna and Herman (the older sons would make their own way out). First, a train ride to Vienna, then to Paris, then Amsterdam, then a ferry to London, and finally a train to Southampton, where they set sail for South Africa.

Their ship, *The Saxon*, left Southampton on 24 December 1920. They travelled second class – a step up from steerage. Some sense of dignity and occasion was possible during the journey.

Erna had her twenty-first birthday on board ship. I hope she celebrated, even if the skies had clouded over.

85 | A Johannesburg 'spinster'

The other shard of Erna's past that she deliberately let slip – intent that we should glimpse it without seeing it in full – concerned some sort of romance she had had on board that ship. She fancied someone, and he fancied her. Even in its brevity, it was an obviously wistful declaration, tinged with loss and regret. For reasons unknown, the encounter did not amount to anything. Erna arrived in Johannesburg an unmarried and uncommitted young woman, aged twenty-one. Nine lean years of longing lay ahead; Erna was a woman who longed for romance.

At least she would be in the bosom of her family, their life somewhat restored after the chaos of the war.

While Erna, her mother and younger brother had been enduring the Romanian version of Czernowitzian life, Karl Mayer was busy rehabilitating his South African life to a version of its previous normality. Arnold Ullman, a German businessman and friend of Alfred's, had married Jenny, Karl's second-oldest daughter, on 21 March 1915 – before the full impact of the war was unleashed on the Mayers. That marriage would become the fulcrum of the Mayers' life once the war ended. Arnold, his twin brother Heinrich and a third brother Anton had gone into business as produce merchants and had done reasonably well. Arnold and his twin were thirty-eight years old when the war began, Anton a few years older, but somehow none of the brothers had been interned, and their business was spared the destruction meted out to others. After the war, Karl joined the Ullman business, regaining an income and a line of work. When he died in 1927, his death certificate gave his occupation as 'produce merchant'; all traces of the *cantineur* had been erased.

Karl and Rosa bought a house at 78 Regent Street, in Yeoville, where they lived with daughters Selma (who married late – in 1938), Erna and their son Herman. After a brief sojourn in Vienna following Alfred's death, Lina returned to Johannesburg with her son. Anna married her long-time beau Emil Epstein in Johannesburg on 4 February 1921 – with both her parents and younger siblings in attendance.

Erna, the youngest of the sisters, was close to all of them. Her dearest friend, Helene, was married to Heinrich Ullman. Following the stress of the war years, the extended family pulled closer and spent much of their leisure time together. When Erna arrived, they drew her into their social circle.

That would likely have included other German-speaking Jewish families living in Yeoville, a suburb that grew rapidly during the 1920s with a large proportion of Jews, both German and Eastern European. As the early Jewish immigrants began to find their financial feet and move out of the poorer areas of the city centre, they took to particular suburbs en masse, rather than dispersing and assimilating among other ethnicities. Synagogues, *mikvahs*, *cheders* (providing Jewish education to children), kosher butcheries and food shops would then mark those areas out as Jewish enclaves. Inside each of these areas, however, the old schisms would take a long time to fade. The German speakers and Eastern Europeans were typically closest to their own, even if the intensity of old antagonisms would begin to wane.[407]

Yeoville became one of the strongholds of Eastern European Jews. How ironic then that Yeoville's member of parliament from 1922 to 1936 was none other than Patrick Duncan, representing the South African Party. His disdain for these 'squat-bodied' Jews had not diminished, but their political support proved useful. Duncan expediently cashed in on the opportunity by 'disguising his class-based antisemitism[408] to secure the Jewish vote. His friends were well aware of his true feelings, however: as he put it in a letter to his close friend Maude Selborne, 'they [the Jews] will have it all soon ... I wish my constituency was not so full of them.'[409]

In the ethnically enclaved environment of Yeoville, Erna surely did not lack opportunities to meet German-speaking men. There was even a Jewish dating agency in Yeoville, Wullfarht's Matrimonial Agency, which had a suitably German ring to it. But either she or potential suitors did not measure up to expectations. As the decade advanced, she remained single and from what I know, without a job.

A woman in waiting, with dwindling options.

Part Seven

86 | Marriage

Maurice and Erna married in the Yeoville synagogue in 1930. She was thirty, he was thirty-three. I don't know how long they had courted, or how they had met.

They were an implausible couple, vastly different in almost every way imaginable: two people with different pasts, different family lives, values and outlooks on the world, different personalities and psyches, different ways of being. They shared very little: both Jewish, neither had attended university, and neither was intellectually inclined – theirs was not a world of issues and ideas. It was not much to build on.

My mother recalls asking Erna several times why she married Maurice. Her answer, repeatedly, was that she had felt sorry for him.

She might well have felt sorry for herself too. At thirty, she was getting on; in those days, if she had wanted a child and a family of her own, there was not much time left.

There are two surviving wedding photographs, both somewhat austere. Erna wore a dark dress, smart enough, but a far cry from the more familiar white froth – a reminder, perhaps, of her age and station, as an older bride grateful for a match but not in a whirl of romance. Her look in the photographs matches her dress: serious, even sombre. Maurice is well turned-out, looking smart and dapper, and pleased with himself. He too had been running out of time if marriage was part of his plan for his life.

By then, Maurice would have had almost no one from his family to witness and celebrate the occasion. Both his parents had died. His half-brother Gershon lived in Johannesburg, but they had no contact; his half-sister Leah was *persona non grata*. Hopefully his half-sister Sarah and her husband Solomon

Maurice and Erna Posel on their wedding day, 1930. Author's collection.

Ginsburg were there to offer their congratulations. Cousin Sam Farfel – back from London, wearing his new medical qualification – might have been there too. By contrast, Erna's extended family in Johannesburg – minus Karl, who had died three years previously – was sizeable. I imagine they were all present at the ceremony, although no photograph has survived to attest to this.

Cultural tensions between German and Russian Jewish families were common. Germans – often more affluent – typically felt superior, judging the Easterners in much the same way as the British Jews had done. It's not surprising then that Rosa Mayer did not warm to her daughter's match. Three of her daughters in Johannesburg had married German speakers who integrated well into a tight familial circle – one of whom was the son of an Austrian noble, no less. Their ways were European, and they thought of themselves as such. Then Maurice came along, a man who spoke like a Britisher, with an excellent command of English, it is true. But this may not have impressed the Mayers one bit, particularly after their devastating wartime experience. Nor would they have warmed to Maurice's Russian lineage: *à la* lower Czernowitz, not the upper reaches.

Maurice would have known full well that he was not their type. For that matter, they would not have been his preferred family either; he had nothing in common with them and would feel judged and excluded as a cultural outsider, with little to show for himself.

I suspect it was generally understood on the Mayer side that Erna had 'married down', but given her shrinking prospects, nothing could be done about it. Life would go on.

How very bleak and depleting for them both. How sad that at that point in their lives, other avenues for more affirming unions had not opened up.

87 | Jewish suburbia

Erna and Maurice became one of the many married couples – offspring of the first generation of immigrants – putting down roots in the White suburbs of Johannesburg. Outwardly, these couples may have looked secure and contented enough, the interior damage of their families' journeying well hidden by a culture of robust secrecy. Stories of loss and pain, shame and grief – the emotional quotients of migration – were seldom told; the injunction was to look ahead and get on with what this new country had to offer.

The second generation was more anglicised than the first, better schooled and more neatly turned out by South Africa's version of the White West. Reactions to what was now on offer were mixed, however. The induction into a hierarchically ordered, racially segregated system of privilege appalled some, who joined the ranks of political activists dedicated to the fight against it. Jews were disproportionately present and prominent in the South African left, and among the lawyers who represented the activists whom the regime sought to prosecute.[410] Others – the majority – slotted comfortably into the tree-lined avenues of Whites-only houses and apartment blocks. The number of Jews attending universities ratcheted up, as did rates of professionalisation – enabled by the dedicated efforts of the first generation to secure their children's opportunities for education. Average incomes would rise; aspirations for personal futures grew bolder.

The sharp edges of the religious, social and ideological differences that had ripped through the first generation of immigrants began to soften – even as schisms and rifts persisted.

Zionism became an increasingly strong glue. An early implant from the Pale of Settlement, a local chapter of the *Chovevei Zion*, prominent in Lithuania, had opened in Johannesburg in 1896, and Zionist organisations multiplied and strengthened through the first half of the twentieth century. It helped that erstwhile Prime Minister Jan Smuts was a supporter and proud advocate of the Balfour Declaration, which he had helped draft. And Afrikaner nationalists, gaining in political ascendancy, were far more likely to be antisemitic than anti-Zionist.[411] The Zionist project offered the promise of a mass departure of Jews; better in their 'homeland' than in a country not their own. By 1948, 'the South African Zionist Federation counted no fewer than three hundred and forty-seven affiliated organisations'.[412] South African Jewish society would become among the most strongly Zionist of the Jewish populations in the diaspora.

Anglicised they may have become, fitting more easily into the colonially fashioned groove, but many Jews continued to pull inwards. Jews were accused of keeping themselves apart, yet not much welcomed when they did otherwise. In many social circles, Jews would remain undesirable and mistrusted – the various clubs they were not permitted to join a persistent reminder.

There were ominous political soundings too. During the 1920s, angry mutterings about the contaminated – and contaminating – influx of Jews from Eastern Europe flared yet again.[413] That eruption was soon eclipsed by a more intensely politicised version of 'the Jewish question' that hit the headlines in the 1930s. As the political star of the National Party (political home of the majority of White Afrikaners) was rising, anti-Jewish rhetoric was prominent and strident, with a condemnation of Jewish immigration at its forefront. The Greyshirts, a neo-Nazi movement on the right of the National Party, were virulent and venomous: 'once a Jew, always an alien … He is repugnant too, and not of one's own. Let him keep to his race, you keep to yours …. He is an Asiatic and NOT a European.'[414] Ever dark.

The hostility would worsen into the 1940s, when World War II created a gruesome spectacle of the unthinkable.

88 | Set in stone

So it was that Maurice and Erna settled into their small apartment in Lydveira Mansions in Hopkins Street, Yeoville, with the weight of their pasts bearing down heavily, snuffing out the fresh air.

Their only child was born in 1932 and received Erna's father's name. The marriage was a contest from the start; this was a significant victory for Erna.

Maurice was proud to have bought the apartment, presumably with the proceeds of his abstemious years of bachelorhood in Johannesburg: he was a property owner, at the very least, and remained so until his dotage. He and Erna lived in that apartment, entirely unchanged, for nearly five decades.

I remember it as a rather oppressive, overcrowded space. It was always perfectly tidy, but in a dead way, as if spared any mess of human habitation. The lounge – the largest room – felt sadly gloomy. A dark bulky couch, punctuated with spotless beige antimacassars, and side tables bearing pot plants on immaculate crocheted doilies, lined one wall; a heavy wooden sideboard, its surface decorated with a few unremarkable *tsatzkes* (trinkets), stood resolutely immovable along the opposite wall.

Throughout his childhood and adolescence, Karl slept in a tiny annex – too small to have become a bedroom. His bed folded up during the day when the space became Maurice's office, with no intrusions permitted.

Maurice worked; Erna devoted herself to the care of their son. Her social life revolved around her extended family; Maurice usually stayed home. Karl recalled spending weekends as a child with his beloved uncle Arnold (married to Erna's sister

Jenny) who taught him to play chess and develop an ear for classical music.

There would be at least one shared outing each year: the three Posels would take an annual holiday, always at Warmbaths. Another win for Erna: 'taking the waters' was one of her family's European ways.

Karl attended King Edward Primary School, and then the high school, distinguishing himself as a bright, even gifted, pupil. His father was gratified but never lifted the pressure. Karl's successes at school – proxies for his less promising father – were the closest Maurice could get to revenge on his first cousin; the *farribel* was alive and well throughout Karl's childhood.

Maurice remained embattled. Early in his married life, he was dismissed from a prized clerical job at the pharmaceutical company Sive and Karnovsky, for reasons unknown. His sense of the unfairness of it, of the lack of appreciation for his skills, never left him. As he saw it, he never received his due. Another knife to the wound.

As Karl's schooling ended, he too would cross his father, refusing to study medicine. He had a love of mathematics and chose to do engineering instead, which launched him into an illustrious academic career. A pioneering scientist, he would acquire two doctorates during his working life – a PhD and then a DSc. But for Maurice, this was not the version of Dr Posel that he had had in mind. It always rankled.

After Karl left school, Erna made a determined effort to create a more fulfilling working day for herself. Like many other married women consigned to full-time domesticity, she longed to get out of the home, so she joined the Union of Jewish Women and undertook voluntary work for the Jewish National Fund (JNF). The JNF had introduced a system of Blue Boxes, donations to which were collected by volunteers and then sent off to Israel in support of its nation-building project. Erna happily trudged the streets day after day, her Blue Box in her bag, visiting friends and associates who might contribute their coins to fill it up.

In her study of Jewish philanthropy during the early years of the twentieth century, Riva Krut has shown the extent to which middle-class women sustained its momentum, by doing much of the organisational legwork.[415] Even the staunchest advocates of stay-at-home wives seemed happy with a philanthropic add-on; it was considered acceptable – even appropriate – that these women should show compassion and dedication to worthy causes beyond the home.[416] This persisted into future decades and enabled Erna to find her niche – as much in breaking out of her stifling domestic routine as in energising friendships, meeting daily for tea and chats with amenable women for what they regarded as a virtuous purpose.

Never an ideologue, Erna's attachment to the Blue Boxes and what they represented was a sentimental rather than a reasoned Zionism. Her brother Hans had escaped from the horror of Romania during the 1920s and fled to Palestine, where he remained for much of his life – almost entirely isolated from his siblings and parents. For Erna, 'collecting money for Israel' was a way of sending money to Hans, to the country that had taken him in when he needed a refuge. She – like many Jews of her generation – had no idea of the painful realities of nationalist conquest, seeing only a land of security and promise for people like her brother. A highlight of her life, she maintained, was her one and only trip abroad to visit Hans and his wife in Israel.

In this, she walked and travelled alone. Maurice was entirely uninterested in the Zionist cause and had no desire to visit Israel, but he permitted Erna to pursue her voluntary work as energetically as she pleased (provided she tailored her schedule to his daily requirements). Had she wanted to find a paying job, I'm sure Maurice would have refused. A wife at work would have added to his shame tally; at the very least, he could support his wife without her requiring an additional salary.

Erna once tried to leave him. She had returned home late – that is, later than he had specified – and in a fit of pique, he locked her out. The humiliation he inflicted, witnessed by neighbours who passed her, embarrassed and helpless in the corridor, proved too much. She spent two nights at our house pondering her possible futures. But then she returned to him; divorce was a step too far. And with the force of that realisation, she never strayed from him again, enduring his insults and injuries.

I return, then, to the prayers that Erna made sure to preserve and pass on, with a fuller understanding of the immense compassion and empathy that she mustered, despite it all. This act of commemoration was surely her way of explaining why she stayed with a man who diminished and wounded her so. She alone understood what he felt himself to be up against; how wounded he had become, made vulnerable and insecure, unsupported and ashamed. By sharing his prayers, she could reveal to others the anguish he tried hard to hide, and his struggles to hold his head up in a world that came crashing down on him. She and Karl were all he had. She could not bring herself to leave him entirely alone with himself.

*

Maurice died in 1982. Erna was then eighty-two years old and moved into a Jewish retirement home in Durban. There, at the age of eighty-six, she found love. It was a romance that lit up her eyes and made her giggle. Isaac was old and frail, but he was witty and lively, attentive and generous. The two of them did whatever they could together: eating breakfast, lunch and supper at their own table in the communal dining room, attending lectures, playing bingo, watching films, going on organised outings, relaxing in the gardens or reading in the communal lounge. I saw them hold hands and kiss, exchange loving smiles, and lean into each other as they sat in adjacent chairs.

Isaac died three years later. Erna was distraught, but she had three more years to cherish the memories. She had found her soulmate.

89 | Archives

In his book *Letters to Camondo*, Edmund de Waal imagines the correspondence he might have with Moise de Camondo, a wealthy Jewish art collector, philanthropist and socialite who lived in Paris during the late nineteenth and early twentieth century. Visiting the old family home, now a museum, De Waal opens a heavy cupboard door on the archive of a lifetime, copiously and neatly filed: 'inventories, carbon copies, auction catalogues, receipts and invoices, memoranda, wills and testaments, telegrams, newspaper announcements, condolence cards, seating plans and menus, opera programmes, sketches, hunting notebooks'[417] – and more. As if nothing was too trivial or ordinary not to be worthy of retention. Did you ever throw anything away? asks De Waal, incredulously.

This was a Jewish family of substance, style and prominence. It hadn't always been that way. Camondo had worked hard to memorialise the accomplishment, in profuse detail. Yet that was not the whole story. That the Camondos were sophisticated and influential Jews caused some offence within the Parisian bourgeoisie. There were accusations of fakery: the pervasive antisemitic trope of Jews masquerading as people they were not. Take, for example, Camondo's interest in horse-riding and hunting, inviting Parisian *hoi polloi* to join him. De Waal writes: 'Who should hunt in these ancient forests? shout the daily anti-Semitic screeds of *La Libre Parole*, the popular newspaper dedicated to exposing the deceit of the Jews. Hunting is an ancient right, writes Drumont in *La France Juise*, and this is trespass. And he goes on: "the spectacle of all those bearers of noble names dragging themselves, under the ironic smiles of the servants, following the hunt with some grotesque Jew from Germany or Russia who kindly invited him".[418] Jews, it was said, did not belong on horseback, pretending to be hunters; in essence, they were – and always would be – the hunted.

Camondo's capacious files included 'hunting journals, the lists of who came, the game you caught, who you sent it to',[419] but omitted any mention of the bitter taunts he had to contend with. The family archive in the cupboard was not comprehensive after all.

Camondo would have had his own personal reasons for the omission, but the logic of his people's history suggests that these could have been measures of his shame: the shame of being judged irredeemably lesser. It cast a shadow on a life's work; this was not something worth archiving.

As I look at it, the logic of erasure among undistinguished Jews from the East may have been similar, even if their life journey was so different from Camondo's.

No doubt there were many Jews who left the Pale with stories to tell, which they passed on to their progeny, who then did likewise. Such stories may or may not have been truthful or complete, and they may or may not have been altered or embellished in the retelling; the mythic version of shtetl life I referred to at the outset is testimony to a lot of that. But there were also many émigres who were far less forthcoming about their Russian pasts.

Maurice was but one among his generation of these immigrant Jews who had none of Camondo's confidence in the weightiness or interest of his or his family's experiences. Like many of his peers, Maurice had no compulsion to stake any historical claim for himself or his parents. His impulse was the opposite: to delete and eliminate, repress and deny, refusing to archive his past. Maurice Posel had become a child of the British Empire and absorbed its judgement on who he had been before and on his parents who had made him so. Nothing of this was worth remembering.

This facet of the lives of Maurice and his ilk urges me to return to the triumphalist narrative of South Africa's Jewish history and look again. It's then that I see a more complex cultural artefact than just a confident retort to antisemitic prejudice. The litany of triumphs is surely a story told for Jewish consumption as much as a rejoinder to hostile others and, as such, a more insecure tale, imprinted by the self-silencing of the many individual Jews who thereby took themselves out of the story. In the aggregate, could the triumphalism have become a communal mask worn by Jews for Jews – a collective repression, omitting what was better left unsaid, and putting as positive a face on things as possible? The experience of antisemitism elicits both.

Historian Milton Shain, who has written extensively on antisemitism in South Africa, has pondered these omissions too. 'I am essentially interested in the way a master narrative of South African Jewish history has evolved which minimizes conflict between Jews and non-Jews. That narrative is one of an immigrant community, upwardly mobile and prosperous, in a land of tolerance and opportunity. It was already evident in an early South African Jewish historiography which, in turn, helped to shape what I believe is a myth of harmony between Jew and non-Jew.'[420]

There's a striking paradox here. Jews do not disclaim suffering, of course; on the contrary, we are defined by it. But the telling is selective, and the terms carefully considered. We are simultaneously triumphant and ever-suffering.

The Eastern migration story – told collectively or individually – usually reveals little of the detail of daily life in the Pale. Like me, most of my contemporaries with Eastern Jewish roots have remained ignorant of the dense everyday realities that the emigrants left behind – largely because we were never informed. There is one exception, however: one mention of which we have all heard. Pogroms. Our ancestors, it is said, were fleeing pogroms. In this telling, the reference to a history of suffering is condensed into a single word. It pulsates. We all understand.

Some of the Jews who arrived in South Africa were indeed fleeing pogroms, but by no means all. The majority of South Africa's Eastern Jews, as mentioned previously, came from northern Lithuania, where there were few pogroms. The single word works as a parable more than fact. It declares the experience of Jewish abjection – no further historical details required – with a version of victimhood that is straightforward and ethically uncomplicated. Life in the Pale was intolerable for Jews because they were put upon, in orgies of violence, by antisemitic Russians, which is why they left. There is no need to remember the deviations and variations of life in the Pale, the mutual pushing and shoving of everyday life, the more complicated versions of Jewish depradation and retaliation.

Once settled in South Africa, the undiluted horror of the Holocaust became the iconic victimhood. South Africans who partook of Nazi thinking or action were regarded as victimisers; their antisemitism was horribly memorable. The Greyshirts, for example – White Hitler-supporting Afrikaners who harassed and attacked Jews during the 1930s. There was less inclination to remember the grinding prejudice and contempt directed towards Eastern Jews from the moment they arrived, largely by the British, and which didn't simply disappear during the apartheid years. Better a redemptive immigration story that focused on the triumphant successes, pitted against the obvious spectacles of collective degradation, and omitting the abiding injuries – less dramatic, more routine – that could wear down the soul.

90 | *Farribels* revisited

Thinking about histories of selective telling, there's more to be said, too, about how Jews tell of suffering inflicted by other Jews – potentially an injury to the image of a cohesive, communal people. How do we deal with Jews as perpetrators of suffering, not merely its victims? What is told, and how? What is omitted or forgotten?

I can suggest a small part of one possible answer, which comes to me as I reflect, again, on the prominence of *farribels* in Jewish lives. *Farribels* are emotional archives, after all. They memorialise and they exclude; they speak and they silence, with a particular logic of expression and exclusion.

As pointed out earlier, *farribels* always tell of injury done to one or more Jews by other Jews, and typically they do so with a strategic vagueness. For both the storyteller and the audience, imprecision or looseness of facts matter little – perhaps not at all, as became clear in the case of Maurice's *farribel*. Its purpose is not a verifiable litany of facts; far more important is to tell a story about an emotional harm that enables those listening to recognise and acknowledge the hurt. The *farribel* chronicles suffering in a way that commiserates wholeheartedly with its victim, communicating very little about the perpetrator other than what is necessary to document his or her wrong-doing, with no ifs and buts.

Anthropologists think of myths as communal stories rooted in shared preoccupations and predispositions. Moral parables rather than literal truths, myths emerge to make sense of the enigmas and challenges of existence, in ways that affirm shared values. In my account, *farribels* function like myths. Listening to a *farribel*'s tale, Jews commiserate readily, partly because in their lack of specifics these stories are predictable, their repertoires entirely recognisable. We Jews know that Jews fall out over money, that they betray each other and inflict hurt, that incorrigible status-seeking brings out the worst. We are neither surprised nor horrified; on the contrary, we are more likely to feel the warmth of cultural recognition.

It's paradoxical. *Farribels* tell of a Jewish propensity to inflict hurt on other Jews, and the pain that ensues. Communities injure their own. Yet these stories do little to damage a Jewish sense of communal cohesion; instead, they become something of a cultural glue.

91 | Dear Maurice

I have reached the end of this story at the limits of the archives I could use. I am left with gaps that I cannot fill, questions that I cannot answer. So, dear Maurice, if you and I were now in conversation, I would have lots to say and put to you.

When you reached your later years, were you as enthralled by the British, and their Britishness, as you were as a younger man? Outwardly, it seemed so, but you were so closed, so emotionally guarded. I wonder what was going on inside, in your hidden reaches: what itched and ached, what flared and burned?

Did you feel entirely grateful for the gift of their civilisation; or were you more mixed about it, even occasionally? When they made you feel even smaller than you already knew yourself to be, did you flex a muscle of indignation or clench an angry fist at them, or was your sense of injury always redirected at fellow Jews?

You longed to be like them; but they never let you think that they recognised you as anything but different. Did you share their judgement: a Jew, never top notch?

Were there any aspects of your Russian past that you grieved for, despite yourself? Did you nurture any memories of your grandfather Itsyk and grandmother Chaia-Sora, of life back then in the shtetl, flashbacks that remained hidden and closeted, secrets that you repeated only to yourself? Was Russia always a part of you, a phantom limb maybe? Or was it easier to turn away entirely, the amputation complete?

And what about your parents? To your son, you were an entirely colonial creation: to him, your parents did not exist. But did you remain your parents' son? You kept your mother's ticket to travel and her permit of entry to the Cape; perhaps you even treasured them. They reshaped your mother into a cut-out of British officialdom; this was the beginning of Beila becoming Betsy. But did Beila remain, hidden in your emotional cupboard? Bere too: did he speak to you, in secret, in Yiddish, as you fathered your own son?

All the Posels who remained in Pumpian were murdered in 1941, annihilated along with the other Pumpian Jews, buried en masse in the graves that they were forced to dig for themselves. I assume you knew. Did you talk about it? Did you ever light a *yarzheit* (memorial) candle to remember your dead? Did you feel a flicker of guilt that you had survived while they had perished? Or did you once pay your last respects – quietly – and then move on without looking back?

In short, dear Maurice, I would like to know: did Sir Carruthers Beattie abandon you, or was he there for you – like Erna – to the end?

Notes

Part One

1. The phrase comes from Anne Michaels, *Fugitive Pieces* (London: Bloomsbury Publishing, 1998), 17.
2. Eric Hobsbawm, *The Age of Capital, 1848–1875* (London: Weidenfeld & Nicolson, 1975), 228.
3. Eric Rosenthal, *Gold! Gold! Gold! The Johannesburg Gold Rush* (London: Macmillan, 1970), 193.
4. A card game of Dutch origin, with international appeal, including among immigrant Jews.
5. My father's childhood nickname.
6. Christopher Bayly, *The Birth of the Modern World, 1780–1914* (Oxford: Blackwell Publishing, 2004), 1.
7. Njabulo Ndebele, *South African Literature and Culture: Rediscovery of the Ordinary* (Manchester: Manchester University Press, 1994), chap. 2.
8. Richard Mendelsohn and Milton Shain, *The Jews in South Africa: An Illustrated History* (Cape Town: Jonathan Ball Publishers, 2008), 91.
9. According to Gideon Shimoni, in 1911, the 47 000 Jews in the country accounted for 3.7% of the White population; by 1936, their numbers had increased to 90 600, which was 4.52% of South African Whites. Gideon Shimoni, 'Review: Milton Shain, *The Roots of Antisemitism in South Africa*', *Modern Judaism* 16, no. 2 (May 1996): 185–188, accessed 15 September 2025, https://muse.jhu.edu/article/21999.
10. Mendelsohn and Shain, *The Jews in South Africa*, 157–159.

NOTES

Part Two

11 Yohanan Petrovsky-Shtern, *The Golden Age Shtetl: A New History of Jewish Life in East Europe* (Princeton: Princeton University Press, 2014), 11–12.

12 Markus Krah, *American Jewry and the Re-Invention of the East European Jewish Past* (Berlin: De Gruyter Oldenbourg, 2017), 6.

13 The word is derived from the Latin 'palus', which meant a stake (as in, a stake placed in the ground). The word Pale signified a bounded territory.

14 Mark Mazower, *What You Did Not Tell: A Russian Past and the Journey Home* (London: Penguin, 2018), 21.

15 Petrovsky-Shtern, *The Golden Age Shtetl*, 2.

16 Petrovsky-Shtern, *The Golden Age Shtetl*, 87.

17 Petrovsky-Shtern, *The Golden Age Shtetl*, 101.

18 Heiko Haumann, *A History of East European Jews* (Budapest: Central European University Press, 2002), 115.

19 Benjamin Bialostotzky, 'From Pumpenai to Kaunas', trans. Sonia Kovitz, in *Lite* Vol. 1, ed. Mendel Sudarsky and Uriah Katzenelenbogen (New York: Jewish-Cultural Society, 1951), accessed 10 June 2022, http://www.jewishgen.org/yizkor/lita/lit1203.html.

20 See Immanuel Etkes, 'Haskalah', in *Yivo Encyclopedia of Jews in Eastern Europe* (New York: Yivo Institute for Jewish Research, 2025), accessed 10 June 2022, https://encyclopedia.yivo.org/article/10. Etkes documents the shifts and variations within the movement over time.

21 James Campbell, 'Beyond the Pale: Jewish Immigration and the South African Left', in *Memories, Realities and Dreams: Aspects of the South African Jewish Experience*, ed. Milton Shain and Richard Mendelsohn (Cape Town: Jonathan Ball Publishers, 2002), 104.

22 Nathaniel Deutsch, *The Jewish Dark Continent: Life and Death in the Russian Pale of Settlement* (Cambridge: Harvard University Press, 2011), 1.

23 Jeffrey Paull and Jeffrey Briskman, 'The Jewish Surname Process in the Russian Empire', Avotaynu Online, August 2015, accessed 10

June 2022, https://avotaynuonline.com/2015/08/the-jewish-surname-process-in-the-russian-empire-and-its-effect-on-jewish-genealogy/. The authors explain that there were tax incentives for Jews to fracture their families into smaller units, by having males take on different surnames. This makes tracking a family's full genealogy difficult.

24 Revealed on a search for the name on Familysearch.org.

25 The information about the Posel family in Pumpian comes from the births, deaths, marriages, taxpayers, voters and passport application sections of the JewishGen Lithuania database. Notes are not provided for every piece of information because the website does not provide web addresses for individual references.

26 Tracy Dennison and Steven Nafziger, 'Living Standards in Nineteenth Century Russia', *Journal of Interdisciplinary History* 43, no. 3 (2011): 398–399, https://www.jstor.org/stable/41678708.

27 Such prices fluctuated between parts of the Pale, so these figures should be treated as impressionistic. See, for example, Petrovsky-Shtern, *The Golden Age Shtetl*, 262.

28 Samuel Kassow, 'Shtetl', in *Yivo Encyclopedia of Jews in Eastern Europe* (New York: Yivo Institute for Jewish Research, 2025), accessed 10 June 2022, https://encyclopedia.yivo.org/article/27.

29 Erica McAvoy, '"To Have and Enjoy": Seating in Boston's Early Anglican Churches, 1686–1732' (Master's thesis, University of Massachusetts, 2020), accessed 10 June 2022, https://scholarworks.umb.edu/cgi/viewcontent.cgi?article=1660&context=masters_theses.

30 Dean Philip Bell, *Jews in the Early Modern World* (Lanham: Rowman and Littlefield Publishers, 2008), 115.

31 Laurance A. Hoffman, *Beyond the Text: A Holistic Approach to Liturgy* (Bloomington: Indiana University Press, 1987), 71.

32 Glenn Dynner, *Yankel's Tavern: Jews, Liquor and Life in the Kingdom of Poland* (New York: Oxford University Press, 2014), 10–11.

33 Personal communication from Yonathan Petrovsky-Shtern, 15 April 2024. The designation in the record on the Jewishgen website does not specify what type of deputy Itsyk was.

34 Personal communication from Yonathan Petrovsky-Shtern, 15 April 2024.

35 Petrovsky-Shtern, *The Golden Age Shtetl*, 125.
36 Petrovsky-Shtern, *The Golden Age Shtetl*, 123.
37 Dynner, *Yankel's Tavern*; Petrovsky-Shtern, *The Golden Age Shtetl*, chap. 4; Ellie Schainker, *Confessions of the Shtetl* (Stanford: Stanford University Press, 2016), chap. 3.
38 Dynner, *Yankel's Tavern*, 10.
39 Petrovsky-Shtern, *The Golden Age Shtetl*, 147.
40 Dynner, *Yankel's Tavern*, 28.
41 Petrovsky-Shtern, *The Golden Age Shtetl*, 130.
42 Dynner, *Yankel's Tavern*, 10 and 16.
43 Dynner, *Yankel's Tavern*, 7.
44 Samuel Kassow, 'Introduction', in *The Shtetl: New Evaluations*, ed. Steven Katz (New York: New York University Press, 2007), 8.
45 Sarah Hamer-Jacklyn, 'My Mother's Grief', in *Found Treasures: Stories by Yiddish Women Writers*, ed. Frieda Forman, et al. (Toronto: Second Story Press, 1994), 67.
46 David Englander, '*Stille Huppah* (Quiet Marriage) among Jewish Immigrants in Britain', *The Jewish Journal of Sociology* 34, no. 2 (1992): 85–109, https://archive.jpr.org.uk/download?id=2259.
47 ChaeRan Freeze, 'Marriage', in *Yivo Encyclopedia of Jews in Eastern Europe* (New York: Yivo Institute for Jewish Research, 2025), accessed 10 June 2022, https://yivoencyclopedia.org/article.aspx/marriage.
48 JewishGen records show that Leah was Bere's first wife's fifth and last child, born on 17 September 1893. Perhaps she died during childbirth; otherwise soon after that. Maurice, the second wife's only child, was born on 8 April 1895. So Bere did not wait long before marrying a second time.
49 Freeze, 'Marriage'.
50 According to Galina Baranova, previously a senior archivist in the Lithuania national archives, marriage and death records for Pumpian are missing for 1910 (email communication, 17 June 2022). Possibly one or both of them died in that year; maybe one or both married in 1910, but they would have been 46 and 39 years old respectively, which makes marriage a very remote possibility at that point.
51 Email communication from Galina Baranova, 17 June 2022.
52 1912 records on JewishGen show Rokha living in a house with three other women. Perhaps by then Yudis had returned to

Pumpian and lived with her other sisters, accessed 10 June 2022, https://www.jewishgen.org/databases/jgdetail_2.php.
53 Personal email communication from Benjamin Nathans, 17 May 2022.
54 Personal email communication from Alice Nakhimovsky, 25 April 2022.
55 Eliyana Adler, 'Rediscovering Schools for Jewish Girls in Tsarist Russia', *East European Jewish Affairs* 34, no. 2 (2004): 144, https://doi.org/10.1080/1350167052000340922.
56 Bialostotzky, 'From Pumpenai to Kaunas'.
57 Nurit Orchan, 'Yiddish: Women's Participation in Eastern European Yiddish Press, 1862–1903', 23 June 2021, accessed 10 June 2022, https://jwa.org/encyclopedia/article/yiddish-womens-participation-in-eastern-european-yiddish-press-1862-1903.
58 Quoted in Norma Fain Pratt, 'Culture and Radical Politics: Yiddish Women Writers 1890–1940', *American Jewish History* 70, no. 1 (1980): 74, http://www.jstor.org/stable/23881991.
59 Elissa Bemporad and Glenn Dynner, 'Introduction: Jewish Women in Modern Eastern and East Central Europe', *Jewish History* 33, no. 1/2, *Special issue: Jewish Women in Modern Eastern and East Central Europe* (March 2020): 2, https://www.jstor.org/stable/48698809.
60 According to Galina Baranova, there are no archival records of people leaving these parts of the Pale until the 1920s. Also, death records are absent for the years 1862–1864, as well as 1910; and there are no marriage records for 1862, 1864 and 1910. Email communication, 17 June 2022.
61 Edward Bristow, *Prostitution and Prejudice: The Jewish Fight against White Slavery, 1870–1939* (New York: Oxford University Press, 1982), 105.
62 On the White slave trade, see Mir Yarfitz, *Impure Migration: Jews and Sex Work in Golden Age Argentina* (New Brunswick: Rutgers University Press, 2019). See also Laura Lammasniemi, '"White Slavery": The Origins of the Anti-trafficking Movement', *openDemocracy* (16 November 2017), accessed 10 June 2022, https://www.opendemocracy.net/en/beyond-trafficking-and-slavery/white-slavery-origins-of-anti-trafficking-movement/.

NOTES

63 Lloyd Gartner, 'Anglo-Jewry and the Jewish International Traffic in Prostitution, 1885–1914', *Association for Jewish Studies Review* 7 (1982): 146, https://doi.org/10.1017/S0364009400000684.

64 Gartner, 'Anglo-Jewry and the Jewish International Traffic in Prostitution, 1885–1914', 139.

65 See ChaeRan Freeze and Jay Harris, eds., *Everyday Life in Imperial Russia: Selected Documents 1772–1914* (Waltham: Brandeis University Press, 2013), 230–231.

66 Elena Keidošiūtė, 'Marginality without Benefits: Converting Jewish Women in Lithuanian Guberniyas', *Jewish History* 33, *Special Issue: Jewish Women in Modern Eastern and East Central Europe* (March 2020): 7–27.

67 Dynner, *Yankel's Tavern*, 19. See also Ellie Schainker, *Confessions of the Shtetl*, chap. 3.

68 Sholem Asch, 'God of Vengeance', in *The Dybbuk and Other Great Yiddish Plays*, ed. Joseph Landis (New York: Bantam, 1966), 98.

69 This was the first Yiddish play to be translated, and performed all over Europe, to packed houses. The first English production was in New York in 1923; it met with rapturous applause from some and outraged declamation from others. Several bannings followed, prompting Asch himself – in 1946 – to withdraw the play from future production.

70 Joseph Sherman, 'Scrutinizing the Shtetl: I.B. Singer's "Tsetyl un Rikl"', *Prooftexts* 15, no. 2 (May 1995): 129–144, http://www.jstor.org/stable/20689415.

71 Deutsch, *The Jewish Dark Continent*, 250–251.

72 His recorded date of birth in the JewishGen records would have made him seven years old when he left for South Africa, not five, as per his mother's ticket for the ship that brought them into Cape Town.

73 Quoted in Haumann, *A History of East European Jews,* 143. See also Deutsch, *The Jewish Dark Continent*, 176.

74 Quoted in Haumann, *A History of East European Jews,* 143.

75 Haumann, *A History of East European Jews*, 143.

76 Deutsch, *The Jewish Dark Continent*, 11.

77 Deutsch, *The Jewish Dark Continent*, 76.

78 Deutsch, *The Jewish Dark Continent*, 14.

79 Yuri Slezkine, *The Jewish Century* (Princeton: Princeton University Press, 2004), 108–109; Petrovsky-Shtern, *The Golden Age Shtetl*, 152.
80 Petrovsky-Shtern, *The Golden Age Shtetl*, 179.
81 Petrovsky-Shtern, *The Golden Age Shtetl*, 156.
82 Petrovsky-Shtern, *The Golden Age Shtetl*, 153.
83 Slezkine, *The Jewish Century*, 108.
84 Petrovsky-Shtern, *The Golden Age Shtetl*, chap. 5.
85 Bialostotzky, 'From Pumpenai to Kaunas'.
86 JewishGen's Cemetery Discovery Project, 'Pumpenai: Kovno', accessed 10 June 2022, http://iajgscemetery.org/eastern-europe/lithuania/pumpenai. See also JewishGen, 'Pumpėnai (Pumpyan)', accessed 10 June 2022, https://www.jewishgen.org/yizkor/lithuania6/lit6_214.html.
87 Darius Staliunas, *Enemies for a Day: Anti-Semitism and Anti-Jewish Violence in Lithuania under the Tsars* (Budapest: Central University Press, 2015), 23.
88 Staliunas, *Enemies for a Day*, 25.
89 Personal email communication from Darius Staliunas, 22 April 2022.
90 See, for example, Hannah Johnson's account of these shifts in *Blood Libel* (Ann Arbor: University of Michigan Press, 2012).

Part Three

91 Archival sources don't produce a completely consistent version of his age. His South African death certificate gives his age at death in 1928 as 75, which would have made him 47 in 1901. But JewishGen records show him as three or four years younger.
92 Leibl Feldman, *The Jews of Johannesburg*, trans. from Yiddish by Veronica Belling (Kaplan Centre, University of Cape Town, 2007), 46. Cohen was living in Johannesburg during a damaging dynamite explosion in 1896. Taking shrewd advice from 'a fellow countryman', he immediately set about selling glass to householders whose windows had been shattered.
93 Riva Krut, 'Building a Home and a Community: Jews in Johannesburg, 1886–1914' (PhD thesis, University of London, 1985), 43–45.

NOTES

94 Andrew Porter, *Victorian Business, Shipping and Imperial Policy* (Suffolk: Boydell Press, 1986), 1.
95 Krut, 'Building a Home and a Community', 56.
96 Krut, 'Building a Home and a Community', 60.
97 I can't find an exact date; his son Aaron says 1890; JewishGen archival documents have Harris in Linkuva in 1893, but not beyond that.
98 FamilySearch, Mr B Posel, 1901, Migration United Kingdom, Outgoing Passenger Lists, 1890-1960, accessed 10 June 2022, https://www.familysearch.org/ark:/61903/1:1:68GW-QTP4.
99 Leah Garrett, *Journeys Beyond the Pale: Yiddish Travel Writing in the Modern World* (Madison: University of Wisconsin Press, 2003), 124.
100 From Lamed Shapiro's Yiddish novella, *Oyfn Yam* (On the Sea), quoted in Garrett, *Journeys Beyond the Pale*, 135.
101 Malka Lee's autobiography, *Durk Kindershe Oygn* (Through the Eyes of Childhood) includes an account of a journey by sea from a shtetl in Galicia to the USA. An extract is included in Frieda Forman, et al., *Found Treasures*, 159–185.
102 Lee, *Through the Eyes of Childhood*, 166.
103 Carmel Schrire and Gwynne Schrire, *The Reb and the Rebel: Jewish Narratives in South Africa, 1882–1913* (Cape Town: University of Cape Town Press, 2016), 57. Leib Schrire is referring to his journey from Vlissengen to the Cape in 1892.
104 Thanks to historian Nick Evans for this information.
105 Nicholas Evans, '"A Strike for Racial Justice?" Transatlantic Shipping and the Jewish Diaspora, 1882–1939', *Jewish Culture and History* 11, nos. 1–2 (2009): 27, https://www.tandfonline.com/doi/abs/10.1080/1462169X.2009.10512113
106 *Standard and Digger News*, 'Steerage to South Africa', *Standard and Digger News*, 13 June 1895, 81, British Library.
107 Gwynne Robins, 'Adapting to a new society: the role of the Cape Town Jewish Philanthropic Society, c. 1900', accessed 10 June 2022, http://www.jcs.org.za/wp-content/uploads/2017/06/CTJPS.pdf.
108 Lee, *Through the Eyes of Childhood*, 168.

109 Tilly Whiteman, interview by L. Levine, UCT Kaplan Centre Oral Histories, May 1985, MSS BC 949.
110 Sally Swartz, *Homeless Wanderers: Movement and Mental Illness in the Cape Colony in the Nineteenth Century* (Cape Town: University of Cape Town Press, 2015), 147.
111 Thanks to historian Nick Evans for this information.
112 William Harry Mitchell and L. A. Sawyer, *The Cape Run: The Story of the Union-Castle Service to South Africa and of the Ships They Employed* (Suffolk: Terence Dalton Ltd, 1987), 24.
113 The demography of the Jewish population has been recounted in great detail by Richard Rowland on the strength of the 1897 population census of the Russian empire in its entirety. See 'Geographical Patterns of the Jewish Population in the Pale of Settlement in the Late Nineteenth Century', *Jewish Social Studies* 48, no. 3 (1986): 207–234, https://www.jstor.org/stable/4467338. He shows that the proportion of Jews to non-Jews varied in different sections of the Pale. In the north of the Pale – including the province of Kovno in what is now Lithuania – Jews were typically in the majority in the shtetls. In some cases, up to 80 per cent.
114 Michael Stanislawski, 'Russian Empire', in *Yivo Encyclopedia of Jews in Eastern Europe* (New York: Yivo Institute for Jewish Research), accessed 10 June 2022, https://encyclopedia.yivo.org/article/25.
115 Nokhem Shtif, *The Pogroms in Ukraine, 1918–19: Prelude to the Holocaust*, trans. Maurice Wolfthal (Open Book Publishers, 2019), para 1, accessed 15 September 2025, https://books.openedition.org/obp/11018?lang=en.
116 JewishGen, 'Pumpenai (Pumpyan)', accessed 10 June 2022, https://www.jewishgen.org/yizkor/lithuania6/lit6_214.html.
117 JewishGen, Pumpenai (Pumpyan)'.
118 JewishGen, 'Pumpenai (Pumpyan)'.
119 See also Bryan Cheyette, 'Neither Black nor White: The Figure of the Jew in Imperial British Literature', in *The Jew in the Text: Modernity and the Construction of Identity*, ed. Linda Nochlin and Tamar Gard (London: Thames and Hudson, 1995), 37.
120 Deutsch, *The Jewish Dark Continent*, 8, quoting Celia Brickman, *Aboriginal Populations in the Mind* (New York: Columbia University

NOTES

Press, 2003), 163. Brickman makes the point that the term 'white negroes' was in circulation in Western Europe during the late nineteenth century.

Part Four

121 *Cape Times*, 25 September 1901, British Library.
122 Elizabeth van Heyningen, 'Public Health and Society in Cape Town 1880–1910' (PhD diss, University of Cape Town, 1989), 311.
123 Van Heyningen, 'Public Health and Society', 332.
124 Van Heyningen, 'Public Health and Society', 333–334.
125 Van Heyningen, 'Public Health and Society', 334.
126 The term 'Polish' was used loosely and would have covered all Jews who had arrived from the East, their dress, language and lifestyle very different from the British or German Jews already settled in the Cape.
127 Quoted in Gwynne Schrire, 'The Bubonic Plague and the Jews in Cape Town', 23 April 2020, accessed 10 June 2022, https://www.sajbd.org/media/the-bubonic-plagueand-the-jews-in-cape-town-1901.
128 The term was usually used to refer to Bantu-speaking peoples, also referred to as 'Natives', as distinct from Cape Malay or Asiatics, but also encompassed indigenous Africans from other parts of the African continent. The collective official category for all three, at the time, was 'non-European'.
129 Joshua Levy, ed., *The Writings of Meyer Dovid Hersch (1858–1953): Rand Pioneer and Historian of Jewish Life in Early Johannesburg* (Johannesburg: Ammatt Press, 2005), 121.
130 Lucien van der Walt, 'Bakunin's Heirs in South Africa: Race and Revolutionary Syndicalism from the IWW to the International Socialist League, 1910–21', *Politikon* 31, no. 1 (May 2004): 72, https://doi.org/10.1080/02589340410001690819
131 Evangelos Mantzaris, 'The Promise of Impossible Revolution: The Cape Town International Socialist League', in *Labour Struggles in South Africa The Forgotten Pages, 1903–1921*, chap. 1, accessed 10 June 2022, https://www.sahistory.org.za/archive/chapter-1-promise-impossible-revolution-cape-town-industrial-socialist-league-1918-1921.

132 *Cape Times*, 23 June 1902, British Library.
133 Eric Rosenthal, 'The Garlicks Story', quoted in Deborah Posel, 'Changes in the Order of Things: Department Stores and the Making of Modern Cape Town', in *Conspicuous Consumption in Africa*, ed. Deborah Posel and Ilana van Wyk (Johannesburg: Wits University Press, 2019), 32.
134 Interview with Hannah Baskin, UCT Libraries, Kaplan Centre Interviews, Series A, A12 BC 949; interview with Louis Fiddel, UCT Libraries, Kaplan Centre Interviews, Series A, A57 BC 949.
135 Interview with Louis Fiddel.
136 Interview with Louis Fiddel.
137 Interview with Louis Fiddel.
138 Interview with Louis Fiddel.
139 Quoted in Baruch Hirson, *The Cape Town Intellectuals: Ruth Schechter and Her Circle, 1907–1954* (Johannesburg: Wits University Press, 2001), 100–101.
140 Letters to the Editor, *Cape Times*, 15 December 1908, British Library.
141 Vivian Bickford-Smith, 'Leisure and Social Identity in Cape Town, British Colony, 1838–1910', *Kronos* 25, no. 9 (1998), 121, https://journals.co.za/doi/pdf/10.10520/AJA02590190_518.
142 Charles van Onselen, *The Fox and the Flies: The Criminal Empire of the Whitechapel Murderer* (London: Vintage Books, 2008), chap. X1V.
143 Vivien Bickford-Smith, 'South African Urban History, Racial Segregation and the Unique Case of Cape Town?', *Journal of Southern African Studies* 21, no. 1 (1995): 63–78, https://www.tandfonline.com/doi/abs/10.1080/03057079508708433.
144 Joerg Baten and Mathias Blum, 'Human Height since 1820', accessed 10 June 2022, https://www.researchgate.net/publication/288657711_Human_height_since_1820.
145 Klaus Hoedl, 'Physical Characteristics of the Jews', accessed 15 September 2022, https://jewishstudies.ceu.edu/sites/jewishstudies.ceu.edu/files/attachment/basicpage/16/01hoedl.pdf.
146 Quoted in Milton Shain, *A Perfect Storm: Antisemitism in South Africa, 1930–1948* (Cape Town: Jonathan Ball Publishers, 2015), 52.

147 Dr A. J. Gregory, quoted in Milton Shain, 'If It Was so Good, Why Was It so Bad?', in Shain and Mendelsohn, *Memories, Realities and Dreams*, 81.
148 Francis Galton, quoted in David Feldman, 'Conceiving Difference: Religion, Race and the Jews in Britain, c.1750–1900', *History Workshop Journal* 76, no. 1 (Autumn 2013): 160–186, https://doi.org/10.1093/hwj/dbt001.
149 The British German philosopher, Houston Stewart Chamberlain, quoted in Deborah Cohen, 'Who Was Who? Race and Jews in Turn-of-the-Century Britain', *Journal of British Studies* 4, no. 4 (2002): 469.
150 Cohen, 'Who Was Who?', 469.
151 Houston Stewart Chamberlain, quoted in Cohen, 'Who Was Who?', 469.
152 Quoted in Cohen, 'Who Was Who?', 482.
153 David Feldman, 'Jews and the British Empire c.1900', *History Workshop Journal* 63, no. 1 (Spring 2007): 86, https://doi.org/10.1093/hwj/dbm027.
154 Jonathan Judaken, 'Mapping the "New Jewish Cultural Studies"', *History Workshop Journal* 51 (2001): 273, https://doi.org/10.1093/hwj/2001.51.269.
155 Milton Shain, *The Roots of Anti-Semitism in South Africa* (Johannesburg: Wits University Press, 1994): 13.
156 *South African Review*, 6 February 1903, quoted in Shain, *The Roots of Antisemitism*, 50.
157 A quote from a letter to the *Cape Times*, cited in Shain, *The Roots of Antisemitism*, 51.
158 A journalist writing in *The Cape*, 3 January 1908, quoted in Shain, *The Roots of* Antisemitism, 51.
159 Shain, *The Roots of Antisemitism*, 52.
160 A quote from the German Jewish press in the USA, quoted in Stephen Birmingham, *Our Crowd: The Great Jewish Families of New York* (London: Longmans, Green and Co Ltd, 1968), 291.
161 Lady Lucie Duff Gordon, *Letters from the Cape* (Cape Town: Maskew Miller Ltd, 1925), 156.
162 Milton Shain, 'Jewry and Cape Society', *Historical Publications Society* (1983): 1–2.

163 Alfred Philipp Bender, 'A Letter on the Jew by Olive Schreiner', 1 July 1906, Bender Papers, Kaplan Centre, UCT Libraries BC 1457.
164 *Cape Times*, 'The Synagogue', *Cape Times*, 9 December 1901, British Library.
165 Alfred Philipp Bender, 'Sermon Preached at the Service in the Synagogue, Durban', *Mayoral Sunday*, 25 August 1912, Bender Papers, Kaplan Centre, UCT Libraries BC 1457.
166 Jewish Board of Guardians, 'History of the Cape Jewish Board of Guardians to Commemorate Centenary Year, 1859–1959', 1963, Cape Provincial Archives (KAB), 296.6, 26.
167 Louis Mirvish, 'Cape Town Jewry in 1910', *Jewish Affairs* (May 1960): 5.
168 *South African Jewish Chronicle*, 3 June 1903, Jacob Gitlin Library, Cape Town.
169 Krut, 'Building a Home and a Community', 69.
170 Hirson, *The Cape Town Intellectuals*, 45–46.
171 *South African Jewish Chronicle*, 5 May 1905, cited in Krut, 'Building a Home and a Community', 151.
172 Suppression of Immorality: Suspected Consignment of Prostitutes, Alexandria, 1906. KAB, AG 1717 6262.
173 See Van Onselen, *The Fox and the Flies*, chap. XV.
174 Van Onselen, *The Fox and the Flies*, 244–245.
175 Rex vs Silver, KAB, AG 1531 12984.
176 Charles van Onselen, 'Jewish Police Informers in the Atlantic World, 1880–1914', *The Historical Journal* 50, no. 1 (2007): 131–132, https://doi.org/10.1017/S0018246X06005942.
177 Van Onselen, *The Fox and the Flies*, 265.
178 Furman, Sandler and Samuel Sandler, Insolvent Liquidation and Distribution Account, 1909, KAB, MOIB 2/3255 1030.
179 Saul Issroff, ed., *Jewish Migration to South Africa*, Vol. 1 (Cape Town: Kaplan Centre, University of Cape Town, 2008), 36.
180 Mirvish, 'Cape Town Jewry in 1910', 6.
181 Posel, Bere. Estate Papers, KAB, MOOC vol 6/9/3346 ref 18907.
182 Millie Pimstone and Milton Shain, *The Jews of District Six: Another Time, Another Place* (Cape Town: Kaplan Centre, University of Cape Town, 2012), 47.

183 Hasia Diner, *Roads Taken: The Great Jewish Migrations to the New World and the Peddlers Who Forged the Way* (New Haven: Yale University Press, 2015): 1.
184 Lorna Levy, *The Hidden Life of a Smous* (Cape Town: Kaplan Centre, University of Cape Town, 2017).
185 Levy, *The Hidden Life of a Smous*, 17.
186 Swartz, *Homeless Wanderers*, 170–173.
187 Harry Ostroff, interview, UCT Libraries, Kaplan Centre Interviews, Series B, A 435, BC 949.
188 Mendelsohn and Shain, *The Jews in South Africa*, 40.
189 Marcia Levenson, *People of the Book: Images of the Jew in South African Jewish Fiction, 1880–1992* (Johannesburg: Wits University Press, 1996), 52.
190 Levenson, *People of the Book*, 152.
191 Francis Brett Young, *City of Gold* (London: Heinemann, 1939), 90–91.
192 Illiquid case, The Table Bay Harbour Board versus Sacks, Chait and Cumes for the Recovery of Money, 1903, KAB, CSC 2/1/1/430 242.
193 For example, see Schrire and Schrire, *The Reb and the Rebel*, 12.
194 Memorial Received. Jacob Cosay. Requesting Letters of Naturalisation, 1898, KAB, CO 4309 C43.
195 Record of Proceedings of Provisional Case. JW Jagger and Co, Ernest Ebert and Co, versus Jacob Cosay, 1899, KAB, CSC 2/2/1/237 80.
196 Sarah Cosay, Insolvent Estate, 1910, KAB, MOIB 2/3339 832.
197 Sarah Cosay, Insolvent Estate, 1910.
198 Application for naturalization, Joseph Jacob Debs, 1/7/1907, KAB, CO 8604 22.
199 Immigration Papers. Jose Taxeira, 1913–1914, KAB, P10 24 2644E.
200 See Veronica Belling, 'Recovering the Lives of South African Jewish Women during the Immigration Years c 1880–1939', chap. 2 (PhD thesis, University of Cape Town, 2013).
201 'Cape Province, South Africa, Civil Deaths, 1895–1972, for Bertha Posel, 1929, Cape Town', reproduced on ancestry.com.au.
202 Betha Padovich, interview, Kaplan Centre Interviews, Series A, A198, UCT Libraries BC 949.

203 Veronica Belling, 'Recovering the Lives of South African Jewish Women', 72–76.

204 Patricia Schonstein Pinnock, *Ouma's Autumn* (Grahamstown: African Sun Press, 1993), 3.

205 Carla Bernardo, 'District Six: Lessons in Remembering', University of Cape Town, 11 February 2021, accessed 10 June 2022, https://www.news.uct.ac.za/article/-2021-02-11-district-six-lessons-in-remembering.

206 Slavery was part of the regime under the Dutch VOC during the eighteenth century. Slaves, arriving from other parts of Africa and the Caribbean, were named by their owners, sometimes drawing on what were deemed biblical names, such as Levy.

207 I visited the museum in 2022, when Noor was working there. He has since passed away.

208 Padovich, interview.

209 Padovich, interview.

210 Louis Herrman, *A History of the Jews in South Africa from the Earliest Times to 1895* (Johannesburg: South African Jewish Board of Deputies, 1935), 258.

211 FamilySearch, Lydia Posel, accessed 10 June 2022, https://www.familysearch.org/ark:/61903/1:1:6ZH5-7WW4.

212 Criminal case, Rex vs Maurice Livingstone, KAB, CSC vol 1/1/1/98, ref 35.

213 Kay McCormick, 'Language in the Jewish Community of District Six, 1880–1940', Jacob Gitlin Library, PMP 194-1, District Six Box, 8.

214 McCormick, 'Language in the Jewish Community of District Six', 5.

215 Hannah Hahn, *They Left It All Behind: Trauma, Loss and Memory among Eastern European Jewish Immigrants and Their Children* (London: Rowman and Littlefield, 2020).

216 Belling, 'Recovering the Lives of South African Jewish Women'.

217 Swartz, *Homeless Wanderers*, chap. 6.

218 Hannah Hahn, *They Left It All Behind*, 44.

219 The saga of Bere's estate is contained in the archival file Posel, Bere: Liquidation and Distribution Account. First and Final, 1929, KAB, MOOC 13/1/6556 1161.

220 Posel, Bere: Liquidation and Distribution Account.
221 Adrienne Baker, 'The Jewish Mother: Is That Why so Many of us Become Counsellors?', *European Judaism* 29, no. 1 (1996): 89, https://www.jstor.org/stable/41444498.
222 Accessed 12 July 2022, www.sacshigh.org.za/about/history.
223 Mirvish, 'Cape Town Jewry in 1910', 5.
224 Tamara Plakins Thornton, *Handwriting in America: A Cultural History* (New Haven: Yale University Press, 1996), xii.
225 Dan Gorman, '"The Character Creed": How Character Shaped the British Imperial Enterprise', *Australasian Journal of Victorian Studies* 4, no. 1 (1998): 127–137, accessed 10 June 2022, https://openjournals.library.sydney.edu.au/AJVS/article/view/13738.
226 Aline Masé, 'Student Migration of Jews from Tsarist Russia to the Universities of Berne and Zurich, 1865–1914', in *East European Jews in Switzerland*, ed. Tamar Lewinsky and Sandrine Mayoraz (Berlin: De Gruyter, 2013), 106–107.
227 Alfred Kazin, *A Walker in the City* (New York: Harcourt Books, 1951), 12.
228 Kazin, *A Walker in the City*, 21–22.
229 Kazin, *A Walker in the City*, 22.
230 Hahn, *They Left It All Behind*, 137.
231 Irving Howe, *World of our Fathers: The Journey of the East European Jews to America and the Life They Found and Made* (New York: Harcourt Brace and Co, 1976), quoted in James Campbell, 'Beyond the Pale: Jewish Immigration and the South African Left', 106.
232 Hahn, *They Left It All Behind*, 138.
233 Hahn, *They Left It All Behind*, 139.

Part Five

234 Slezkine, *The Jewish Century*, 1.
235 Slezkine, *The Jewish Century*, 41.
236 Slezkine, *The Jewish Century*, 28.
237 Slezkine, *The Jewish Century*, 2.
238 Slezkine, *The Jewish Century*, 1.
239 George T. Hutchinson, *From the Cape to the Zambesi* (London: John Murray Publishers, 1905), 190.

240 Claudio Lomnitz, *Nuestra America: My Family in the Vertigo of Translation* (New York: Other Press, 2021), 1–3.
241 Gideon Reuveni, 'Prologomena to an "Economic Turn" in Jewish History', in *The Economy in Jewish History: New Perspectives on the Interrelationship between Ethnicity and Economic Life*, ed. Gideon Reuveni and Sarah Wonick-Segev (New York: Berghahn Books, 2011), 4.
242 Catherine Chatterley, 'The Antisemitic Imagination', in *Global Antisemitism: A Crisis of Modernity*, ed. Charles Asher Small (Leiden: Brill Publishers, 2013), 80.
243 'Zionism, Antisemitism and the Left: An Interview with Moishe Postone', accessed 10 June 2022, https://www.workersliberty.org/files/100205postone.pdf.
244 Martin Meredith, *Diamonds, Gold and War* (London: Pocket Books, 2007), 173–174.
245 Rosenthal, *Gold! Gold! Gold!*, 193.
246 Feldman, *The Jews of Johannesburg*, 20.
247 Quoted in Clive Chipkin, *Johannesburg Style: Architecture and Society, 1880s–1960s* (Cape Town: David Philip, 1993), 9.
248 Van Onselen, *The Fox and the Flies*, 148.
249 Van Onselen, *The Fox and the Flies*, 148.
250 Chipkin, *Johannesburg Style*, 15.
251 Gerhard-Mark van der Waal, *From Mining Camp to Metropolis: The Buildings of Johannesburg 1886–1940* (Pretoria: HSRC, 1987), 29.
252 *Guide to South Africa for the Use of Tourists, Sportsmen, Invalids and Settlers* (Cape Town: Juta and Co, 1893), 224.
253 James A. Cavanagh, *Adventures of an Insurance Agent* (Cape Town: Juta and Co, 1924), 41–42.
254 Van der Waal, *From Mining Camp to Metropolis*, 38.
255 *Guide to South Africa for the Use of Tourists*, 91.
256 Feldman, *The Jews of Johannesburg*, 35.
257 Richard Mendelsohn, *Sammy Marks: 'The Uncrowned King of the Transvaal'* (Cape Town: David Philip, 1991), 14. Thanks to Clive Glaser for the pointer.
258 Feldman, *The Jews of Johannesburg*, 36.
259 Georgina Jaffee, *Joffe Marks: A Family Memoir* (Johannesburg: Sharp Media, 2001), 68.
260 Feldman, *The Jews of Johannesburg*, 35–39.
261 Feldman, *The Jews of Johannesburg*, 36.

262 Eric Rosenthal, *Other Men's Millions* (Cape Town: Howard Timmins, 1959), 84.

263 *The Star*, 10 January 1890, British Library.

264 Richard Lewinsohn, *Barney Barnato: From Whitechapel Clown to Diamond King* (London: George Routledge and Sons Ltd, 1937), 197.

265 Mendel Kaplan, *Jewish Roots in the South African Economy* (Cape Town: C. Struik Publishers, 1987), 29.

266 Personal email communication from Gordon Pirie, 30 December 2021.

267 The Corporal, *An Imperial Yeoman at War* (London: Elliot Stock, 1901), 82. According to the British Museum, the author (The Corporal) is P. E. Bodington.

268 Jonathan Coopersmith, *The Electrification of Russia, 1880–1926* (New York: Cornell University Press, 1992), chap. 3.

269 Schrire and Schrire, *The Reb and the Rebel*, 68.

270 Mrs Lionel Phillips [Florence], *Some South African Recollections* (London: Longmans, Green and Co, 1899), 48.

271 Hutchinson, *From the Cape to the Zambesi*, 187–188.

272 Phillips, *Some South African Recollections*, 48–49.

273 Maurice Harbord, *Froth and Bubble* (London: Edward Arnold, 1915), 237.

274 *Standard and Digger News*, 'Kaffirs and their money', *Standard and Digger News*, 22 June 1895, British Library.

275 *The Star Weekly Edition*, 'Terrible Tragedy at Klip River', *The Star Weekly Edition*, 14 May 1904, British Library.

276 Lawrence E. Neame, *City Built on Gold* (Cape Town: CNA, 1960), 75.

277 Charles van Onselen, 'The World the Mineowners Made: Social Themes in the Economic Transformation of the Witwatersrand 1886–1914', *Review* 3, no. 2 (Fall, 1979): 319, https://www.jstor.org/stable/40240837.

278 Quoted in Krut, 'Building a Home and a Community', 73.

279 *Cape Times Special Supplement*, 6 April 1877, British Library.

280 *Cape Times Special Supplement*, 6 April 1877, British Library.

281 Francis Wilson, *Dinosaurs, Diamonds and Democracy: A Short, Short History of South Africa* (Johannesburg: Penguin Random House, 2011), 73.

282 Union of SA, *Union Statistics for 50 years, 1910–1960*, 1960, A-5.

283 Patrick Harries, *Work, Culture and Identity: Migrant Labourers in Mozambique and South Africa, c. 1860–1910* (London: James Currey, 1994), 174.

284 Joseph Sherman, 'Serving the Natives: Whiteness as the Price of Hospitality in South African Yiddish Literature', *Journal of Southern African Studies* 26, no. 3 (2000): 505, https://www.tandfonline.com/doi/abs/10.1080/713683588.

285 Joshua Levy, *The Writings of Dovid Meyer Hersch*, 133.

286 William Pimlott, 'The Yiddish Press and the Making of South African Jewry in the British World: Exclusion, Libel and British Nationalism, 1890–1914', *Jewish Historical Studies* 55, no. 1 (2024): 15, https://doi.org/10.14324/111.444.jhs.2024v55.02.

287 *South African Jewish Chronicle*, 5 May 1905, cited in Krut, 'Building a Home and a Community', 151.

288 Alice Rallis and Ruth Gordon, *Daughter of Yesterday: A Pioneer Child Looks Back at Early Johannesburg* (Cape Town: Howard Timmins, 1975), 56.

289 Driefontein 148, enlargement of stand 157, Gordon and Posel, TAB, MMB 126 ref MCK 534/09.

290 Personal communication from Judy Le Grange, archivist at Jeppe Boys High School.

291 William Charles Scully, *The Ridge of White Waters* (London: Stanley Paul and Co, 1911), 77.

292 Milton Rugoff, *America's Gilded Age: Intimate Portraits from an Era of Extravagance and Change, 1850–1890* (New York: Henry Holt and Co, 1989), 41–42.

293 Rugoff, *America's Gilded Age*, 71.

294 Schrire and Schrire, *The Reb and the Rebel*, 74.

295 Rosenthal, *Other Men's Millions*, 71–72.

296 Edward Frederick Knight, *South Africa After the War* (London: Longmans, Green and Co, 1903), 203.

297 Hutchinson, *From the Cape to the Zambesi*, 184.

298 Cavanagh, *Adventures of an Insurance Agent*, 45.

299 Scully, *The Ridge of White Waters*, 77.

300 Rosenthal, *Other Men's Millions*, 74.

301 Quoted in Eric Rosenthal, *Meet Me at the Carlton* (Cape Town: Howard Timmins, 1972), 33.

302 Quoted in Rosenthal, *Meet Me at the Carlton*, 31 and 33.

NOTES

303 Quoted in Rosenthal, *Meet Me at the Carlton*, 47.
304 The origin of the term 'Peruvian' is uncertain. Some think the word originated as an 'acronym for Polish and Russian Jews'; others, as 'a specifically Transvaal colloquialism' that then travelled. See Krut, 'Building a home and a community', 90–91.
305 Levy, ed., *The Writings of Meyer Dovid Hersch*, 133.
306 Charles van Onselen, *Studies in the Social and Economic History of the Witwatersrand, 1886–1924, Volume One: New Babylon* (Johannesburg: Ravan Press, 1982), 74.
307 Margot Rubin, 'The Jewish Community of Johannesburg, 1886–1939' (MA thesis, University of Pretoria, 2004), 71.
308 Quoted in Jillian Carman, *Uplifting the Colonial Philistine: Florence Phillips and the Making of the Johannesburg Art Gallery* (Johannesburg: Wits University Press, 2006), 44.
309 Henry Weinberg, 'The Image of the Jew in Late Nineteenth Century French Literature', *Jewish Social Studies* 45, no. 3 (1983): 242, https://www.jstor.org/stable/4467228.
310 Carman, *Uplifting the Colonial Philistine*, 44–45.
311 Rosenthal, *Gold! Gold! Gold!*, 236.
312 Michael Stevenson, *Art and Aspirations: The Randlords of South Africa and their Collections* (Cape Town: Fernwood Press, 2002), 21 and 24.
313 Quoted in Stevenson, *Art and Aspirations*, 30.
314 Keith Surridge, ' "All You Soldiers Are What We Call Pro-Boer": The Military Critique of the South African War', *History* 82, no. 268 (1997): 585, https://doi.org/10.1111/1468-229X.00052.
315 Quoted in Surridge, ' "All You Soldiers Are What We Call Pro-Boer" ', 589.
316 Shain, *The Roots of Antisemitism in South Africa*, 62.
317 Scully, *The Ridge of White Waters*, 79–80.
318 Schrire and Schrire, eds., *The Reb and the Rebel*, 84.
319 Krut, 'Building a Home and a Community', 110.
320 Krut, 'Building a Home and a Community', 72. See also Campbell, 'Beyond the Pale'.
321 *South African Jewish Chronicle*, 'Congregational Rivalry', 1924, 483. Jacob Gitlin Library, Cape Town.
322 See Krut, 'Building a Home and a Community', 140–143 for a detailed account of the back and forth that all this entailed.

323 Krut, 'Building a Home and a Community', 71.
324 Martin Murray, *City of Extremes: The Spatial Politics of Johannesburg* (Durham: Duke University Press, 2011), 46.
325 Feldman, *The Jews of Johannesburg*, 48–49.
326 Bernard Sachs, *Personalities and Places* (Johannesburg: The Dial Press, 1965), 35.
327 The *chevraleit* referred to here were pimps party to the White slave trade.
328 Sachs, *Personalities and Places*, 78.
329 Quoted in Rubin, 'The Jewish Community of Johannesburg', 90.
330 Feldman, *The Jews of Johannesburg*, 192.
331 Sachs, *Personalities and Places*, 38.
332 Feldmann, *The Jews of Johannesburg*, 49.
333 Susan Parnell, 'Race, Power and Urban Control: Johannesburg's Inner-City Slum-Yards, 1910–1923', *Journal of Southern African Studies* 29, no. 3 (2003): 626, https://doi.org/10.1080/03057070306219.
334 Quoted in Parnell, 'Race, Power and Urban Control', 630.
335 Parnell, 'Race, Power and Urban Control', 626.
336 Claims for compensation. Foreign Subjects. Johannesburg. Barnett Cumes, 1903, National Archives (SAB), TAB CJC 311, ref CJC 1496.
337 Potatoes imported by Sacks, Chiat and Cumes, National Archives, TAB DCU 72 471/06, 13/10/05.
338 Unlike the regular African townships, Sophiatown was a freehold area, in which Africans could buy their own homes.
339 Cumes, Barnett. Estate Papers, 1948, KAB, MOOC 6/9/15270, 4097/48.
340 Feldman, *The Jews of Johannesburg*, 46.
341 Ann Rabinowitz, 'South Africa Rand Steam Matzah Ltd', accessed 10 June 2022, https://groups.jewishgen.org/g/main/message/612605.
342 Rabinowitz, 'South Africa Rand Steam Matzah Ltd'.
343 Kosher rules forbade cooking on the sabbath; *cholent* referred to dishes prepared the day before and cooked on a fire, also pre-prepared, that stayed warm during the day of the sabbath.
344 Feldman, *The Jews of Johannesburg*, 48.

NOTES

Part Six

345 Sergeant Gerome, Komatipoort, 5 November 1909, to Chief Immigration Officer, National Archives, SAB, IND, 920 E17260.
346 Andrew MacDonald, 'Forging the Frontiers: Travellers and Documents on the South Africa-Mozambique Border, 1890s–1940s', working paper, academia.edu. Also, Andrew MacDonald, 'Colonial Trespassers in the Making of South Africa's International Borders 1900 to c. 1950' (PhD thesis, St John's College, Cambridge, 2012).
347 MacDonald, 'Colonial Trespassers', 102.
348 Chief Immigration Officer to Sergeant in Charge, Komatipoort, 11 November 1909, SAB, IND, 920 E17260.
349 Office of the Transvaal Agent, Lourenco Marques, 10 November 1909, to Chief Immigration Officer, Pretoria, SAB, IND, 920 E17260.
350 Karolina Koziura, 'The Spaces of Nostalgia(s) and the Politics of Belonging in Contemporary Chernivitsi, Western Ukraine', *East European Politics and Societies and Cultures* 33, no. 1 (February 2019): 219, https://doi.org/10.1177/0888325418777060.
351 Sue Ann Harding, 'The Jews of Chernivitsi', accessed 10 June 2022, https://kehilalinks.jewishgen.org/sadgura/jqharding.html.
352 Daniel Unowsky, *The Pomp and Politics of Patriotism: Imperial Celebrations in Hapsburg Austria, 1848–1916* (West Lafayette: Purdue University Press, 2005), 11 and 19.
353 The first Edict of Tolerance, in 1781, lifted previous restrictions on Jewish economic opportunities in the trades, crafts and professions – although they could not own land and were restricted in the areas in which they could settle. They were no longer required to wear items of clothing or emblems that marked them out as Jewish. As a quid pro quo, a German secular education became compulsory, one of several ways in which Jews were expected to integrate as citizens of the empire. See Daniel Rechter, *Becoming Hapsburg: The Jews of Austrian Bukovina 1774–1918*, Littman Library of Jewish Civilization (Liverpool: Liverpool University Press, 2013), 26–32.
354 Unowsky, *The Pomp and Politics*, 77.

355 Unowsky, *The Pomp and Politics*, chap. 5.
356 Edmund de Waal, *The Hare with Amber Eyes: A Hidden Inheritance* (London: Picador, 2011), 132.
357 Stefan Zweig, *The World of Yesterday*, trans. Anthea Bell (Lincoln: University of Nebraska Press, 2009), 33.
358 Aharon Appelfeld, 'A City That Was and Is No Longer', accessed 10 June 2022, http://czernowitz.ehpes.com/czernowitz12/testfile2008/1451.html.
359 Zweig, *The World of Yesterday*, 27.
360 Rechter, *Becoming Hapsburg*, 142.
361 Cited in De Waal, *The Hare with Amber Eyes*, 130.
362 Cited in De Waal, *The Hare with Amber Eyes*, 131.
363 De Waal, *The Hare with Amber Eyes*, 130.
364 Rechter, *Becoming Hapsburg*, 7.
365 Koziura, 'The Spaces of Nostalgia(s)', 223.
366 Rechter, *Becoming Hapsburg*, 2.
367 Rechter, *Becoming Hapsburg*, 115–116.
368 Quoted in Rechter, *Becoming Hapsburg*, 142.
369 Rechter, *Becoming Hapsburg*, 176.
370 Personal communication from a cousin, Lois Shevel, who was told by her grandmother, a daughter of Chave Posel and therefore Maurice's first cousin.
371 Peter C. Appelbaum, *Hapsburg Sons: Jews in the Austro-Hungarian Army 1788–1918* (Boston: Academic Studies Press, 2022), viii.
372 Appelbaum, *Hapsburg Sons*, viii.
373 Appelbaum, *Hapsburg Sons*, viii.
374 Appelbaum, *Hapsburg Sons*, viii.
375 Annemarie Steidl, 'Migration Patterns in the Late Hapsburg Empire', in *Migration in Austria*, ed. Gunter Bischof and Dirk Rupnov (New Orleans: University of New Orleans Press, 2017), 69.
376 G. Neyer, 'Austrian Emigration from the Mid Nineteenth Century to the Present', *Demographic Information*, 1995, abstract, accessed 10 June 2022, https://pubmed.ncbi.nlm.nih.gov/12321139/.
377 Robert Goodrich, 'Conflicted Loyalties: Austro-Hungarian Immigrants in Michigan and the Great War', *Proceedings of Armistice and Aftermath, 28-9 September 2018*, 1A16, accessed 10 June 2022, https://digitalcommons.mtu.edu/cgi/viewcontent.cgi?article=1006&context=ww1cc-symposium.

378 Tvrtko Mursalo, 'Croatians in the South of Africa', *Werkwinkel* 3, no. 12008, 176.
379 MacDonald, 'Colonial Trespassers', 100.
380 Montague George Jessett, *The Key to South Africa: Delagoa Bay* (London: T. Fisher Unwin, 1899), 25.
381 MacDonald, 'Colonial Trespassers', 100.
382 'Levy's Kiosque, Lourenço Marques, 1900', in *The Graphic*, 24 March 1900, cited in MacDonald, 'Colonial Trespassers', 185.
383 MacDonald, 'Colonial Trespassers', 183.
384 'The Jewish Community of Lourenco Marques, Maputo, Mozambique, 1899–2021', accessed 10 June 2022, https://www.africanjewishcongress.com/Mozambique2.htm.
385 'The Jewish Community of Lourenco Marques'.
386 Jessett, *The Key to South Africa*, 71.
387 Rubin, 'The Jewish Community of Johannesburg', 107.
388 H. B. M. Consulate General to Commercial Intelligence Branch, Board of Trade, London, 28 April 1915, SAB GG 9/64/166.
389 My thanks to Paul von Zwiklitz – Alfred's grandson – for sharing this with me.
390 Tilman Dedering, ' "Avenge the Lusitania": The Anti-German Riots in South Africa in 1915', *Immigrants and Minorities* 31, no. 3 (2013): 256, https://doi.org/10.1080/02619288.2013.781811.
391 Dedering, ' "Avenge the Lusitania" ', 7.
392 A. von Zwiklitz. Released on Parole 1/5/1915. ES 70/2085/14, 29/4/1915. SAB BNS 1/8/62 2282.
393 Form of Parole, 5 July 1919, SAB BNS 1/8/6 265.
394 Neame, *City Built on Gold*, 199.
395 *Sunday Times*, 16 May 1915, 'Anti-German Riots', in *A Century of Sundays: 100 Years of Breaking News in the Sunday Times*, ed. Nadine Dreyer (Cape Town: Zebra Press, 2006), 42.
396 Neame, *City Built on Gold*, 198–199.
397 Neame, *City Built on Gold*, 200.
398 Zweig, *The World of Yesterday*, 246.
399 Rechter, *Becoming Hapsburg*, 176.
400 Rechter, *Becoming Hapsburg*, 177.
401 Rechter, *Becoming Hapsburg*, 177.
402 Sigmund Freud, quoted in Anton Cebalo, 'There Once Was an Empire', *Novum Newsletter*, 20 November 2023, accessed

10 June 2022, https://novum.substack.com/p/there-once-was-an-empire.
403 Ludwig Wittgenstein, quoted in Anton Cebalo, 'There Once Was an Empire'.
404 William Brustein and Amy Ronnkvist, 'The Roots of Antisemitism: Romania before the Holocaust', *Journal of Genocide Research* 4, no. 2 (2002): 211, https://doi.org/10.1080/14623520220138047.
405 Hirsch, Marianne and Leo Spitzer. *Ghosts of Home: The Afterlife of Czernowitz in Jewish Memory* (Los Angeles: University of California Press, 2010), 72–73.
406 Andrei Corbea-Hoisie, 'Chernivitsi', *Yivo Encyclopaedia of Jews in Eastern Europe*, accessed 10 June 2022, https://encyclopedia.yivo.org/article/914.
407 Rubin, 'The Jewish Community of Johannesburg', 142.
408 Deborah Lavin, ed., *Friendship and Union: The South African Letters of Patrick Duncan and Maud Selborne 1907–1943* (Cape Town: Van Riebeeck Society for the Publication of Southern African Historical Documents, 2010), 70.
409 Patrick Duncan to Lady Selborne, 31 October 1922, Letter number 70, in *Friendship and Union*, ed. Deborah Lavin, 381.

Part Seven

410 Campbell, 'Beyond the Pale', 157.
411 Campbell, 'Beyond the Pale', 108–109.
412 Campbell, 'Beyond the Pale', 110.
413 Shain, *A Perfect Storm*, 11.
414 Quoted in Gwynne Robins, 'Greyshirts on the Grand Parade', *Cape Jewish Chronicle*, 1 July 2020, accessed 10 June 2022, https://cjc.org.za/2020/07/01/greyshirts-on-the-grand-parade/.
415 Krut, 'Building a Home and a Community', chap. 4.
416 Krut, 'Building a Home and a Community', 214.
417 Edmund de Waal, *Letters to Camondo* (London: Vintage Press, 2022), 3.
418 De Waal, *Letters to Camondo*, 44.
419 De Waal, *Letters to Camondo*, 44.
420 Shain, '"If It Was so Good, Why Was It so Bad?"'.

Acknowledgements

This book took shape over several years, and always in conversation with generous and insightful family, friends and colleagues. A chunk of the social history that I have written draws on research done in the British Library. My access to that remarkable resource during 2018/9 was thanks to a Leverhulme Visiting Professorship at the Institute for Advanced Study at UCL, London. The Institute's then director, Tamar Garb, was an engaging and enabling host. In the early stages of writing, when I was uncertain about the project, enthusiastic encouragement from Hilary Janks, Karen Lazar and Karin Shapiro kept me going. As the text took shape, through various iterations, the perspectives and suggestions of several willing readers were helpful and formative. Thanks to Robin Cohen, Jean Comaroff, Clive Glaser, Hilary Janks, Diana Jimenez Thomas, Karen Lazar, Wahbie Long, Clare Loveday, Irwin Manoim, David Medalie, Howard Phillips, Karin Shapiro, Martin Smith, Jonny Steinberg, Hedley Twidle and Ilana van Wyk for taking the time to engage with my text. I'm grateful to South African colleagues Tilman Dedering, Howard Phillips, Andrew MacDonald and Gordon Pirie for sharing their expertise, and to Alice Nakhimovsky, Benjamin Nathans, Yohanan Petrovsky-Shtern, David Rechter and Darius Staliunas for replying so obligingly to email queries from a complete stranger. Thanks also to the Lithuanian archivist Galina Baranova for useful responses to my questions, to Jacqui Rogers and her staff at the Gitlin Library for their efficient and helpful support and to Michal Singer and Katie Garrun, archivists at University of Cape Town Libraries, for fielding queries and enabling access to invaluable resources. Long and animated conversations with Cathy Michelson and Micky Stern helped bring the psychological complexities of the story into clearer focus. Talking and walking with Brahm Fleisch, Orenna Krut, Richard Moultrie, Joanna Taylor and Nick Taylor helped draw the book to a close.

I am endebted to my cousin Paul von Zwiklitz for access to his family archive, and for his savvy assistance with piecing together aspects of the Austro-Hungarian family story. Another cousin, Lois Shevel, added some indispensable details. Grateful thanks to Max Posel's daughters Carol and Sandra (neither of whom I had met before embarking on this book), Max's grandson – fellow historian Keith Shear – as well as Max's niece Francie Jowell, for sharing their reflections and memories.

Special thanks to Hilary Janks and Karin Shapiro for their astute and close interest in the project throughout. Veronica Klipp and her team at Wits University Press have been wonderfully enthusiastic and professional, including Inga Norenius and Alison Paulin, who sweated the detail with me through to the end.

Max, Jess and Ilan Price – my very dearest – believed in the project from the get-go, and gave the loving and fervent prods I needed to get it done. Their astute insights and questions too have opened my eyes and shaped my thinking.

Bibliography

Adler, Eliyana. 'Rediscovering Schools for Jewish Girls in Tsarist Russia'. *East European Jewish Affairs* 34, no. 2 (2004). https://doiI:10.1080/1350167052000340922.

Appelbaum, Peter C. *Hapsburg Sons: Jews in the Austro-Hungarian Army 1788–1918*. Boston: Academic Studies Press, 2022.

Appelfeld, Aharon. 'A City That Was and Is No Longer'. Accessed 10 June 2022, http://czernowitz.ehpes.com/czernowitz12/testfile2008/1451.html.

Asch, Sholem. 'God of Vengeance'. In *The Dybbuk and Other Great Yiddish Plays*, edited by Joseph Landis, 69–113. New York: Bantam, 1966.

Baker, Adrienne. 'The Jewish Mother'. *European Judaism* 29, no. 1 (1996): 89. https://www.jstor.org/stable/41444498.

Baskin, Hannah. Interview. UCT Libraries, Kaplan Centre Interviews, Series A, A 12, BC 949.

Baten, Jeorg and Mathias Blum. 'Human Height since 1820'. Accessed 10 June 2022, https://www.researchgate.net/publication/288657711_Human_height_since_1820.

Bayly, Christopher. *The Birth of the Modern World, 1780–1914*. Oxford: Blackwell Publishing, 2004.

Bell, Dean Philip. *Jews in the Early Modern World*. Lanham: Rowman and Littlefield Publishers, 2008.

Belling, Veronica. 'Recovering the Lives of South African Jewish Women during the Immigration Years c 1880–1913'. PhD thesis, University of Cape Town, 2013.

Bemporad, Elissa and Glenn Dynner. 'Introduction: Jewish Women in Modern Eastern and East Central Europe'. *Jewish History* 33, no. 1/2, *Special Issue: Jewish Women in Modern Eastern and East Central Europe* (March 2020): 2. https://www.jstor.org/stable/48698809.

Bender, Alfred Philipp. 'A Letter on the Jew by Olive Schreiner', 1 July 1906. Bender Papers, Kaplan Centre, UCT Libraries BC 1457.

Bender, Alfred Philipp. 'Sermon Preached at the Service in the Synagogue, Durban', *Mayoral Sunday*, 25 August 1912. Bender Papers, Kaplan Centre, UCT Libraries BC 1457.

Bernardo, Carla. 'District Six: Lessons in Remembering', University of Cape Town, 11 February 2021. Accessed 10 June 2022, https://www.news.uct.ac.za/article/-2021-02-11-district-six-lessons-in-remembering.

Bialostotzky, Benjamin. 'From Pumpenai to Kaunus'. Translated by Sonia Kovitz. In *Lite* Vol 1, edited by Mendel Sudarsky and Uriah Katzenelenbogen. New York: Jewish Cultural Society, 1951. Accessed 10 June 2022, http://www.jewishgen.org/yizkor/lita/lit1203.html.

Bickford-Smith, Vivian. 'Leisure and Social Identity in Cape Town, British Colony, 1838–1910', *Kronos* 25, no. (1998): 103–128, https://journals.co.za/doi/pdf/10.10520/AJA02590190_518.

Bickford-Smith, Vivian. 'South African Urban History, Racial Segregation and the Unique Case of Cape Town?', *Journal of Southern African Studies* 21, no. 1 (1995): 63–78. https://www.tandfonline.com/doi/abs/10.1080/03057079508708433.

Birmingham, Stephen. *Our Crowd: The Great Jewish Families of New York*. London: Longmans, Green and Co Ltd, 1968.

Brett Young, Francis. *City of Gold*. London: Heinemann, 1939.

Brickman, Celia. *Aboriginal Populations in the Mind*. New York: Columbia University Press, 2003.

Bristow, Edward. *Prostitution and Prejudice: The Jewish Fight Against White Slavery 1870–1939*. New York: Oxford University Press, 1982.

Brustein, William and Amy Ronnkvist. 'The Roots of Antisemitism: Romania before the Holocaust'. *Journal of Genocide Research* 4, no. 2 (2002): 211–235. https://doi.org/10.1080/14623520220138047.

Campbell, James. 'Beyond the Pale: Jewish Immigration and the South African Left'. In *Memories, Realities and Dreams: Aspects of South African Jewish Experience*, edited by Milton Shain and Richard Mendelsohn, 104. Cape Town: Jonathan Ball Publishers, 2002.

Carman, Jillian. *Uplifting the Colonial Philistine: Florence Phillips and the Making of the Johannesburg Art Gallery*. Johannesburg: Wits University Press, 2006.

Cavanagh, James A. *Adventures of an Insurance Agent*. Cape Town: Juta and Co, 1924.

Cebalo, Anton. 'There Once Was an Empire'. *Novum Newsletter*, 20 November 2023. Accessed 10 June 2022, https://novum.substack.com/p/there-once-was-an-empire.

Chatterley, Catherine. 'The Antisemitic Imagination'. In *Global Antisemitism: A Crisis of Modernity*, edited by Charles Asher Small, 77–82. Leiden: Brill Publishers, 2013.

Cheyette, Bryan. 'Neither Black nor White: The Figure of the Jew in Imperial British Literature'. In *The Jew in the Text: Modernity and the Construction of Identity*, edited by Linda Nochlin and Tamar Gard, 37. London: Thames & Hudson, 1995.

Chipkin, Clive. *Johannesburg Style: Architecture and Society, 1880s–1960s*. Cape Town: David Philip Publisher, 1993.

Cohen, Deborah. 'Who Was Who? Race and Jews in Turn-of-the-Century Britain'. *Journal of British Studies* 4, no. 4 (2002): 469. https://doi.org/10.1086/341438.

Coopersmith, Jonathan. *The Electrification of Russia, 1880–1926*. New York: Cornell University Press, 1992.

Corbea-Hoisie, Andrei. 'Chervinitzi'. In *Yivo Encyclopaedia of Jews in Eastern Europe*. New York: Yivo Institute for Jewish Research, 2025. Accessed 10 June 2022, https://encyclopedia.yivo.org/article/914.

The Corporal [P. E. Bodington]. *An Imperial Yeoman at War*. London: Elliot Stock, 1901.

Dedering, Tilman. '"Avenge the Lusitania": The Anti-German Riots in South Africa in 1915'. *Immigrants and Minorities* 31, no. 3 (2013): 256–258. https://doi.org/10.1080/02619288.2013.781811.

Dennison, Tracy and Steven Nafziger. 'Living Standards in Nineteenth Century Russia'. *Journal of Interdisciplinary History* 43, no. 3 (2011): 398–399. https://doi.org/10.1162/JINH_a_00424.

Deutsch, Nathaniel. *The Jewish Dark Continent: Life and Death in the Russian Pale of Settlement*. Cambridge: Harvard University Press, 2011.

De Waal, Edmund. *Letters to Camondo*. London: Vintage Press, 2022.

De Waal, Edmund. *The Hare with Amber Eyes: A Hidden Inheritance*. London: Picador, 2011.

Diner, Hasia. *Roads Taken: The Great Jewish Migrations to the New World and the Peddlers who Forged the Way*. New Haven: Yale University Press, 2015.

Dreyer, Nadine, ed. *A Century of Sundays: 100 Years of Breaking News in the Sunday Times*. Cape Town: Zebra Press, 2006.

Duff Gordon, Lady Lucie. *Letters from the Cape*. Cape Town: Maskew Miller Ltd, 1925.

Dynner, Glenn. *Yankel's Tavern: Jews, Liquor and Life in the Kingdom of Poland*. New York: Oxford University Press, 2014.

Englander, David. '*Stille Huppah* (Quiet Marriage) among Jewish Immigrants in Britain'. *The Jewish Journal of Sociology* 34, no. 2 (1992): 85–109. Accessed 10 June 2022, https://archive.jpr.org.uk/download?id=2259.

Etkes, Immanuel. 'Haskalah'. In *Yivo Encyclopaedia of Jews in Eastern Europe*. New York: Yivo Institute for Jewish Research, 2025. Accessed 10 June 2022, https://encyclopedia.yivo.org/article/10.

Evans, Nicholas. '"A Strike for Racial Justice?" Transatlantic Shipping and the Jewish Diaspora, 1882–1939'. *Jewish Culture and History* 11, nos. 1–2 (2009): 27. https://www.tandfonline.com/doi/abs/10.1080/1462169X.2009.10512113.

Feldman, David. 'Conceiving Difference: Religion, Race and the Jews in Britain c.1750–1900'. *History Workshop Journal* 76, no. 1 (Autumn 2013): 160–186. https://doi.org/10.1093/hwj/dbt001.

Feldman, David. 'Jews and the British Empire c.1900'. *History Workshop Journal* 63, no. 1 (Spring 2007): 70–89. https://doi.org/10.1093/hwj/dbm027.

Feldman, Leibl. *The Jews of Johannesburg*. Translated from the Yiddish by Veronica Belling. Kaplan Centre, University of Cape Town, 2007.

BIBLIOGRAPHY

Fiddel, Louis. Interview. UCT Libraries, Kaplan Centre Interviews, Series A, A57 BC 949.

Forman, Frieda, Ethel Raicus, Sarah Silberstein Swartz and Margie Wolfe, eds. *Found Treasures: Stories by Yiddish Women Writers*. Toronto: Second Story Press, 1994.

Freeze, ChaeRan. 'Marriage'. In *Yivo Encyclopedia of Jews in Eastern Europe*. New York: Yivo Institute for Jewish Research, 2025. Accessed 10 June 2022, https://yivoencyclopedia.org/article.aspx/marriage.

Freeze, ChaeRan and Jay Harris, eds. *Everyday Life in Imperial Russia: Selected Documents 1772–1914*. Waltham: Brandeis University Press, 2013.

Garrett, Leah. *Journeys Beyond the Pale: Yiddish Travel Writing in the Modern World*. Madison: University of Wisconsin Press, 2003.

Gartner, Lloyd. 'Anglo-Jewry and the Jewish International Traffic in Prostitution, 1885–1914'. *Association for Jewish Studies Review* 7 (1982). https://doi.org/10.1017/S0364009400000684.

Goodrich, Robert. 'Conflicted Loyalties: Austro-Hungarian Immigrants in Michigan and the Great War'. *Proceedings of Armistice and Aftermath, 28–9 September 2018*, 1A16. Accessed 10 June 2022, https://digitalcommons.mtu.edu/cgi/viewcontent.cgi?article=1006&context=ww1cc-symposium.

Gorman, Dan. '"The Character Creed": How Character Shaped the British Imperial Enterprise'. *Australasian Journal of Victorian Studies* 4, no. 1 (1998): 127–137. Accessed 10 June 2022, https://openjournals.library.sydney.edu.au/AJVS/article/view/13738.

Guide to South Africa for the Use of Tourists, Sportsmen, Invalids and Settlers. Cape Town: Juta and Co, 1893.

Hahn, Hannah. *They Left It All Behind: Trauma, Loss and Memory among Eastern European Jewish Immigrants and Their Children*. London: Rowman and Littlefield, 2020.

Hamer-Jacklyn, Sarah. 'My Mother's Grief'. In *Found Treasures: Stories by Yiddish Women Writers*, edited by Frieda Forman, Ethel Raicus, Sarah Silberstein Swartz and Margie Wolfe, 67. Toronto: Second Story Press, 1994.

Harbord, Maurice. *Froth and Bubble*. London: Edward Arnold, 1915.

Harding, Sue Ann. 'The Jews of Chernivitsi'. Accessed 10 June 2022, https://kehilalinks.jewishgen.org/sadgura/jqharding.html.

Harries, Patrick. *Work, Culture and Identity: Migrant Labourers in Mozambique and South Africa, c. 1860–1910*. London: James Currey, 1994.

Haumann, Heiko. *A History of East European Jews*. Budapest: Central European University Press, 2002.

Herrman, Louis. *A History of the Jews in South Africa from the Earliest Times to 1895*. Johannesburg: South African Jewish Board of Deputies, 1935.

Hirsch, Marianne and Leo Spitzer. *Ghosts of Home: The Afterlife of Czernowitz in Jewish Memory*. Los Angeles: University of California Press, 2010.

Hirson, Baruch. *The Cape Town Intellectuals: Ruth Schechter and Her Circle, 1907–1954*. Johannesburg: Wits University Press, 2001.

Hobsbawm, Eric. *The Age of Capital, 1848–1875*. London: Weidenfeld & Nicolson, 1975.

Hoedl, Klaus. 'Physical Characteristics of the Jews'. Accessed 15 September 2025, https://jewishstudies.ceu.edu/sites/jewishstudies.ceu.edu/files/attachment/basicpage/16/01hoedl.pdf.

Hoffman, Laurance A. *Beyond the Text: A Holistic Approach to Liturgy*. Bloomington: Indiana University Press, 1987.

Howe, Irving. *World of Our Fathers: The Journey of the East European Jews to America and the Life They Found and Made*. New York: Harcourt Brace and Co, 1976.

Hutchinson, G. T. *From the Cape to the Zambesi*. London: John Murray Publishers, 1905.

Issroff, Saul, ed. *Jewish Migration to South Africa*, Vol 1. Cape Town: Kaplan Centre, University of Cape Town, 2008.

Jaffee, Georgina. *Joffe Marks: A Family Memoir*. Johannesburg: Sharp Media, 2001.

Jessett, Montague George. *The Key to South Africa: Delagoa Bay*. London: T. Fisher Unwin, 1899.

Jewish Board of Guardians. 'History of the Cape Jewish Board of Guardians to Commemorate Centenary Year, 1859–1959', 1963. Cape Provincial Archives (KAB), 296.6, 26.

Johnson, Hannah. *Blood Libel*. Ann Arbor: University of Michigan Press, 2012.
Judaken, Jonathan. 'Mapping the "New Jewish Cultural Studies"'. *History Workshop Journal* 51 (2001): 269–277. https://doi.org/10.1093/hwj/2001.51.269.
Kaplan, Mendel. *Jewish Roots in the South African Economy*. Cape Town: C. Struik Publishers, 1987.
Kassow, Samuel. 'Introduction'. In *The Shtetl: New Evaluations*, edited by Steven Katz, 8. New York: New York University Press, 2007.
Kassow, Samuel. 'Shtetl'. In *Yivo Encyclopedia of Jews in Eastern Europe*. New York: Yivo Institute for Jewish Research, 2025. Accessed 10 June 2022, https://encyclopedia.yivo.org/article/27.
Kazin, Alfred. *A Walker in the City*. New York: Harcourt Books, 1951.
Keidošiūtė, Elena. 'Marginality without Benefits: Converting Jewish Women in Lithuanian Guberniyas'. *Jewish History* 33. *Special Issue: Jewish Women in Modern Eastern and East Central Europe* (2020): 7–27. https://doi.org/10.1007/s10835-019-09347-x.
Knight, Edward Frederick. *South Africa After the War*. London: Longmans, Green and Co, 1903.
Koziura, Karolina. 'The Spaces of Nostalgia(s) and the Politics of Belonging in Contemporary Chernivitsi, Western Ukraine'. *East European Politics and Societies and Cultures* 33, no. 1 (February 2019): 218–237. https://doi.org/10.1177/0888325418777060,
Krah, Markus. *American Jewry and the Re-Invention of the East European Jewish Past*. Berlin: De Gruyter Oldenbourg, 2017.
Krut, Riva. 'Building a Home and a Community: Jews in Johannesburg, 1886–1914'. PhD thesis, University of London, 1985.
Lammasniemi, Laura. '"White Slavery": The Origins of the Anti-trafficking Movement', *openDemocracy* (16 November 2017). Accessed 10 June 2022, https://www.opendemocracy.net/en/beyond-trafficking-and-slavery/whiteslavery-origins-of-anti-trafficking-movement/.
Lavin, Deborah, ed. *Friendship and Union: The South African Letters and Maud Selborne, 1907–1943*. Cape Town: Van Riebeeck Society for the Publication of Southern African Historical Documents, 2010.
Lee, Malka. *Durk Kindershe Oygn* (Through the Eyes of Childhood). In *Found Treasures: Stories by Yiddish Women Writers*, edited by Frieda

Forman, Ethel Raicus, Sarah Silberstein Swartz and Margie Wolfe, 159–185. Toronto: Second Story Press, 1994.

Levenson, Marcia. *People of the Book: Images of the Jew in South African Jewish Fiction, 1880–1992*. Johannesburg: Wits University Press, 1996.

Levy, Joshua, ed. *The Writings of Dovid Meyer Hersch: Rand Pioneer and Historian of Jewish Life in Early Johannesburg*. Johannesburg: Ammatt Press, 2005.

Levy, Lorna. *The Hidden Life of a Smous*. Cape Town: Kaplan Centre, University of Cape Town, 2017.

Lewinsohn, Richard. *Barney Barnato: From Whitechapel Clown to Diamond King*. London: George Routledge and Sons Ltd, 1937.

Lomnitz, Claudio. *Nuestra America: My Family in the Vertigo of Translation*. New York: Other Press, 2021.

MacDonald, Andrew. 'Colonial Trespassers in the Making of South Africa's International Borders, 1900 to c.1950'. PhD thesis, St John's College, Cambridge, 2012.

MacDonald, Andrew. 'Forging the Frontiers: Travellers and Documents on the South Africa-Mozambique border, 1890s–1940s'. Working paper, Academia.edu. Accessed 10 June 2022, https://www.academia.edu/4872917/Forging_the_Frontiers_Travellers_and_Documents_on_the_South_Africa_Mozambique_Border_1890s_1940s_WORKING_PAPER_.

Mantzaris, Evangelos. 'The Promise of Impossible Revolution: The Cape Town International Socialist League'. In *Labour Struggles in South Africa The Forgotten Pages, 1903–1921*, chap. 1. Accessed 10 June 2022, https://www.sahistory.org.za/archive/chapter-1-promise-impossible-revolution-cape-town-industrial-socialist-league-1918-1921.

Masé, Aline. 'Student migration of Jews from Tsarist Russia to the Universities of Berne and Zurich, 1865–1914'. In *East European Jews in Switzerland*, edited by Tamar Lewinsky and Sandrine Mayoraz, 106–107. Berlin: De Gruyter, 2013.

Mazower, Mark. *What You Did Not Tell: A Russian Past and the Journey Home*. London: Penguin, 2018.

McAvoy, Erica. '"To Have and Enjoy": Seating in Boston's Early Anglican Churches, 1686–1782'. Master's thesis, University of

Massachusetts, 2020. Accessed 10 June 2022, https://scholarwo rks.umb.edu/cgi/viewcontent.cgi?article=1660&context=masters _theses.

McCormick, Kay. 'Language in the Jewish Community of District Six, 1880–1940'. Jacob Gitlin Library, PMP 194-1, District Six Box, 8.

Mendelsohn, Richard. *Sammy Marks: 'The Uncrowned King of the Transvaal'*. Cape Town: David Philip, 1991.

Mendelsohn, Richard and Milton Shain. *The Jews in South Africa: An Illustrated History*. Cape Town: Jonathan Ball Publishers, 2008.

Meredith, Martin. *Diamonds, Gold and War*. London: Pocket Books, 2007.

Michaels, Anne. *Fugitive Pieces*. London: Bloomsbury Publishing, 1998.

Mirvish, Louis. 'Cape Town Jewry in 190'. *Jewish Affairs* (May 1960): 5.

Mitchell, William Harry and L. A. Sawyer. *The Cape Run: The Story of the Union-Castle Service to South Africa and of the Ships They Employed*. Suffolk: Terence Dalton Ltd, 1987.

Murray, Martin. *City of Extremes: The Spatial Politics of Johannesburg*. Durham: Duke University Press, 2011.

Mursalo, Tvrtko. 'Croatians in the South of Africa'. *Werkwinkel* 3, no. 1 (2008): 176.

Ndebele, Njabulo. *South African Literature and Culture: Rediscovery of the Ordinary*. Manchester: Manchester University Press, 1994.

Neame, Lawrence E. *City Built on Gold*. Cape Town: CNA, 1960.

Neyer, G. 'Austrian Emigraton from the Mid Nineteenth Century to the Present'. *Demographic Information*, 1995. Abstract. Accessed 10 June 2022, https://pubmed.ncbi.nlm.nih.gov/12321139/.

Orchan, Nurit. 'Yiddish: Women's Participation in East European Yiddish Press, 1862–1903'. The Shalvie/Hyman Encyclopedia of Jewish Women, Jewish Women's Archive. Accessed 10 June 2022, https://jwa.org/encyclopedia/article/yiddish-womens-participat ion-in-eastern-european-yiddish-press-1862-1903.

Ostroff, Harry. Interview. UCT Libraries, Kaplan Centre Interviews, Series B, A 435, BC 949.

Padovich, Betha. Interview. UCT Libraries, Kaplan Centre Interviews, Series A, A198, BC 949.

Parnell, Susan. 'Race, Power and Urban Control: Johannesburg's Inner-City Slum-Yards, 1910–1923'. *Journal of Southern African*

Studies 29, no. 3 (2003): 615–637. https://doi.org/10.1080/03057070306219.

Paull, Jeffrey and Jeffrey Briskman. 'The Jewish Surname Process in the Russian Empire'. Avotaynu Online, 21 August 2015. Accessed 10 June 2022, https://avotaynuonline.com/2015/08/the-jewish-surname-process-in-the-russian-empire-and-its-effect-on-jewish-genealogy/.

Petrovsky-Shtern, Yohanan. *The Golden Age Shtetl: A New History of Jewish Life in East Europe*. Princeton: Princeton University Press, 2014.

Phillips, Mrs Lionel [Florence]. *Some South African Recollections*. London: Longmans, Green and Co, 1899.

Pimlott, William. 'The Yiddish Press and the Making of South African Jewry in the British World: Exclusion, Libel and British Nationalism, 1840–1914'. *Jewish Historical Studies* 55, no. 1 (2024): 1–26. https://doi.org/10.14324/111.444.jhs.2024v55.02.

Pimstone, Millie and Milton Shain. *The Jews of District Six: Another Time, Another Place*. Cape Town: Kaplan Centre, University of Cape Town, 2012.

Porter, Andrew. *Victorian Business, Shipping and Imperial Policy*. Suffolk: Boydell Press, 1986.

Posel, Deborah. 'Changes in the Order of Things: Department Stores and the Making of Modern Cape Town'. In *Conspicuous Consumption in Africa*, edited by Deborah Posel and Ilana van Wyk, 32. Johannesburg: Wits University Press, 2019.

Pratt, Norma Fain. 'Culture and Radical Politics: Yiddish Women Writers 1890–1940'. *American Jewish History* 70, no. 1 (1980): 68–90. http://www.jstor.org/stable/23881991.

Rabinowitz, Ann. 'South African Rand Steam Matzah Ltd'. Accessed 10 June 2022, https://groups.jewishgen.org/g/main/message/612605.

Rallis, Alice and Ruth Gordon. *Daughter of Yesterday: A Pioneer Child Looks Back at Early Johannesburg*. Cape Town: Howard Timmins, 1975.

Rechter, Daniel. *Becoming Hapsburg: The Jews of Austrian Bukovina, 1774–1918*. Littman Library of Jewish Civilization. Liverpool: Liverpool University Press, 2013.

Reuveni, Gideon. 'Prologomena to an "Economic Turn" in Jewish History'. In *The Economy in Jewish History: New Perspectives on the Interrelationship between Ethnicity and Economic Life*, edited by Gideon Reuveni and Sarah Wonick-Segev, 1–20. New York: Berghahn Books, 2011.

Robins, Gwynne. 'Adapting to a New Society: The Role of the Cape Town Jewish Philanthropic Society c.1900'. Accessed 10 June 2022, http://www.jcs.org.za/wp-content/uploads/2017/06/CTJPS.pdf.

Robins, Gwynne. 'Greyshirts on the Grand Parade'. *Cape Jewish Chronicle*, 1 July 2020. Accessed 10 June 2022, https://cjc.org.za/2020/07/01/greyshirts-on-the-grand-parade/.

Rosenthal, Eric. 'The Garlicks Story'. Quoted in Deborah Posel, 'Changes in the Order of Things: Department Stores and the Making of Modern Cape Town'. In *Conspicuous Consumption in Africa*, edited by Deborah Posel and Ilana van Wyk, 32. Johannesburg: Wits University Press, 2019.

Rosenthal, Eric. *Gold! Gold! Gold! The Johannesburg Gold Rush*. London: Macmillan, 1970.

Rosenthal, Eric. *Meet Me at the Carlton*. Cape Town: Howard Timmins, 1972.

Rosenthal, Eric. *Other Men's Millions*. Cape Town: Howard Timmins, 1959.

Rowland, Richard. 'Geographical Patterns of the Jewish Population in the Pale of Settlement in the Late Nineteenth Century'. *Jewish Social Studies* 48, no. 3 (1986): 207–234. https://www.jstor.org/stable/4467338.

Rubin, Margot. 'The Jewish Community of Johannesburg, 1886–1939'. MA thesis, University of Pretoria, 2004.

Rugoff, Milton. *America's Gilded Age: Intimate Portraits from an Era of Extravagance and Change, 1850–1890*. New York: Henry Holt and Co, 1989.

Sachs, Bernard. *Personalities and Places*. Johannesburg: The Dial Press, 1965.

Schainker, Ellie. *Confessions of the Shtetl*. Stanford: Stanford University Press, 2016.

Schonstein Pinnock, Patricia. *Ouma's Autumn*. Grahamstown: African Sun Press, 1993.

Schrire, Carmel and Gwynne Schrire. *The Reb and the Rebel: Jewish Narratives in South Africa, 1892–1913*. Cape Town: University of Cape Town Press, 2016.

Schrire, Gwynne. 'The Bubonic Plague and the Jews in Cape Town', 23 April 2020. Accessed 10 June 2022, https://www.sajbd.org/media/the-bubonic-plagueand-the-jews-in-cape-town-1901.

Scully, William Charles. *The Ridge of White Waters*. London: Stanley Paul and Co, 1911.

Shain, Milton. 'If It Was so Good, Why Was It so Bad?' In *Memories, Realities and Dreams: Aspects of South African Jewish Experience*, edited by Milton Shain and Richard Mendelsohn, 81. Cape Town: Jonathan Ball Publishers, 2002.

Shain, Milton. 'Jewry and Cape Society'. *Historical Publications Society* (1983): 1–2.

Shain, Milton. *A Perfect Storm: Antisemitism in South Africa, 1930–1948*. Cape Town: Jonathan Ball Publishers, 2015.

Shain, Milton. *The Roots of Antisemitism in South Africa*. Johannesburg: Wits University Press, 1994.

Sherman, Joseph. 'Scrutinizing the Shtetl: I.B. Singer's "Tsetyl un Rikl"'. *Prooftexts* 15, no. 2 (May 1995): 129–144. http://www.jstor.org/stable/20689415.

Sherman, Joseph. 'Serving the Natives: Whiteness as the Price of Hospitality in South African Yiddish Literature'. *Journal of Southern African Studies* 26, no. 3 (2000): 505–521. https://www.tandfonline.com/doi/abs/10.1080/713683588.

Shimoni, Gideon. 'Review: Milton Shain, *The Roots of Antisemitism in South Africa*'. *Modern Judaism* 16, no. 2 (May 1996): 185–188. Accessed 15 September 2025, https://muse.jhu.edu/article/21999.

Shtif, Nokhem. *The Pogroms in Ukraine, 1918–19: Prelude to the Holocaust*. Translated by Maurice Wolfthal. Open Book Publishers, 2019. Accessed 10 June 2022, https://books.openedition.org/obp/11018?lang=en.

Slezkine, Yuri. *The Jewish Century*. Princeton: Princeton University Press, 2004.

South African Jewish Chronicle, 3 June 1903. Jacob Gitlin Library, Cape Town.

South African Jewish Chronicle. 'Congregational Rivalry', 1924. Jacob Gitlin Library, Cape Town.

Staliunas, Darius. *Enemies for a Day: Anti-Semitism and Anti-Jewish Violence in Lithuania under the Tsars*. Budapest: Central University Press, 2015.
Standard and Digger News. 'Kaffirs and their Money'. 22 June 1895. British Library.
Standard and Digger News. 'Steerage to South Africa'. 13 June 1895. British Library.
Stanislawski, Michael. 'Russian Empire'. In *Yivo Encyclopedia of Jews in Eastern Europe*. New York: Yivo Institute for Jewish Research, 2025. Accessed 10 June 2022, https://encyclopedia.yivo.org/article/25.
The Star Weekly Edition. 'Terrible Tragedy at Klip River'. 14 May 1904. British Library.
Steidl, Annemarie. 'Migration Patterns in the Late Hapsburg Empire'. In *Migration in Austria*, edited by Gunter Bischof and Dirk Rupnov, 69–86. New Orleans: New Orleans University Press, 2017.
Stevenson, Michael. *Art and Aspirations: The Randlords of South Africa and their Collections*. Cape Town: Fernwood Press, 2002.
Surridge, Keith. '"All You Soldiers Are What We Call Pro-Boer": The Military Critique of the South African War'. *History* 82, no. 268 (1997): 582–600. https://doi.org/10.1111/1468-229X.00052.
Swartz, Sally. *Homeless Wanderers: Movement and Mental Illness in the Cape Colony in the Nineteenth Century*. Cape Town: University of Cape Town Press, 2015.
Thornton, Tamara Plakins. *Handwriting in America: A Cultural History*. New Haven: Yale University Press, 1996.
Unowsky, Daniel. *The Pomp and Politics of Patriotism: Imperial Celebrations in Hapsburg Austria, 1848–1916*. West Lafayette: Purdue University Press, 2005.
Van der Waal, Gerhard-Mark. *From Mining Camp to Metropolis: The Buildings of Johannesburg 1886–1940*. Pretoria: HSRC, 1987.
Van der Walt, Lucien. 'Bakunin's Heirs in South Africa: Race and Revolutionary Syndicalism from the IWW to the International Socialist League, 1910–12'. *Politikon* 31, no. 1 (May 2004): 67–89. https://doi.org/10.1080/02589340410001690819.
Van Heyningen, Elizabeth. 'Public Health and Society in Cape Town 1880–1910'. PhD diss., University of Cape Town, 1989.

Van Onselen, Charles. *The Fox and the Flies: The Criminal Empire of the Whitechapel Murderer.* London: Vintage Books, 2008.
Van Onselen, Charles. 'Jewish Police Informers in the Atlantic World, 1880–1914'. *The Historical Journal* 50, no. 1 (2007): 131–132. https://doi.org/10.1017/S0018246X06005942.
Van Onselen, Charles. *Studies in the Social and Economic History of the Witwatersrand, 1886–1924, Volume One: New Babylon.* Johannesburg: Ravan Press, 1982.
Van Onselen, Charles. 'The World the Mineowners Made: Social Themes in the Economic Transformation of the Witwatersrand, 1886–1914'. *Review* 3, no. 2 (Fall 1979): 289–323. https://www.jstor.org/stable/40240837.
Weinberg, Henry. 'The Image of the Jew in Late Nineteenth Century French Literature'. *Jewish Social Studies* 45, no. 3 (1983): 241–250. https://www.jstor.org/stable/4467228.
Whiteman, Tilly. Interview by L. Levin. UCT Kaplan Centre Oral Histories, May 1985, MSS BC 949.
Wilson, Francis. *Dinosaurs, Diamonds and Democracy: A Short, Short History of South Africa.* Johannesburg: Penguin Random House, 2011.
Yarfitz, Mir. *Impure Migration: Jews and Sex Work in Golden Age Argentina.* New Brunswick: Rutgers University Press, 2019.
Zweig, Stefan. *The World of Yesterday.* Translated by Anthea Bell. Lincoln: University of Nebraska Press, 2009.

Archives consulted

Ancestry, https://www.ancestry.com/
British Library, London
Jacob Gitlin Library, Cape Town
Jeppe High School for Boys Archive, Johannesburg
JewishGen, https://jewishgen.org/
Kaplan Centre, UCT Libraries, Cape Town
National Archives and Records Service, Pretoria
South African College Archive, Cape Town
Western Cape Archives and Records Service, Cape Town

www.ingramcontent.com/pod-product-compliance
Lightning Source LLC
Chambersburg PA
CBHW020515080526
44583CB00013B/607